A Long Road
How Quakers Made Sense of God and the Bible
by T. Vail Palmer, Jr.

BARCLAY PRESS
Newberg, OR 97132

A Long Road
How Quakers Made Sense of God and the Bible

©2017 by T. Vail Palmer, Jr.

BARCLAY PRESS
Newberg, Oregon
www.barclaypress.com
www.barclaypress.com/vailpalmer

All rights reserved. No part may be reproduced for any commercial purpose by any method without permission in writing from the copyright holder.

Unless otherwise noted, scripture quotations are taken from *The New Revised Standard Version*, copyright 1989, 1995 by the Division of Christian Education of the National Council of the Churches of Christ in the United States of America. Used by permission. All rights reserved.

Printed in the United States of America

COVER DESIGN BY DARRYL BROWN

ISBN 978-1-59498-042-8

To

Izzy

Warm, tender, loving, and faithful, even yet,

my very present comfort and strength.

And to the memory of

T. Canby Jones

Mentor and firm friend,

splendid example of a Christian on pilgrimage, with a vision.

Contents

Introduction	7
1. Friends and God: The Great Deviations	25
2. Friends and the Bible: A Nineteenth-Century Sampler	45
3. Friends, the Bible, and God: Holiness and Modernist Friends	95
4. Friends and the Bible: Quaker Bible Scholars	177
Epilogue	249
Notes	251
Bibliography	283
Index	295
Old Testament	295
New Testament	296
Subject Index	297

Introduction

In my first book, *Face to Face: Early Quaker Encounters with the Bible*, I describe how I discovered that some of the earliest seventeenth-century Friends—George Fox, Edward Burrough, Margaret Fell—read the Bible with empathy. They identified themselves with the ancient Hebrews and earliest Christians and looked at the world from within their thought and lifeworlds. This is a way of understanding the Bible that emphasizes its personal narratives and its rich use of symbols and metaphors. This approach contrasts sharply with the widespread view of the Bible as a legal constitution, filled with propositions from which Christian theology and moral rules may be deduced. The empathetic understanding of the Bible is well summed up by second-generation Quaker theologian Robert Barclay:

> God hath seen meet that herein we should, as in a looking-glass, see the conditions and experiences of the saints of old; that finding our experience answer to theirs, we might thereby be the more confirmed and comforted, and our hope of obtaining the

same end strengthened; that observing the providences attending them, seeing the snares they were liable to, and beholding their deliverances, we may thereby be made wise unto salvation.[1]

Nearly all of the earliest Friends were unsophisticated in linguistics and philosophy. They did not themselves use such terms as "empathy" or "metaphor." This may be one of the reasons why their way of looking at the Bible nearly disappeared after the first generation. The one exception found in my first book is John Woolman, who on occasion referred to his "near sympathy" with biblical prophets. But even Woolman mostly used other principles in his arguments from the Bible.

During the eighteenth century, Friends ministers and reformers showed astonishing differences in the ways they used and understood the Bible, even as they worked together toward eliminating slaveholding among Friends, discovering innovative ways of opposing war, expressing a mystical spirituality known as Quietism, and trying to protect Quakerism from outside influences.

By the beginning of the nineteenth century, the effort to keep outside influences from impacting Quaker spirituality was clearly failing. Two major worldviews were sweeping through Western society—the evangelical movement and the Enlightenment. Many Friends were impressed by the Enlightenment emphasis on reason in religion and commitment to religious and political freedom. Others were caught up in the deep Christian enthusiasm and commitment to social justice of evangelicalism. Friends on both sides mistakenly believed that they were dedicated to the very spirituality, commitment, and thinking that had been expressed in the lives of the first Quakers.

Evangelical Friends, such as Henry Tuke and Stephen Grellet, accepted the Bible as a legal constitution, in which they found clear, not-to-be-questioned doctrines and ethical rules. Enlightenment Friends varied in their approaches to the Bible. Grammarian John Comly recognized the importance of figurative speech, symbols, and metaphors in biblical writings. The dynamic, popular preacher Elias Hicks looked on the Bible as a secondary rule; he insisted "that we cannot believe what we do not understand."[2] He openly recognized that there were inconsistencies within the Bible.

By 1822, influential elders in Philadelphia had become alarmed at the popularity of Hicks's ministry, and attempted to prevent this visiting minister from speaking at meetings in Philadelphia, but failed. During the next few years, evangelical Quaker attempts to silence Hicks intensified. In the 1827 sessions of Philadelphia Yearly Meeting, a plan was adopted, over the objections of John Comly and many of his friends, to appoint a committee to judge the soundness of the preaching of recorded ministers. Many of those who objected met three times in another location, where they accepted Comly's proposal to "retreat from these scenes of confusion." Comly's hope that this "retreat" would be temporary was doomed; too many evangelical leaders, like Stephen Grellet, were adamant in their refusal to compromise on issues of sound doctrine.

In the following year, Elias Hicks's own yearly meeting, New York, and several other yearly meetings followed Philadelphia's example and split. There were now two rival branches of Friends in America, who called their opposing parties "Orthodox" and "Hicksite." The depth of their division was not simply due to differences in understanding and using the Bible; there were sociological causes, which Larry Ingle has masterfully described in his book *Quakers in Conflict*. At the ideological level, two especially contentious issues centered around creeds and atonement. I begin this volume with an in-depth look at these two issues in the history of Quaker thought.

On these issues, Hicksite and Orthodox Friends were not only in sharp conflict with each other, but both branches also believed they were affirming Quaker tradition and the views of the first Friends. In actuality, neither understood the position of the earliest Friends, and therefore they differed as much from such Friends as George Fox, Robert Barclay, and William Penn as they did from each other.

The contrasting attitudes toward creeds or formal statements of belief, especially between seventeenth-century Friends and nineteenth-century Orthodox Friends, were rooted in their widely differing understandings of the point or purpose of God's revelation to humankind. In 1824 and 1825, English Friend Joseph John Gurney published two books that were widely accepted among Orthodox Friends as brilliant and masterful expressions of their understanding of Quakerism as a Christian body. In one of these books he wrote: "The principal object of the revelations acknowledged by Christians, was to unfold certain doctrines, and to promulgate certain moral principles."[3] In short, the point of divine revelation is that we may *know about* God.

For George Fox and Robert Barclay, the point of revelation is that we may *know* God. For Fox, Friends were united through dwelling together in the power of God, the power that was made known in the series of historical events from Abraham to Moses to the prophets to the Christian apostles—to the Friends themselves. These events have been portrayed in narratives that can best be understood if they are read with empathy. Fox rejected creeds because they are attempts to abstract this knowledge from history and to express it in timeless, rational propositions. Creeds are dead, cold, and frozen. God's revelation is alive and dynamic, warm and personal.

For nineteenth-century Hicksites, in general, revelation came through immediate, individual religious experience or through the mind's rational activity. They insisted on preserving "the right of private judgement" in regard to religious beliefs.[4]

After the Great Separation, Orthodox Friends were quick to establish formal statements of faith. In 1829 their representatives prepared a detailed statement that was promptly accepted by seven Orthodox yearly meetings. Belief in the total content of this statement was required in order to remain members in good standing. Throughout the nineteenth century, Orthodox yearly meetings (after the second round of separations, Gurneyite yearly meetings) continued to adopt increasingly formal and elaborate statements of belief. The ultimate conclusion of this process was the 1887 fourteen-page Richmond Declaration of Faith, which was adopted by nearly all Gurneyite yearly meetings.

Hicksite Friends increasingly insisted, through the nineteenth century and into the twentieth, that *what* individual Friends believe is not essential. This finally emerged into a conviction that it is not even essential *that* individual Friends believe—even in God. This conclusion to their process can be seen in the example of an influential member of a Hicksite meeting, an innovative college president, who told his monthly meeting at the age of ninety that after long, honest search he had never found evidence for the existence of God, nor had belief in God been revealed to him.

Between the twelfth century and the early twentieth century, Christians generally accepted that there were two major ways of understanding Christ's atonement—what Jesus had accomplished in his life, death, and resurrection. Examples of the first way were the satisfaction theory (articulated by St. Anselm in the eleventh century) and the substitutionary theory (articulated by John Calvin in the sixteenth century). These are sometimes called forensic theories, because they make use of ideas drawn from courts of law. Basic tenets of these theories are sin requires a heavy penalty from God, and satisfaction must be made for sin. This satisfaction could only be made by a human being, so Christ, who was fully God, became a human. By enduring the punishment for our sin, he provided the needed satisfaction on our behalf—substituting for us. Our sins were imputed—or transferred—to Christ, and Christ's righteousness is imputed to us.

The second way, first developed (in opposition to Anselm) by Peter Abelard, is often referred to as "subjective" or "moral influence" theories of the atonement. The emphasis is on the impact of Christ's life and work on people's hearts and behavior.

Joseph John Gurney clearly traced out a summary of the satisfaction theory; he insisted that such a theory is essential to Christian faith and that belief in it is necessary for our present and everlasting welfare.

John Comly and Elias Hicks both argued strongly against the substitutionary theory. There is clear evidence in his letters that Hicks held to the moral influence type of atonement theory.

George Fox and Robert Barclay clearly rejected the Calvinist idea of imputed righteousness, which is a central part of the forensic theories. Neither Fox nor Barclay used the term atonement very much. Can we determine what view they actually held to?

In 1930, Swedish Lutheran theologian Gustaf Aulén published his finding that there has long since been a third major way of looking at the atonement, which lay at the heart of theories proposed by church fathers in the earliest centuries of Christianity. The basic idea in this third view is that God, through Christ, has delivered humankind from captivity to the devil, and so gained victory over death and the forces of evil. Aulén popularized this view in the phrase "Christus Victor." This view was never fully developed into a satisfactory theory until the beginning of the twenty-first century, when Mennonite theologian J. Denny Weaver published *The Nonviolent Atonement*, in which he called his theory "narrative Christus Victor." Another twenty-first century theory, a "covenant theory," was spelled out by a Methodist professor at George Fox Evangelical Seminary, R. Larry Shelton, in his book *Cross and Covenant*. In this theory, the work of Christ was God's initiative in making the covenant with humans and establishing and maintaining the covenant community.

There is much in Fox's writings that is strongly consistent with a Christus Victor view of the atonement. He frequently referred to Genesis 3:15 (King

James Version, of course), which he understood to be looking forward to Jesus Christ, using such language as "Christ [the Seed] bruises satan the serpent's head." The Lamb's War theme, in the thought of Fox, Edward Burrough, and James Nayler, was a powerful and original extension of the Christus Victor way of viewing the work of Christ. The concept of covenant was also a favorite for Fox.

There is evidence that John Comly would readily accept a moral influence theory or even a covenant view of Christ's atonement. Clearly Elias Hicks emphasized the idea of Christ's mission and death as a powerful moral example; there are hints that he also believed that Christ established a new covenant.

In sum, leaders of the Orthodox faction held firmly to the substitutionary theory—completely at odds with the original Quaker view of the atonement. Hicksite leaders struggled to find a meaningful understanding of the atonement. Thus, after adding creeds and atonement to the major theme of this work—interpretation of the Bible—I return to a look at Quaker thought during the main part of the nineteenth century, examining the views of six Friends, three Orthodox and three Hicksite: Orthodox Friends Joseph John Gurney, John Wilbur, and Jonathan Dymond; and Hicksite Friends Edward Hicks, Lucretia Mott, and Abraham Lawton.

Joseph John Gurney looked on the Bible as a handbook or legal constitution. He began his arguments by using biblical texts as cognitive information, then built up his doctrines upon this foundation. Even though this approach was radically different from that of the earliest Friends, Gurney managed to find legalistic, biblical explanations for nearly all the ways in which Friends differed from other British Christians in their way of worship, style of life, and specific moral standards. On one major issue, this attempt broke down: the ministry of women. He suggested that there were areas of ministry forbidden to women. He insisted that men held authority over women in church government, as evidenced by some very doubtful statements of historical fact, such as: "While it belonged to the brethren only to form rules for the government of the Society, and ultimately to carry them into effect, the women's meetings were established . . . exclusively . . . for the purpose of exercising a wholesome care over their own sex."[5]

John Wilbur agreed with early Friend Robert Barclay that the Spirit of God is the highest authority, with the scriptures holding second place and the writings of the early Friends following closely behind. He looked at the

Introduction

Bible as a sourcebook for doctrinal statements. He agreed with evangelicals like Gurney that sound Christian doctrine was essential; in practice he took the writings of first-generation Friends as the criteria for determining soundness of doctrine. It was this difference that led to the split of Orthodox Friends in several American yearly meetings (beginning in 1845 with Wilbur's own New England Yearly Meeting) into Wilburite (or Conservative) and Gurneyite branches.

On one major theological issue, Wilbur opposed "trusting in a mere imputed righteousness for salvation, without regard to obedience."[6] He (with Barclay) stood in opposition to an important point in the satisfaction theory of the atonement.

English Friend Jonathan Dymond wrote about principles of morality and Christian ethics. He affirmed the supreme authority of scripture on questions of morality—specifically that the New Testament alone expresses God's will for Christians. He also recognized the subordinate authority of such principles as natural law, "the authority, in moral affairs, of what are called natural instincts and natural rights,"[7] and utility, "the endeavor to produce the greatest sum of happiness,"[8] or what utilitarian philosophers called "the greatest happiness of the greatest number" of people.

As I read through his reasoning, I found numerous uncertainties and inconsistencies in the ways in which he applied and related these various principles. The only consistency I could find was in the conclusions that he reached: on every issue, he ended up affirming and supporting the established beliefs and practices of the Society of Friends. (He never explicitly admitted that Quaker practice was the authority or even a reason for affirming or rejecting a specific form of action.) Specifically, he did not always affirm positions taken in Fox's and Barclay's generation, but rather the practices of Quakers in his own time. His basic, unstated starting point was that the authoritative source for our knowledge of God's will is the received tradition of the Society of Friends.

An admirer of eighteenth-century Quaker reformers John Woolman and John Churchman, Edward Hicks readily followed reforming Friends Churchman, Samuel Fothergill, and Job Scott in their sometimes unconventional ways of interpreting the Bible. In his own time, he was a sharp critic not only of the too-strict theology of the Philadelphia elders (he sided with his cousin Elias Hicks during the 1827–28 split), but also of many Hicksite Friends who he felt went too far in rejecting the authority of the Bible or the saviorhood of Jesus.

A failure as a farmer, Edward Hicks found that he was good at sign painting and desperately needed the income it brought in. But he followed the reformers in his strong belief in the importance of strict adherence to Quaker traditions, which included rejection of the arts. This dichotomy produced inward stress—which may be reflected in the fact that he never mentioned in his *Memoirs* the sixty-some *Peaceable Kingdom* paintings for which he is so widely admired today.

Lucretia Mott and her husband James were actively involved in the abolitionist movement, often working with ministers from other denominations in their anti-slavery work. Many Friends, following the lead of Elias and Edward Hicks, looked with suspicion on such activities. Lucretia went on to become a pioneer in the women's suffrage movement. She was one of a small group who called together the Seneca Falls Convention in 1848—the formal beginning of that movement in the United States. She firmly believed in "the divine gift of reason,"[9] and that human history was a story of advance and progress.

George Fox and Margaret Fell read the Bible empathetically; Lucretia Mott emphasized reading the Bible intelligently. One result of her effort to read the Bible intelligently was that she distinguished between the divinely inspired quality of some parts of the Bible and the merely human, fallible origin of other parts. She did not simply use her own unaided reason in interpreting the Bible, but was also ready to utilize the findings of critical biblical scholarship that was beginning to flourish. Mott was sure that great truths can be found not only in the Hebrew and Christian scriptures, but also in "the testimonies of many other servants of God, . . . recorded in every age and in every condition of life."[10]

Mott repeatedly rejected the idea of Christ's "vicarious atonement." It seems clear that what she was actually rejecting was the satisfaction or substitutionary theory of the atonement. She gave no evidence that she was aware of the possibility of any other viable view or theory of the atonement.

In the 1860s Abraham Lawton made one of the earliest attempts to bring all groups of Friends together. His writings consist of such a cascade of biblical pictures and metaphors, I often find it difficult to determine just what points he was trying to make. A couple of his passages resound with the language of the early Quaker Lamb's War, and tie this theme into a view of Christ as victor.

Late in the nineteenth century, two movements made a dramatic impact

Introduction

on the direction of Gurneyite Quakerism, especially in America but also to a significant extent in Great Britain. These were the Holiness movement and the modernist movement. Three prominent leaders of the Holiness movement among Friends were David B. Updegraff, Dougan Clark Jr., and Luke Woodard.

Central to the Holiness movement is the belief that a true Christian life centers around two separate experiences: first, a conversion experience in which the individual accepts Jesus Christ as personal savior, and is thereby freed from the eternal punishment that is the consequence of sin; and second, an experience of sanctification, in which the Holy Spirit enables the believer to live without sinning in this life.

For over two hundred years, Quakers who allowed themselves to be baptized with water were violating strict Quaker discipline and were regularly disowned (removed from membership). David Updegraff, a minister in Ohio Yearly Meeting, was baptized in water by a Baptist pastor in 1882. In 1885, Ohio Yearly Meeting took action, officially "tolerating" this departure from Quaker tradition. In 1887, the conference of all Gurneyite yearly meetings published the Richmond Declaration of Faith, which included an assertion that true Christian baptism "is not an outward baptism with water." Ohio Yearly Meeting therefore did not adopt the Richmond Declaration. When the Five Years Meeting was organized in 1902, Ohio Yearly Meeting did not join that body, thus becoming the first evangelical yearly meeting to separate from the larger body of Gurneyite Friends.

In 1894, Dougan Clark was a recorded minister in Indiana Yearly Meeting and head of the Bible department at Earlham College. In that year, at the memorial service in Ohio for Updegraff, Clark "felt led to take on water baptism."[11] In consequence, his status as a recorded minister was revoked, and the president of Earlham College maneuvered him out of his position on Earlham's faculty.

Updegraff assumed that every statement in the Bible is literally true. He and Luke Woodard rejected historical and literary criticism of the Bible, which they dismissed as "higher criticism." Updegraff openly appealed to proof texts in his application of the Bible to specific situations. He, along with Clark and Woodard, clearly used the Bible as a handbook or legal constitution.

William Penn developed the idea that human history, under God, went through a sequence of "dispensations": (1) the dispensation of angels, beginning with Abraham, (2) the dispensation of the Law, from Moses through John the Baptist, and (3) the dispensation of Christ, the Son of God, beginning with Jesus. Through the next couple of centuries, many Friends followed Penn in this interpretation. Updegraff, Clark, and Woodard all adopted this scheme, but with some variations. Updegraff collapsed the first two dispensations into one—the dispensation of the Father. The second dispensation, the dispensation of the Son, lasted only briefly through the ministry, resurrection, and ascension of Christ. Then, beginning at Pentecost, came "the last and most glorious *dispensation of the Holy Ghost*,"[12] or "the Dispensation of the Spirit."[13]

Updegraff, Clark, and Woodard all argued vigorously in favor of the ministry of women. For the Holiness movement, the account of the gift of the Holy Spirit at Pentecost was the key to their whole understanding of scripture. Along that line, Acts 2:16–18 was for Updegraff the foundation text for his interpretation of the Bible on the issue of women's ministry. This was modeled, in his own experience, by the example of his mother, Rebecca Taylor Updegraff, who was a recorded Friends minister and influential revival preacher. Clark stood firmly with Updegraff in making Acts 2:16–18 and Galatians 3:28 the key texts in his biblical arguments. Woodard appealed to the living example of a biblical person—Mary Magdalene—as well as making logical deductions from propositional statements in the Bible.

Updegraff vehemently rejected the moral influence theory of the atonement; he claimed that this view was false Christianity and subversive of the doctrine of the atonement. Clark opposed the ancient ransom theory, which he called "the Satan theory."[14] Woodard regarded both the ransom and the moral influence theories as being opposite to the true, scriptural theory.

All three of these Holiness ministers firmly believed in a forensic view of the atonement. Updegraff used terms such as "satisfaction," "substitutional," and "judicial" in describing the atonement. Clark insisted on "the propitiatory and substitutional theory of the Bible."[15] Woodard, in his discussion of the atonement, also used language of the forensic theories: "substitution," "satisfaction," "imputed righteousness," and "penalty of sin." Woodard did bring forth some powerful images when he focused on the resurrection: Christ "destroyed him that had the power of death, that is the devil,"[16] and again: "Christ vanquished all the hosts of darkness, and bruised Satan utterly under His feet."[17] Here we see strong echoes of George Fox's Christus Victor language; it has only been in the twenty-first century

Introduction

that we have fully recognized the inconsistency between that language and the satisfaction/substitution views of the atonement.

Woodard expressed "the conviction that our early Friends were guided by the Holy Spirit, and that the principles which they enunciated were sound."[18] He lamented one exception to this generalization: William Penn's essay, *Sandy Foundation Shaken*, which he regarded as "seriously defective, and . . . very unfortunate . . . for the reputation" of the Quaker movement.[19] In that essay Penn strenuously rejected the doctrines of satisfaction and of imputed righteousness. Early Friends such as Fox and Barclay also rejected imputed righteousness; they did not use terms such as "substitution," "satisfaction," or the "penalty of sin." It seems clear that Woodard assumed most early Quaker leaders promoted a forensic theory of the atonement—an assumption that was seriously mistaken.

I find at least one other example of a Holiness leader being mistaken in believing that their own views agreed with those of the first Friends. Updegraff attacked traditional Quaker Quietism by appealing to the preaching and practice of the earliest Friends. He insisted that "Fox . . . and his compeers . . . had come to an experimental knowledge of Christ enlightening and saving . . . souls. . . . They were witnesses unto a personal Christ."[20] I have found no evidence that Fox and Burrough showed any interest in "soul saving," in individuals going to heaven or hell after death, or even in a "personal Christ."

A milepost in the rise of the modernist movement in Quakerism was a conference, authorized by London Yearly Meeting, which met in Manchester, England, in 1895. A number of young modernist Friends were among those who presented papers they had written. For the first time, some felt that their questioning of the prevailing evangelicalism among British Friends was recognized as a legitimate alternative. They were inspired in their thinking by the emerging biblical criticism and rejection of biblical infallibility, and were repelled by such evangelical doctrines as the substitutionary theory of the atonement. Other views held by many modernist Friends include the innate goodness of human nature, the inevitability of progress, and the "social gospel"—the belief that the message of Jesus and the biblical prophets centered on social justice and peace.

Even before the Manchester Conference, a few Friends had already published modernist ideas—in particular, Rufus M. Jones in America and Caroline Stephen and J. Rendel Harris in England. Rufus Jones, as a student at the Friends School in Providence, Rhode Island, learned from his science teacher that the creation account in Genesis was not literally true science, but a great poetic story. Caroline Stephen rejected the idea that the Bible is literally infallible. J. Rendel Harris also rejected the infallibility of the words of scripture and wholeheartedly supported historical and literary criticism of the Bible.

In his study of the writings of Ralph Waldo Emerson while at Haverford, Jones learned from Emerson that George Fox was a mystic and as such was in a great company of the world's outstanding spiritual leaders. Jones was becoming conscious that mysticism lay at the heart of Quaker religion. Even though this discovery came to him in the 1880s, he did not publish these views until he became editor and publisher of the Gurneyite *Friends Review* in 1893–94. In 1890 Stephen published her conviction that the early Friends were mystics, and that mysticism was central to Quakerism. She did not state where or how she came to this conclusion, but did not leave the impression that she was introducing a radically new idea.

In 1884–85 Jones was a senior at Haverford College, where Harris had recently joined the faculty. During that year the two men began a deep and flourishing friendship that was to have significant impact on the emerging Quaker modernist movement.

Stephen was convinced that one of the strengths of the early Quaker movement was their vigorous rejection of substitutionary atonement.

From the time of the Manchester Conference, John Wilhelm Rowntree was the accepted leader of the modernist Friends in Great Britain. In the summer of 1897, Jones had been visiting Friends in England. From there he and Harris went to Switzerland on a walking trip, planning to meet a party of Friends, including members of the Rowntree family. On a rainy Sunday, Jones and Rowntree spent hours talking together: "Here began our immortal friendship. . . . Monday we climbed the Schilthorn—a ten thousand foot peak—and all the time we talked and talked of our future joint work for the Society of Friends,"[21] which would include a major project of writing the history of Quakerism and its mystical and spiritual predecessors.

In 1902 a new educational institution, devoted to critical biblical studies and the special views of Friends, was founded at Woodbrooke, just south of Birmingham. Harris became the first director of studies at Woodbrooke.

Rowntree died in 1905. Jones met with a small group of English

Introduction

Friends and worked out a new plan for the writing project. William Charles Braithwaite wrote two volumes on seventeenth-century Quakerism, and Jones wrote (one volume included some co-authors) the history of the later centuries. The outcome was the massive seven-volume Rowntree series, with the final volumes published in 1921.

Rowntree was enthusiastic about potential gains from biblical criticism. He hinted that biblical criticism would lead to the discovery of fresh new ways of understanding and interpreting Quaker heritage. Edward Grubb argued that higher criticism enables us to establish the actual facts, so that the Spirit can then reveal the meaning of the facts. He understood that biblical revelation was a process of progressive revelation. Elbert Russell began with the accepted results of historical and literary criticism of the Bible.

Rowntree clearly rejected the forensic basis of the satisfaction and substitutionary theories of the atonement. He found in the parable of the prodigal son the basis for the moral theory of the atonement. Jones's views on the atonement did not neatly match any of Gustaf Aulén's types. Theologian Gregory Love has modified this typology by proposing a variety of atonement models. Jones's emphasis on mystical experience fit easily into Love's "enlightenment model" of salvation. Grubb saw in the resurrection the assurance that victory was really won. Grubb disapproved of the substitutionary and ransom theories. He looked especially favorably on a version of the moral influence theory formulated by nineteenth-century American Horace Bushnell. Russell did see signs of Christ's victory and the covenant community. More clearly, he subscribed to the subjective, moral influence view of the atonement.

For Caroline Stephen the Quaker rejection of creeds rested on the conviction that verbal statements of faith are "mere opinion." Grubb, as a Friend, saw no necessity for creeds, because salvation does not depend on theology.

Since the late nineteenth century, a surprising number of Friends—especially considering what a tiny fraction of the Christian church consists of Friends—have become solid and influential biblical scholars, making significant contributions to the field of biblical scholarship. In the late nineteenth century, many scholars believed that the Gospels and other biblical writings had not been written until the second century. Studies by J. Rendel Harris were among the important contributions to the present-day consensus that the Gospels and Acts were indeed written in the first century.

Harris also proposed that one of the earliest written sources for the Gospels was a small "book of testimonies," quotations from the Old Testament collected as proofs that Jesus was the Messiah. At the time, this hypothesis was not widely accepted among New Testament scholars. When the Dead Sea Scrolls were discovered in the 1940s and later, they included collections of Old Testament quotations used to prove the Essenes' claims for their own leaders—which lent high support to Harris's idea that the early Christians had followed a similar method themselves!

In his 1927 work, *The Making of Luke-Acts*, Henry J. Cadbury was the first New Testament scholar to analyze the gospel of Luke and the book of Acts as a unified two-volume work. As late as the 1980s, most Old Testament scholars believed that the sufferings of the Jews in the Babylonian exile were not deep enough to be characterized as slavery. Daniel Smith-Christopher provided strong evidence to prove that conditions in Babylon and even under the later Persian rule were severe enough that they indeed amounted to slavery.

Three Friends served actively on committees responsible for two major twentieth-century translations of the Bible. Cadbury was a valued member of the committee that produced the Revised Standard Version of the New Testament. H. G. Wood was the representative of the Society of Friends on the committee that oversaw the translation of the New English Bible. He served from 1947 until he was incapacitated in 1959 by his last illness. Friends then appointed George H. Boobyer as his successor; Boobyer served until the New Testament portion of the New English Bible was published in 1961.

Wood advocated a "prophetic interpretation of history," based on the teaching of the New Testament and the facts of history. During and after World War I, he and Cadbury warned against a spirit of blind revenge and a self-righteous goodness that led to the harshness of the Versailles treaty toward the defeated enemy. Cadbury and Wood were exercising the gift of true prophecy in foreseeing the terrible consequences that followed this vindictive spirit: "They sow the wind, and they shall reap the whirlwind" (Hosea 8:7).

Decades later, Howard Macy plumbed other depths of biblical understanding. Building on his mentor's discovery of the humor of Christ, which had been expressed in pedestrian, sobersides language, Macy explored humor throughout the Bible with a light and delightfully funny approach that was far more appropriate to the subject-matter—let the medium match the message!

Several Quaker Bible scholars have examined evidence relevant to theories or views of the atonement. Elbert Russell, in *The Message of the Fourth Gospel*, argued that the gospel of John provides no basis for a forensic—satisfaction or substitutionary—theory of the atonement. In *The Making of Luke-Acts*, Cadbury implied that, at the very least, Acts and the gospel of Luke offered no basis for satisfaction and substitutionary atonement theories. In *Belief and Unbelief Since 1850*, Wood wrote: "The idea of appeasing God's anger had no place in the New Testament. . . . The time is ripe for a reformulation of the nature of the atonement in the light of our present-day scholarship."[22] In his 1920 Swarthmore Lecture, Wood had already recognized a sinful connection between satisfaction doctrines of the atonement and the insistence by most Christians on punitive justice in human society. In his entry, "Paul the Apostle," in *The Interpreter's Dictionary of the Bible*, Alexander Purdy supplied evidence to suggest that the ancient ransom theory and the modern Christus Victor and perhaps covenant (the new humanity) theories can find support in Paul's writings; on the other hand, Purdy saw little in Paul's thinking to support the forensic (satisfaction and substitutionary) theories or the moral influence theory of the atonement.

Two scholars have pioneered in showing how their Quaker heritage and faith can lead to creative innovation in biblical studies. Purdy, in his *Interpreter's Bible* study of the letter to the Hebrews, looked carefully at the potentially off-putting emphasis on the importance of priests and sacrifices. He showed that, in actuality, the point of that language was to show that there is no need for priest or sacrifice within Christianity, because Christ was the "priest to end all priests" who made the "sacrifice to end all sacrifices." In this, he was harking back to early Friends like George Fox, for whom Hebrews was a favorite letter, showing that "Christ's sacrifice ends all other sacrifices."[23]

The early "peace churches"—Anabaptists, Quakers, Church of the Brethren—were the first to systematically challenge the marriage of Christendom and the political establishment. Daniel Smith-Christopher took seriously the claim by Mennonite scholars that Christian thought had made this fateful turn when the Roman emperor Constantine co-opted the Christian church in the fourth century. For Smith-Christopher, this challenge found biblical rootage in Micah's critique of the kingdom's sponsorship of the Hebrew religion—a critique that was followed up and expanded when the experience of exile led Jewish writers to take seriously the possibility of a viable faith community not tied to the power of the monarchy.

Smith-Christopher carried this analysis a Quaker-like step further in his essay in the *Festschrift* for Arthur O. Roberts, where he claimed that Ezra and Nehemiah, realistically assessing this situation, advocated neither violent revolt nor passive submission, but rather "a faithful non-violent resistance to any idea that Persian power or authority is greater than God's spiritual armament of the faithful."[24] In his commentary on the book of Daniel in *The New Interpreter's Bible*, Smith-Christopher argued effectively that the book of Daniel was written in condemnation of the strategy of violent revolt followed by the Maccabees in the second century BCE. According to Smith-Christopher, the author of the book of Daniel was urging non-violent resistance and civil disobedience in response to tyranny and oppression. The book was indeed a call to fight the Lamb's War!

As we go through this rapid summary of this volume, we may well wonder why the story matters. This account of Quaker religious thinking, particularly in the nineteenth and early twentieth centuries, paints a picture of a long, rocky, even muddy road, interrupted by a few points of high achievement. What, if anything, does this all mean?

This is not the first time that the story has been told. We can read *The Faith and Practice of the Quakers* by Rufus Jones, *The Rich Heritage of Quakerism* by Walter Williams, *Portrait in Grey* by John Punshon, and *Holiness: The Soul of Quakerism* by Carole Spencer. Each author highlights certain events and personalities; each author has his or her unique interpretation of what has taken place. As we read these side by side, we recognize that each interpretive approach adds to our understanding and appreciation of this history.

What I offer, then, is yet another approach, another interpretation of the history of Quaker thinking. More specifically, we note the dismal story of a series of separations and divisions since 1827. As I write this, we are going through one more set of divisions in one yearly meeting after another. For those going through the trauma, it may seem that the issues are new and unique. What I have found is that many of the underlying issues have been similar from one generation to the next—if anything, becoming more intense and intractable. It may be too late to prevent the new splits from becoming final, but we may at least here gain some perspective on what is happening among us today.

Introduction

The story of these Quaker Bible scholars may add a dimension of hope. It shows that somehow, through everything—even though some Friends today may give little credence to the Bible—underlying our history there has been a deep understanding and appreciation of the importance of the Bible. Just as Quakerism has produced a disproportionate number of scientists and innovators in business and industry, so it has also produced a disproportionate number of outstanding Bible scholars. This is a current that can nourish the vitality of Quakerism on into the future, even through all the rocks and bumps of our story.

My first volume, *Face to Face*, and the first chapter of this volume suggest some of the deep resources on which we can draw. This volume is in a sense a transitional volume carrying the story forward, while in the third volume I suggest ways we might move into the future.

1
Friends and God: The Great Deviations

Joseph John Gurney's first wife died in 1822. During that decade he had reached the height of his spiritual and intellectual power. He wrote what may well be the two most important of his many publications. *Observations on the Religious Peculiarities of the Society of Friends* was published in 1824. *Essays on the Evidences, Doctrines, and Practical Operation of Christianity* was published in 1825. Even though these books were written and published at a time when the controversy in America over the ministry of Elias Hicks was seething, I have found no evidence that these books were written in response to that crisis.

Ten editions of *Observations* were printed in Great Britain and America. Gurney added significant new material to the seventh edition in 1834; for that edition he also changed its title to *Observations on the Distinguishing Views and Practices of the Society of Friends*. The seventh edition was reprinted in 1979 with an introduction by Donald Green and a new title: *A Peculiar People: The Rediscovery of Primitive Christianity*.

> Like his direct ancestor, Robert Barclay, Joseph John Gurney presented his thought in a clearly organized manner. . . . Thus it is relatively easy to pin down and draw out the basic directions of his thought.
>
> Gurney's very organization of his thought into two areas—the area common to all Christians (including Quakers), and the area peculiar to Quakerism—is instructive.[1]

Early Friends generally emphasized the uniqueness of the Quaker vision of the Christian faith and directed sharp polemics against alternative understandings of Christianity. Only in a few writings, such as George Fox's epistle to the governor of Barbados, did they spell out the beliefs that they held in common with other Christian groups. Quietist Friends also asserted the peculiarities of Quaker beliefs and practices, to the point of insisting on completely isolating themselves from other Christian churches and from society at large. Gurney broke from this approach; he worked closely with many non-Quaker Christians. In his writings he spelled out a large number of basic beliefs that he was convinced Friends shared with all other Christians.

In the preface to his volume on Christianity as a whole, he clearly stated his intentions in that work:

> Throughout the present volume, I have endeavoured to avoid the discussion of any of those points in religion, which can with any reason be regarded as *peculiar* or *sectarian*. I have considered it to be, on the present occasion, my sole duty to arrange and unfold the testimonies borne in Scripture, to those *primary religious principles* which the generality of the Christian world unite, not merely in believing to be true, but in regarding as of *essential* importance to their present and everlasting welfare.[2]

It is remarkable that Gurney was able to devote over five hundred pages to an exposition of beliefs he believed to be *essential* to the Christian faith and on which he believed Christians generally united. In this very emphasis he went far beyond anything ever attempted by early Friends.[3]

How well would the views of early Friends have fit into the extensive set of essential Christian principles that Gurney developed in this volume? I found that early Friends would have agreed with many of these doctrines and ethical principles.

But I found a few very important points on which early Friends would not have fit into Gurney's consensus on Christian essentials. A basic point is the purpose of God's revelation to humans. Gurney wrote: "The principal object of the revelations acknowledged by Christians, was to unfold certain doctrines, and to promulgate certain moral principles."[4]

Gurney's emphasis on revelation as unfolding doctrines and promulgating moral principles is in sharp contrast with Robert Barclay's understanding of the intent of divine revelation: "The height of all happiness is placed in the true knowledge of God."[5] "Inward and immediate revelation is the only sure and certain way to attain the true and saving knowledge of God."[6] In short, for Barclay the point of divine revelation is that we may know God.[7]

I also find in George Fox's *Works* a number of passages that point strongly in the direction Barclay has summed up:

> That which brings to know God, is the revelation of the spirit of God.[8]
>
> It is clear the Son must reveal himself and his Father to people, if they know them, and they are not known but by revelation.[9]
>
> And none know the gospel, but who know immediate revelation; for the gospel is the power of God unto salvation.[10]
>
> You all with the Light may see the one faith, which Christ is the author and the finisher of. Then you may all see the end of your faith, the salvation of your souls with that which gives you victory over the world. . . .
>
> They that come to believe in the Light, hear the Voice of the Son of God . . . and live over death, the grave and hell, and so come to Life.[11]

I find it safe to affirm that for Fox, as for Barclay, "the point of revelation (whether through Scripture, through the history of God's action, or through immediate experience) is, indeed, that we may *know God*."[12]

Late in the eighteenth century, Job Scott affirmed the same principle:

> If it is necessary we should know God and our duty, which will not be questioned, it is certainly attainable: if it is not attainable by all the searchings, conceivings and reasonings of mere natural wisdom and learning, as it is not, then some other help is necessary; and if necessary, it is certainly afforded, and that through

God's shining in our hearts to give us this necessary knowledge. Here is a ground of certainty; without this we may read, contend, dispute and reason all our days and never know God, or ourselves.[13]

In contrast to Barclay, Fox, and Scott, "For Gurney, the point of divine revelation is that we may *know about God*. The difference is, if I may use Gurney's own term, essential! And there is at least one significant consequence of this difference."[14] George Fox himself strongly suggested this consequence:

And none know salvation, but by the immediate teaching and revelation of Christ Jesus the son of God, the salvation. And if men have all the scriptures given forth from God, they themselves are not able to make men wise unto salvation without faith, . . . and so they are not able of themselves "to guide men to salvation." Neither are they a rule of faith, but Christ is the author of faith, and the spirit the rule that gave them forth.[15]

If the words of scripture cannot be a rule of faith, what about the words of a creed?

In the earliest decades, individual Friends and groups of Friends did write statements of faith. These included Edward Burrough's *Declaration to All the World of Our Faith* in 1657, George Fox's 1671 letter to the governor of Barbados, and *The Christian Doctrine and Society of the People Called Quakers*, published in 1693 by George Whitehead and several other Friends. But, as Arthur Mekeel insisted,

They did not consider their declarations in the light of official creeds as the other Christian groups of their day did, but merely as testimonies of certain fundamental aspects of their faith. . . .

These early declarations . . . were issued in defence of the Society and thus often stressed controverted points, giving a distorted and incomplete view of Quaker belief.[16]

Members of the Society of Friends were not required to subscribe to any of these statements. When Friends were disowned, it was because of the danger that their behavior would reflect badly on the good name of the church. Serious controversies that threatened the unity of the Society were about matters of Christian practice, such as the establishment of women's meetings for business, or whether all Friends present must take off their hats when one member vocally addressed the Lord in prayer. Leaders such as George Fox, William Penn, and Robert Barclay differed in their statements of Christian belief and their ways of interpreting the Bible; but they continued to be very close friends, traveled together harmoniously in the ministry, and strongly supported each other when controversies arose within the Quaker body.

George Fox had something to say about creeds. When an opponent wrote, "The whole word of God in general is summed up in the apostles' creed," Fox replied, "Where hast thou got the word creed, but out of the mass-book, and pope's canon-book? not out of the apostles' epistles."[17] A page later, he made his point more inclusive: "The scripture doth not teach us those words, as sacrament and creed, but the old mass-book."[18]

Fox rejected not only creeds, but also certain words and phrases in the creeds of the churches—such as trinity, God in three persons, and the human nature of Christ—because they were not in the Bible:

> As for the word trinity, and three persons, we have not read it in the Bible, but in the common-prayer-book, or mass-book, which the pope was the author of.[19]

> Where doth the scripture speak of human? . . . We do not deny that Christ, according to the flesh, was of Abraham, but deny the word human. Christ's nature is not human, which is earthly, for that is the first Adam.[20]

But we have a problem. Fox was egregiously inconsistent in following the principle of rejecting everything in the creeds that could not be found in scripture:

> So are not people to hear this Comforter, this Holy Ghost, that proceeds from the Father and the Son?[21]

> And this spirit of truth doth all the true christians witness which proceeds from the Father and the Son; and this spirit of truth leads us out of all error into all truth, all such as are led, and guided, and taught by it, up to God from whence it comes.[22]

Fox asserted more than twenty times in his eight-volume *Works* that the Holy Spirit proceeds from the Father and the Son—not only in controversial works but also in his epistles to Friends—from an early 1656 epistle: "Everyone with the Light . . . shall see Christ and shall see the Father through the Spirit that proceeds from the Father and the Son."[23]—to a late 1685 epistle: "Pray in the holy ghost, which proceeds from the Father and the Son."[24]

The phrase "and the Son" is a translation of the Latin word *filioque*, which the Western, Roman Church added to the Nicene Creed in CE 589. The Eastern Orthodox Church never agreed to the addition of this word. In John 15:26 (KJV) we read of "the Comforter, . . . the Spirit of truth, which proceedeth from the Father," but the Bible says nowhere that the Holy Spirit proceeds from the Son or from Christ.

Why did Fox affirm some nonbiblical terms from the ancient creeds and reject others, as well as the word "creed" itself? I searched more deeply to tease out hints as to why George Fox and the first Friends found it inappropriate to summarize their knowledge of God by way of a creed.

Beginning with this quotation, which I have already noted, "None know the gospel, but who know immediate revelation; for the gospel is the power of God unto salvation,"[25] I have been searching through Fox's epistles for further clues he may have given to the faithful about the connection between knowing God and the power of God. In 1656 he wrote to Edward Burrough and Francis Howgill:

> In the Power of the Lord Jesus Christ preach the everlasting Gospel, that by his Power the sick may be healed, the leprous cleansed, the dead raised, the blind eyes opened and the devils cast out. . . . Speak, to bring up all into the head Christ and into the Life, which gave forth the Scriptures.[26]

In a 1664 epistle to all Friends, George Fox told how the power of God was made known up to their own day through a succession of historical events:

> Look upon the valiant prisoners [who] stood with the Lord and for the Lord and followed and obeyed his movings, motions and commands. With the victory they had, how they triumphed over that which was against the Lord. By faith Abraham forsook his country, his father's house and his national worship. . . . By the Faith, Power and Wisdom of God did Moses go down and speak to Pharaoh, the king of Egypt. And through the Power, hand and arm of God he led them out of Egypt. . . .
>
> Whilst they stood in the Power of God, what victories they had over their enemies! As instance, Samson, David and Saul. . . .

> And also remember how the Prophets were imprisoned, put into dungeons and stocks, etc; particular[ly] Jeremiah, and how they were mocked, scoffed at and reproached, for declaring against the sins and wickedness of the times. . . . And yet, by the Power of God they were carried through and over all. . . .
>
> Look upon the Apostles and consider how they suffered . . . [who] bore testimony to the Substance. . . .
>
> Come to see the Power and be in it, . . . Which Power gives them dominion over them all, and to see to the very Apostle's days, what they were in. . . .
>
> But now the Bride is coming up out of the wilderness, the Prophet is arisen and arising and the everlasting Gospel shall be and is preached again to all nations, kindreds, tongues and peoples . . . that dwell upon the earth. . . .
>
> True prophets and true witnesses are rising and risen. Sing, triumph and rejoice! . . .
>
> So the measuring line of Righteousness is in this known. Also, the state now wherein the Lamb and the saints shall have the victory.[27]

In a 1655 epistle to "all Friends everywhere," Fox had already summed up:

> As you are moved of the Lord God, . . . that reaches to that of God in others and is effectual. Nor none stop writing or speaking, when you are moved with the Spirit of the Lord God. . . .
>
> And the Gospel you shall be shod with. Standing and dwelling in the Power of God, there the shield of faith you will receive, that gives victory over the world with which you have all access to God, which mystery of faith is held in pure conscience. So, in the Power of God . . . live in the Lamb's authority, in the Lamb's dominion and victory through him over all the world . . . to answer that of God in all consciences. . . .
>
> And all Friends, in the Life and Power that stands in God, dwell that you may have unity with God and one with another.[28]

For Fox, Friends' unity came through dwelling in the power of God, the power that was demonstrated in the series of historical events from Abraham to Moses to the prophets to the apostles to the Friends themselves. I believe he was striving to express a truth that was phrased, perhaps more clearly for us today, by twentieth-century biblical theologian G. Ernest Wright. Wright, a Presbyterian, expressed "great respect" for his own communion's Westminster Confession of Faith. Nevertheless, he insisted:

> A tension will always exist between the Bible and our attempts to communicate its faith in rational language at a given historical period. The faith is greater than our attempts to express it and deeper than any one individual can conceive in his historical finitude. Furthermore, the creeds of the Church . . . are not in themselves a substitute for the Bible. They are not sacrosanct in the sense that they bear the same authority as the Bible itself. The faith of the Church must constantly be reformed and illumined on the basis of fresh study of the Bible. . . .
>
> The suspicion still remains that the systematic presentation of abstract dogma cannot and should not be the primary teaching method of the Church. In part this is because propositional dogmatics lacks the colour, the flexibility, the movement of the Bible and because it attempts to freeze into definite, prosaic, rationality that which was never intended by the Bible so to be frozen and which by its very nature cannot be so construed.[29]

Wright quoted a definition of God from the Westminster Confession, and then went on:

> By its very cold, abstract, and tight nature such a definition of God somehow separates us from his living, active and warm Presence which we come to know by contemplation of what he has done and by seeing ourselves as the recipients of his gracious work. What is here said may all be true and very important, and yet it does not quite introduce us to the Biblical God. . . . Is this accidental, or does our dull abstractness betray our separation from Biblical faith, in which the nature of God is taught us by the narration of what he has done? Is there not always the danger of focusing attention by abstraction upon the being of God in and for himself and thus separating ourselves from the Bible with its serious attention to history in which God alone is known? If so, then the Church's theology must always beware of the scholastic tendency to become unhistorical.[30]

What George Fox and G. Ernest Wright recognized was that our knowledge of God comes through historical events. It is best expressed in narrative form. But creeds are attempts to abstract this knowledge from history and to express it in timeless, rational propositions. Creeds are dead; God's revelation is alive and dynamic. Creeds are cold and frozen; God's revelation is warm and personal.

"For Fox, . . . perhaps even more than for Barclay, the point of revelation (whether through scripture, through the history of God's action, or through immediate experience) is, indeed, that we may *know God*."[31] Joseph John Gurney took it as his starting point that the purpose of revelation (through scripture) is to provide us with doctrines and moral principles. In summary,

> For Gurney, the point of divine revelation is that we may *know about God*. And there is at least one significant consequence of this difference. If the main point is personal, saving knowledge *of* God, then all cognitive statements of faith (creeds, in short) must remain provisional and can never be regarded as binding, or—essential. If the main point, on the other hand, is knowledge *about* God, then the more cognitive information, the better. It is hardly surprising, then, that Gurney himself could insist on 500+ pages of essential Christian belief.[32]

By the 1820s, Friends had forgotten their original insight that revelation comes through God's action in history—through historical events, portrayed in narratives that can best be understood if they are read with empathy. The only options seemed to be that revelation comes through the written words of scripture, or through immediate, individual religious experience, or through the mind's rational activity. The outcomes may have been unavoidable.

As soon as the separations of 1827 and 1828 occurred:

> All orthodox-minded bodies hastened to issue declarations of their position. These delineated those elements of Christian doctrine which they considered fundamental. . . . If any member voiced beliefs considered contrary to fundamental doctrine, he was immediately labored with and, if persistent in his ideas, was disowned.[33]

This was not sufficient for Orthodox Friends; their yearly meetings appointed representatives

> who met in Philadelphia in August, 1829, and prepared an

inclusive declaration of faith. This document . . . consists to a great extent of quotations from, and references to, the scriptures and the works of early Friends. . . .

Within a short time after its publication it was approved and accepted by the Yearly Meetings of Ohio, Baltimore, North Carolina, Philadelphia, New York, Virginia, and New England.[34]

The Hicksite attitude can be summarized in Elias Hicks' dictum, "We cannot believe what we do not understand,"[35] and in the claim made at the January 1823 meeting of Philadelphia's Meeting for Sufferings, for "the right of private judgement"[36] in regard to religious beliefs. In the Hicksite yearly meetings since the Great Separation,

No declarations of faith are formulated, and those drawn up by the various Orthodox bodies are viewed somewhat askance as being contrary to the traditions of Friends. The liberal tone of the "Hicksite" groups discouraged any attempt to circumscribe freedom of thought on religious matters.[37]

Through the nineteenth century, Orthodox yearly meetings and, after the second round of separations, the Gurneyite yearly meetings in particular continued to adopt increasingly formal and elaborate statements of faith. The final dead end of the Gurneyite deviation from the original Quaker understanding of revelation and creeds was the Richmond Declaration of Faith. This fourteen-page document was written in 1887 at a conference of representatives from the Gurneyite yearly meetings. It was adopted by nearly all of the Gurneyite yearly meetings.

Hicksite Friends continued to believe that revelation must be consistent with reason, and eventually with science. Their increasing insistence, that *what* individual Friends believe is not essential, finally became for many a conviction that it is not essential *that* individual Friends believe—even in God. The final dead end of the Hicksite deviation from the original Quaker understanding of creeds and revelation can be seen in the person of Arthur Morgan (1878–1975), civil engineer, first chairman of the Tennessee Valley Authority, innovative president of Antioch College, and influential Hicksite Friend. Morgan can fairly be called an atheist—or at least a nontheist; he told his monthly meeting on his ninetieth birthday, "I have not seen evidence which has led me to know of any order of existence beyond that of matter-energy. . . . The idea he [the believer in God] holds has not been revealed to me, though I have endeavored to search honestly."[38]

"Another point, on which Gurney's 'Christian consensus on essentials' would have excluded early Friends, is his view of the nature of Christ's atonement."[39] For my understanding of what is going on here, I have been greatly helped by a typology developed by Gustaf Aulén. Aulén was a twentieth-century Swedish Lutheran bishop and theologian. He proposed that there have been three types of ideas (or theories) of Christ's atonement.

> Aulén calls one type the Latin type. This type of atonement theory was first fully developed by St. Anselm of Canterbury (ca. A.D. 1033–1109) and has been popular in Protestant orthodox thought, from John Calvin on. Basic aspects of this type of theory are that sin requires a heavy penalty, and that satisfaction must be made for sin.[40]

This satisfaction could only be made by a human being; and so Christ, both fully God and fully human, endured the punishment for our sin and provided the needed satisfaction on our behalf. Our sins were imputed, or transferred, to Christ, and so Christ's righteousness is imputed to us.

> The second type, according to Aulén, is the "subjective" type, including various "moral influence" theories of the atonement. This type of theory was first developed, in opposition to Anselm, by Peter Abelard (A.D. 1079–1142). It has become popular among "liberal" Protestant thinkers in the nineteenth and twentieth centuries. The emphasis in these theories is on the subjective impact of Christ's work on the hearts and behavior of men and women.[41]

Aulén argued that there is a third type, which he called the "classic" idea of the atonement. Early church Fathers often described Christ's death as a ransom paid to the devil. Sometimes they even used the image of Christ as the bait that deceived the devil into being caught on a fishhook and into being taken captive by God. The basic idea is that God, through Christ, delivers humankind from captivity to the devil, and so gains the victory over death and the forces of evil:

> This type of view may be described . . . as the "dramatic." Its central theme is the idea of the Atonement as a Divine conflict and victory; Christ—Christus Victor—fights against and triumphs over the evil powers of the world, the "tyrants" under which mankind is in bondage and suffering, and in Him God reconciles the world to Himself.[42]

In the light of this typology, I look at the views of Joseph John Gurney. He argued in great detail for his understanding of the atonement:

> The incarnation, humiliation, sufferings, and propitiatory sacrifice, of Christ, were ordained by the Father himself as *the means* through which, in his own infinite knowledge and wisdom, he saw fit to provide for the satisfaction of his justice; and at the same time for the pardon and restoration of a lost and sinful race of his creatures.[43]

> This inherent righteousness or holiness is inscribed for our instruction, . . . on the doctrine of the propitiatory sacrifice of Jesus Christ; not only because while the sinner was forgiven the penalty of sin was exacted, but because the burthen of that penalty was borne by no less a person than the SON OF GOD.[44]

> *Our* sinfulness may properly be said to have been *imputed* to Christ, because when he underwent the penalty which that sinfulness demanded, he was dealt with as if he had been himself the sinner; and it is, I apprehend, on a perfectly analogous principle that *his* righteousness is said to be imputed to us; because, through the boundless mercy of God, *we* are permitted to reap the fruits of it.[45]

We can hardly have a clearer summary of the Latin type of theory. "Given the premises of his book, Gurney is clearly arguing that the Latin, 'satisfaction' theory of the atonement is *essential* to the Christian faith and to salvation, and that any other views are therefore outside the pale."[46]

What about seventeenth-century Friends? Do they fit into the consensus on which Gurney insisted? In a recent article on the atonement, I reviewed evidence from the writings of early Friends, and critically examined the interpretations of contemporary scholars. My conclusion was: "Without doubt, George Fox, Robert Barclay, and William Penn rejected the satisfaction and substitutionary theories of the atonement. . . . George Fox's views were strongly consistent with a Christus Victor view of the atonement."[47] These early Friends simply did not fit into Gurney's consensus on the essential Christian beliefs, in regard to the atonement. "How could this be? We may guess that Gurney simply assumed that Fox and Barclay held to the satisfaction theory, without carefully examining their views on this issue."[48]

In my atonement article I found that contemporary scholars such as

Timothy Gorringe, in *God's Just Vengeance*, and Gregory Anderson Love, in *Love, Violence, and the Cross*, have strongly reinforced Fox's, Barclay's, and Penn's—and my own—rejection of satisfaction and substitutionary (or "forensic") theories of the atonement. I also proposed the outline of a contemporary Quaker theory of the atonement. I began this outline with an affirmation of two twenty-first century theories: J. Denny Weaver's "narrative Christus Victor," in *The Nonviolent Atonement*, and R. Larry Shelton's covenant theory, in *Cross and Covenant*:

> Denny Weaver's narrative Christus Victor theory adds a more extended narrative emphasis to the earlier classic views of the atonement and develops them into a more complete and consistent theory. I am convinced that Weaver's theory also coheres significantly with Shelton's view of the atonement as initiating and maintaining the covenant relationship. To read both of these views in the context of a biblical theology movement framework adds a strong systematic framework to this coherence. This framework brings in the understanding that the mighty acts of God are events in which God takes the initiative in forming the covenant with humans and establishing and upholding the covenant community. The victory over the forces of evil, which God gains (non-violently!) in his acts in history, results in the healing of all broken relationships and the creation of a new, loving community bond. This growing, healing bond is universal in its thrust. Its ultimate goal is *anakèphalaiôsasthai ta panta* (Eph. 1:10)— "to gather up all things in ... Christ" (NRSV), "bring everything together under Christ, as head" (NJB), "all ... might be brought into a unity in Christ" (NEB).[49]

I have found clear evidence that

> George Fox was committed to a Christus Victor way of viewing the work of Christ. In their writings about the Lamb's war, Fox, Edward Burrough, and James Nayler came up with a powerful and original extension of that view. Fox, William Penn, and Robert Barclay realised that at least one major part of the substitutionary theory of the atonement was incompatible with the Quaker understanding of Christian faith and life. At the very least, these seventeenth-century Friends—especially George Fox—strikingly foreshadowed the combination of narrative

Christus Victor theory with aspects of a covenant theory of the atonement, that I am . . . proposing in outline form.[50]

Recent developments in my own thinking about Christ's atonement have increased my appreciation of the ways in which some Friends in the past have dealt with this question. I have new understanding of what they have been getting at—particularly George Fox, Edward Burrough, and James Nayler in the seventeenth century, and John Comly in the early nineteenth century.

As I read the writings of eighteenth-century Quietist Friends, I ran across a few passages in which they reaffirmed some of George Fox's and Robert Barclay's thinking in regard to the atonement. Anthony Benezet used Christus Victor language in one of his letters:

> Human nature . . . has neither faculties, nor organs, to see into the deeply humbling mystery of Divine love; God becoming man, letting the whole power of hell spend its wrath upon him, and being finally made perfect through suffering, this being the means ordained by the wisdom of God, by which a deadly blow is struck to the very root and being of sin.[51]

Samuel Fothergill argued against imputed righteousness in a discourse that he spoke in Bristol, England, in 1767:

> CHRIST was more than a prophet. I repeat my belief, that he suffered, died, ascended, and is now come "the second time, without sin, to salvation," (*Heb. ix. 28.) in order to reconcile the world to himself. I know many are willing to admit that he died for all, as all were in a state of death; and that, by the imputation of his righteousness, all are justified in the sight of GOD. Whereas I think it more just to proceed in the language of the holy inspired apostle; that "they which live, should not henceforth live to themselves; but to him who died for them and rose again;" that there may be an effectual redemption, a thorough change; not the imputation of righteousness, without works; but a real substantial righteousness in the heart and life; which may operate upon and regulate the mind and will, and lead us to a conformity to his divine nature: not a righteousness imputed to us from what Christ did and suffered without us; but a righteousness raised by him within us, through our surrendering

ourselves to his government, and yielding entire submission to his heart-cleansing, refining power.[52]

Job Scott gave consideration to the atonement in his book, *The Knowledge of the Lord*, published in 1824:

> What bitterness and persecution, what bloodshed and butchery, as well as false doctrines and absurd opinions, has this ever ready, ever restless and active disposition, caused in the earth! Yea, doctrines which have induced, perhaps millions, to rest the eternal salvation of their immortal souls upon a mere broken reed, upon "imputed righteousness" without regeneration; or to set down at ease, upon some other foundation, equally imaginary, equally dangerous; covering themselves with a covering, and not of God's Holy Spirit.[53]
>
> The whole scope of salvation by Christ, is that of a real bruising of satan under us, destroying his power in us, binding the strong man, casting him out, utterly spoiling all his goods, granting us remission of sins that are past, preservation in righteousness and true holiness all the days of our lives, and union and communion with God, the fountain of all good, here and hereafter for ever.[54]

In one passage, Scott even combined Barclay's anti-imputation argument with Fox's ideas about Christ's victory over the devil:

> What reconciliation does man stand in need of?—What has separated him from God?—Has any thing but sin?—Will God then be reconciled to him again *in* sin? No verily: that which doth let and separate, will for ever let and separate, till it be removed out of the way.
>
> It is removed, these imputarians may say, by Christ. I grant it is, where Christ destroys the works of the devil in the soul, and no where else.[55]

These eighteenth-century Friends did not pay much attention to theories about the atonement. When they did, they were satisfied to reassert Christus Victor themes from Fox and Barclay. I found no evidence that they showed any affirmative interest in satisfaction theories of the atonement.

What about Joseph John Gurney's contemporaries, John Comly and Elias Hicks? In one untitled essay or memorandum, Comly wrote an extended argument against the substitutionary theory of the atonement:

> Priestcraft has fabricated, in the darkness of selfish reasoning, a system of debt and credit between God and man. Priestcraft declares, on behalf of the God of mercy and love, that his justice must be satisfied for the debt contracted by our first parents in the garden, when they eat the forbidden fruit. Priestcraft says, our first parents, by their disobedience, contracted a debt to Divine Justice which must be paid. But the exaction of this debt was deferred in consequence of its being assumed to be paid by another at a future period. They say Jesus Christ became surety for the payment of this debt, and Divine Justice was satisfied by the crucifixion of Jesus as the surety and substitute for the sin of Adam and Eve. This, if true, is a flat contradiction of Ezekiel's doctrine, for it makes the soul of Jesus Christ bear the sin of Adam—the righteous life of Christ to die for the wickedness of man. It says, in fact, that the righteousness of the righteous is not upon himself, nor does the wickedness of the wicked rest upon himself.
>
> If Divine Justice keeps accounts of debt and credit with man on the dark principles which Priestcraft ascribes to the God of mercy and love, then it follows that when men sin they incur a debt, and this debt is thenceforward due to Divine Justice until it is paid, either by themselves or some one else on their behalf. This appears to be the kind of foundation on which the common notions of salvation by the death and atonement of Jesus Christ is founded. Man sinned and contracted the debt; Jesus Christ assumed the responsibility and payment thereof, and by his actual death upon the cross cancelled or balanced the account. Oh! shocking ignorance of the benignity, mercy, and love of the adorable Fountain of all goodness.[56]

Comly went on to clinch his argument by appealing to the teachings of Jesus:

> But, of all the parables and doctrines of the blessed Messiah, illustrating the Divine character as the God of mercy and love, and eminently confirming the exhibition of his equal and just dealings with mankind, as declared by Ezekiel the prophet, there is none more clear and emphatic than that of the father's

conduct toward the prodigal son. Here, if the notion of debt and credit, and the satisfaction for past sins before forgiveness had any foundation whatever, certainly Jesus would have adverted to it in some way. But no, not a word about atonement, or vicarious sacrifice, or paying off the old debt first. But mercy, love, pardon, free grace, flow forth toward the repentant, returning, humbled son, and shine forth conspicuously in their transcendant purity in the character of the benevolent Father. None of the transgressions of the penitent wanderer are mentioned to him, no allusion to original sin nor total depravity, but love, pure love, meets the returning prodigal with evidences of affection and acceptance. The best robe, the ring, the feast of the fatted calf, and all the demonstrations of joy and peace portray the attributes of the God of mercy, compassion, and love, with whom we have to do.[57]

Does Comly's comment that Jesus never used the word "atonement" imply that he completely opposed the idea of Christ's atonement? He would have been familiar with George Fox's practice of rejecting certain terms because they could not be found in the Bible. A good example would be the word "trinity." Fox rejected the word, but he affirmed most of the theological ideas about the relationships between Father, Son, and Holy Spirit that are implied in the use of that word. Similarly, John Comly's insistence on the mercy, compassion, and pure love of God is compatible with Larry Shelton's emphasis that "we see by God's sending of Christ that he is already merciful and gracious. Love is his nature. His covenant promises of love never change.... God does not need to be reconciled."[58] Or it fits well with the moral influence theories of the atonement, which include, according to Shelton, "Abelard's subjective emphasis of divine love" or "positive aspects of Christ's identification and sympathy with human suffering and sin."[59]

I can see that Comly would readily accept a moral influence theory or even a covenant theory of Christ's atonement. When Comly acclaimed God's essential nature as being love and mercy, he was echoing the assurances that George Fox repeatedly gave to Friends in his letters:

The God of power and love keep all Friends in power, in love, that there be . . . pure refreshing in the unlimited love of God.[60]

Dear Friends, whom deaths, bonds nor the outward creature can separate from the Love of God in Christ Jesus, live in Peace and Love with one another.[61]

> Friends, consider you that have known the mercies of the Lord God and of Jesus Christ.[62]
>
> My desire is, that all Friends may prize the Mercies of the Lord, and live in humility, in his Power that is over all.[63]

Fox had even tied God's love in with the victory that was won in Christ's atonement: "Live and walk in the Lamb which has the Victory. . . . In the Love of God all dwell. . . . And this Love will enable you to bear all things whatever wicked men can do unto you."[64]

One of the most severe complaints that Orthodox Friends leveled against Elias Hicks was that he denied Christ's atonement. This judgment was continued in the late nineteenth century by evangelical Friends. Even well into the twentieth century, evangelical Friend and historian Walter Williams complained of Hicks that "his teachings included no atonement for sin."[65]

We can indeed find quotations in letters that Hicks wrote that would make this accusation seem plausible:

> I readily acknowledge, I have not been able to see or understand, how the cruel persecution and crucifixion of Jesus Christ, by the wicked and hard-hearted Jews, should expiate my sins.[66]
>
> Much more might be produced to show the wickedness and absurdity of the doctrine, that would accuse the perfectly just, all-wise, and merciful Jehovah, of so barbarous and cruel an act, as that of slaying his innocent and righteous Son, to atone for the sins and iniquities of the ungodly.[67]

A quotation from another one of Hicks' letters should clarify that his real complaint was specifically against the substitutionary theory of Christ's atonement:

> I have faithfully and honestly borne testimony against those false and unscriptural, though generally acknowledged and applauded doctrines, of . . . the impossibility of God's pardoning sinners without a plenary satisfaction; and the justification of impure persons by an imputative righteousness.[68]

He made the same point, in regard to the "imputed righteousness" aspect of the substitutionary theory, in his *Journal*, where he emphasized "the danger that some of my fellow professors of the Christian name are exposed to by placing their chief dependence for justification and salvation on the imputative righteousness of Christ performed without them."[69]

The subjective or moral influence theories of Christ's atonement often emphasize the idea that Christ's life, mission, and death serve as a powerful moral example. This example encourages and strengthens us to live better lives. We can find evidence in the letters of Hicks that he held to this type of atonement theory:

> This is the true atonement, which the creature cannot effect for himself, only as he submits to the operation of the life and spirit of Christ, which will enable the willing and obedient to do it. And the outward atonement was a figure of it, which, with the outward example of Jesus Christ in his righteous works and pious death, gives strength to be faithful to make this necessary offering and sacrifice unto [God], by which his sins are blotted [out], and he again reconciled to his Maker.[70]

> By what means did Jesus suffer? . . . Did God send him into the world purposely to suffer death by the hands of wicked men? By no means; but to live a righteous and godly life, . . . and thereby be a perfect example to such of mankind as should come to the knowledge of him and of his perfect life.[71]

> He set an example to all his followers, that, in order to be saved, they must surrender themselves, as he had done, a willing offering to God. And we must suffer the fire of his divine word in us, to burn as an oven, . . . until all the chaff, and every thing in us and of us that the controversy of God is against, is burned up and consumed, and the soul made pure and clean, a fit receptacle for his holiness to dwell in; and even our natural lives must likewise be surrendered to his holy will. This comprehends the true atonement.[72]

Hicks followed up this last statement with a paragraph in which he argued that the effect of Christ's atonement was to initiate the new covenant:

> That the death of Christ . . . was an atonement, . . . I rested it principally on *the effects of his mission and death*. . . . The design of his mission . . . was purposely to put an end to that law and covenant, and to introduce a better: . . . an inward one, agreeably to the prophecy of Jeremiah.[73]

In another letter we find further evidence that he was moving toward a covenant theory of the atonement, in a statement that Christ became "qualified to enter upon his gospel mission, and usher in the new covenant, . . . being the son of God, with power according to the spirit of holiness."[74]

Early in his *Journal*, Hicks described the work of Christ in terms both of moral influence and of establishing the new covenant: "We have a better and higher example than David—the Lord Jesus Christ, who is the mediator of a better covenant." In referring to the "self-denying apostles" of Jesus, he added that "we are by them exhorted . . . to walk as we have them for example, and to follow them as they follow Christ."[75]

Without doubt, Hicks did believe in and affirm Christ's atonement. What he denied was the substitutionary theory. The problem was that many Orthodox and evangelical Friends believed that theory was the only valid understanding of the atonement.

Friends in the early nineteenth century had completely lost sight of the original Quaker understanding of the atonement. Even the Lamb's War was no longer part of their understanding of Quakerism or Christianity. Deviations from the original view were inevitable.

Leaders of the Orthodox faction held firmly and uncompromisingly to the substitutionary theory, which was completely at odds with the original Quaker view of the atonement. Hicksite leaders struggled to find a meaningful understanding of the atonement. Even in their deviations from the core of the original Quaker position, I can hear a few echoes of some of George Fox's insights.

2
Friends and the Bible: A Nineteenth-Century Sampler

Joseph John Gurney

In his book, now titled *A Peculiar People*, Joseph John Gurney explained the "religious peculiarities" or the "distinguishing views and practices" of the Society of Friends. There is a vast difference between his approach to these Quaker distinctives and the way in which the earliest Friends saw Quaker testimonies as being an integral part of their radically distinctive understanding of the Christian message. Fox, Burrough, and Fell read the Bible with empathy instead of using it as a handbook from which doctrines, rules, and precedents could be deduced. In contrast, for Gurney the central purpose of biblical revelation was to unfold doctrines and to set forth moral principles:

> The result is that he inevitably used the Bible as a handbook, always starting with biblical texts as cognitive information, and building up his doctrines upon this foundation. He therefore saw Christian faith as based on a substantial foundation (500+ pages worth!) of common doctrines shared by all Christians (including

Quakers), and the radically different behavior of Friends as a superstructure, based on a particular reading of selected biblical passages, but not absolutely essential to Christian faith or salvation.[1]

In spite of these basic differences in biblical interpretation, Gurney managed to find biblical explanations for nearly all of the ways in which Friends differed from other British Christians in their worship practices, style of life, and specific moral standards. In two areas of moral practice—oaths and war—he followed those Friends, from William Penn to Henry Tuke, who used the idea of dispensations to account for differences between the Old Testament and the New Testament. But Gurney had an interesting innovation in his understanding of the dispensations, which shows up clearly when I compare his thought with that of Henry Tuke.

For Tuke, the difference in the dispensations was primarily the time periods in which the successive dispensations represented God's will for his people. He did refer to "the most glorious dispensation of the gospel"[2] and affirm that the present dispensation is "much more excellent" than "the former dispensations of God to mankind."[3] But he did not explain in what ways the present dispensation is more glorious or excellent than the earlier ones. His emphasis was on the succession of time periods in which the dispensations held sway; he insisted that God's reasons for this succession or for the changes in God's moral law are completely beyond human understanding.

Gurney was readier to venture an explanation for the differences in the dispensations. In his discussion of oaths, he stated

> that the *moral law*—the law of practice—was less fully developed, and less properly understood, under the Mosaic, than it is under the Christian dispensation. In condescension to a state of comparative ignorance and weakness, many things were permitted, and even temporarily enjoined, which the full light of Christian truth has evinced to be now unlawful.[4]

In his consideration of war and peace, Gurney explained that the Old Testament prophets had looked forward "to the superior spirituality, and to the purer morality of that system of religion, of which the law, with all its accompaniments, was only the introduction." He concluded: "The objection of Friends to every description of military operation is founded principally, *on that complete revelation of the moral law of God which distinguishes the dispensation of the Gospel of Christ.*"[5] Gurney's emphasis was on a developmental difference, rather than a simple time difference, between the dispensations. He suggested that God's revelation had to unfold in developmental stages for a reason—a reason that was spelled out more fully by John Comly seven years after Gurney originally published these words. This reason was expressed briefly in Jesus' statement that the earlier laws were written "for the hardness of your heart" (Mark 10:5 KJV).

There was one major issue on which Gurney's attempt to explain Quaker practices, by using the Bible as a handbook for basic doctrines and moral principles, broke down. This issue was the ministry of women. In his chapter on that topic, Gurney cited several authorities, including John Locke, on the historical background and the interpretation of Paul's letters. And in fact Gurney followed Locke's interpretation fairly closely. On the matters disputed by eighteenth-century Friends Benjamin Coole and Josiah Martin, Gurney agreed with Martin in identifying prophecy with preaching, but he followed Coole in finding areas of ministry forbidden to women and in insisting on a hierarchy of gender in church government and authority. He did this by giving weight to the passage in 1 Timothy 2, which was largely passed over by those earlier authors. And, like Locke, he completely ignored Galatians 3:28:

> When the apostle Paul said, "I suffer not a woman to teach," he added *"nor to usurp authority over the man."* (1 Tim. ii, 12.) Had the women, in the church of Ephesus, after receiving this injunction, assumed the office of pastors; had they attempted that description of teaching, which was immediately connected with the government of the church; they would have been guilty of infringing the apostle's precept, and would have usurped an improper authority over their brethren: but, as long as their ministry was the result of the immediate influence of the Holy Spirit, and consisted in the orderly exercise of the prophetic gift, so long must they have been free from any imputation of that nature. Women who speak, in assemblies for worship, under such an influence, assume thereby no *personal authority* over others.[6]

In developing his biblical interpretation on this issue, Gurney drew on the writings of Oxford and Cambridge biblical scholars and of philosophers Hugo Grotius and John Locke, but he overlooked the possibility of seeing George Fox as a resource for interpreting the Bible. Gurney quoted 1 Timothy 2:12; Fox had placed this quotation in its fuller context:

> Let the woman learn in silence, with all subjection. But I suffer not a woman to teach, nor to usurp authority over the man, but to be in silence. For Adam was first formed, then Eve. And Adam was not deceived, but the woman being deceived was in the transgression (1 Timothy 2:11–14 KJV).

In his tract, "The Woman Learning in Silence," Fox opened with this passage, but then overwhelmed it with counter-examples of early Christian women who did preach and act as leaders in the church. In his *Journal*, in response to a Friend who opposed the setting up of women's meetings for business, he dealt more directly with the reasoning presented in the first letter to Timothy:

> Though the apostle said, "I permit not a woman to teach nor usurp authority over the man," as also saith the law (for Eve was first in transgression, and such teaching as Eve taught her husband, and usurped authority over the man, is forbidden); yet the apostle also says that daughters and handmaids should prophesy, which they did both in the time of the law and the Gospel; and man and woman were meet-helps (before they fell) and the image of God and righteousness and holiness; and so they are to be again in the restoration by Christ Jesus.[7]

The subjection of women to men was part of God's curse on humanity and nature, imposed because of the disobedience in the Garden of Eden (Genesis 3:16); connected to the curse was the flaming sword that prevented any return to the Garden (Genesis 3:24). Fox's claim was that "now was I come up in spirit through the flaming sword into the paradise of God. . . . I was come up to the state of Adam which he was in before he fell."[8] Friends were in "the restoration by Christ Jesus," where the curse was revoked, and women and men were restored to their original condition of equality and mutuality:[9]

> God was the first teacher, in Paradise. . . . The serpent was the second, and when man followed his teaching he came into misery, into the fall from the image of God, from righteousness and holiness, and from the power that they had over all that God had made, even the serpent. Christ Jesus was the third teacher; of whom God saith, "This is my beloved Son, in whom I am well pleased, hear ye him"; . . . he bruises the head of the serpent that is the false teacher. . . . So that man and woman come up again

to God and are renewed up into his image and righteousness and holiness by Christ, by which he comes up into the Paradise of God, as man was before he fell; and into a higher state than that, to sit down in Christ that never fell.[10]

Fox triumphantly summed up his argument in a 1677 "Epistle to be read in the Men and Women's Meetings":

> All your Men and Women's Meetings everywhere, keep in the Power of the Lord Jesus Christ in his Gospel . . . so that all the faithful men and women may in the Lord's Power be stirred up in their inheritances of the same Gospel, to labor in it, helps-meet in the Restoration, as Man and Woman was before the Fall in the Garden of God. . . .
>
> And now, you women, though you have been under reproach, because Eve was first in Transgression . . . here comes the reproach to be taken off from woman, which was first in transgression, who are not suffered to speak in the Church; but Mary did speak and believe that which was spoken to her. And also, the reproach and transgression [are] taken off men, that believe in the Seed, Christ Jesus, who bruises the head of the Serpent. . . . Christ destroys both him and his works and redeems man and woman up into the Image of God, as they were in before they fell. . . .
>
> All are now to labor in the Garden of God, that are in the Power and Image of God, being brought into it by Christ Jesus . . . so that Christ Jesus may be Head in all men and women, every man and woman may act from him their holy Head.[11]

Joseph John Gurney failed to see the Christus Victor theology and the empathetic reading of the Bible that shine through in these quotations from George Fox, and so he was stuck with only a partial appreciation of the full gospel freedom of women in their ministry.

We see how narrow a corner into which Gurney had painted himself when he let his interpretive method lead him to some very doubtful statements of historical fact. In his concluding essay on church government in the earliest church and in early Quakerism, he made this statement about the Christian church in the first century:

> Since *women* were not permitted to speak in the churches, except

under the immediate influence of the Spirit, and since they were forbidden to "usurp authority over the man," I conclude that no active part was assigned to them in public assemblies for the settlement of the affairs of the church.[12]

We can contrast this with a more recent historical statement: "In the early Christian communities . . . women were seen as equal to men and participated in every level of church activity."[13] Gurney, of course, did not have the benefit of the later work of historical criticism, which has established with high probability that the pastoral epistles (to Timothy and Titus) were not written until the second century CE, and so cannot be taken as evidence of first-century Christian practice.

When it came to early Friends, Gurney claimed:

> George Fox was led to recommend the setting up of *women's meetings*. . . . While it belonged to the brethren only to form rules for the government of the Society, and ultimately to carry them into effect, the women's meetings were established for the purpose of exercising a wholesome care over their own sex."[14]

His statement probably better described the actual situation among British Friends in the eighteenth and nineteenth centuries: "The London Women's Yearly Meeting only began in 1784. . . . In 1896 Men's Yearly Meeting decided that women should be able to serve on Meeting for Sufferings and that important decisions at Yearly Meeting should be considered jointly."[15]

The situation was somewhat better from the outset among Friends in the American colonies. Women's yearly meetings had been established in Baltimore in 1672 and in Philadelphia in 1681.[16] Even in England, in the seventeenth century at least such meetings as the Swarthmoor Women's Monthly and Quarterly Meetings, and the London women's meetings set up by Edward Burrough, exercised authority well beyond the scope claimed for them by Joseph John Gurney.[17]

Edward Hicks

Edward Hicks was born in Attleborough, Bucks County, Pennsylvania, in 1780. He noted in his *Memoirs*: "My parents were Isaac and Catharine Hicks, both regularly descended from Thomas Hicks, . . . as was also my late distinguished kinsman, Elias Hicks."[18] I calculate, from the genealogy in the appendix to Bliss Forbush's biography,[19] that Isaac and Catharine were second cousins to Elias Hicks. Catharine, a pious Episcopalian, died when Edward was still an infant. His father asked a Quaker couple, Elizabeth and David Twining, "to take his poor little son as a boarder."[20] They raised him as an adopted son. At the age of thirteen, he was apprenticed to a coach painter.

After a short period in the Army, he joined Friends in 1803. Later that year, he married a Friend, Sarah Worstall. They had at least one son and three daughters. "Edward Hicks tried farming and failed miserably. Burdened with debt, . . . he turned back to . . . making and painting coaches."[21] "From the painting of coaches and houses he moved on through sign posts to tavern signs."[22] Friends—especially strict Friends—had always avoided the arts. Painting signs was perilously close to visual art, and Edward himself had qualms about sign painting, but he was good at it and desperately needed the income that it brought in.

In 1812, Edward Hicks was recorded as a minister in Middletown Monthly Meeting. "In 1815 he helped to found Newtown Preparative Meeting, where he remained a member and minister for the rest of his life."[23] Beginning about 1820, and continuing to the end of his life, Hicks produced sixty or more paintings, most of them repeating his famed "peaceable kingdom" theme. In the foreground of these paintings were the creatures named in Isaiah 11:6–9—wolf and lamb, leopard and kid, calf and lion and ox, little child, cow and bear, and asp and cockatrice (adder or viper). In the background of most of them, William Penn was making his treaty with the Indians. Half a dozen, beginning in 1827, pictured instead a pyramid of Quakers bearing a banner: "peace on earth, good will to men." George Fox, William Penn, and Robert Barclay have been identified at the peak; Elias Hicks and George Washington (!) are easy to recognize in the front row.

Edward Hicks was never censured or disciplined by his fellow Quakers for this departure from Quaker tradition. He never mentioned his paintings in his *Memoirs*. *Memoirs* does include a long discourse, based on a sermon he preached at Goose Creek Meeting in Virginia in 1837. In this discourse he expounded in great detail on Isaiah 11:6–9. He began by summing up his basic themes:

> The divinely inspired prophet Isaiah held forth this language when alluding to the fulness of the glorious gospel dispensation: "The wolf also shall dwell with the lamb, and the leopard shall lie down with the kid;" "The cow and the bear shall feed; their young shall lie down together; and the lion shall eat straw like the ox." Now the prophet was not only a righteous man, but a true philosopher, and understood the astonishing variety embraced in the wonderful creature called man, viewing him, no doubt, as he ought to be viewed.[24]

> This is the death that Adam died the day he transgressed the Divine command, having lost that life that is hid with *Christ* in GOD; the stream of heavenly light and love that united him to his Heavenly Father, which constituted the only substantial source of rational happiness in time and eternity, was cut off, and his soul fell from its dignified station in the divine harmony, (when it governed the animal man with all its propensities, making them subservient to the purposes for which they were intended,) and became a slave to that cruel, selfish nature, emblematically described by the wolf, the leopard, the bear, and the lion; having lost the innocent angelic covering of GOD's righteousness, in vain did he attempt to hide his nakedness with a patched covering of fig-leaves;—there was nothing now so suitable to his state and condition as to be clothed with the skins of beasts. Therefore the Lord's prophet was bid to make use of the interesting figure contained in the text. The lamb, the kid, the cow, and the ox, are emblems of good men and women—while the wolf, the leopard, the bear, and the lion, are figures of the wicked. These last, we know, if they were confined in a small enclosure, would cruelly destroy each other, while the four innocent animals in the same enclosure would dwell harmoniously together. It was the innocent nature of the lamb that ruled in Abel, that made his offering so acceptable to God, while the cruel, carnivorous nature of the wolf was producing in Cain jealousy, envy, hatred, and murder; so that it was marked in the very lines and configuration of his face. . . . It was this wrathful, selfish, cruel, carnivorous

nature that so increased and predominated over all good in the antediluvial world, that mankind became so dreadfully wicked that they were destroyed by an awful deluge.

Noah and his family, in whom the most of the innocent nature reigned, was saved to re-people the earth; and notwithstanding his own uprightness, the same evil genius made its appearance in his family. The same was prefigured in Ishmael and Esau, as allegorically alluded to by the apostle Paul, and therefore the paradoxical difficulties that some have discovered in the writings of that truly spiritually-minded saint, with respect to the Almighty's loving Jacob and hating Esau, is easily understood; Jacob being in the innocent nature of the lamb, while Esau was in that of the wolf, the leopard, the bear, and the lion, where cursed self reigns with all its cruel, bloodthirsty violence—the fountain of hatred, envy, jealousy, and all those malevolent passions and propensities that make man the enemy of man; producing not only bloody and destructive war, but all that dark catalogue of crime that characterises a fallen world of intelligent beings separated from the Divine harmony.[25]

When we view his paintings, the obvious meaning would be that Edward Hicks saw William Penn's dealings with the American Indians and the succession of "true" Quakers, from George Fox to Elias Hicks, as historical events or movements that fulfilled Isaiah's prophecy. In his discourse, in contrast, he interpreted the beasts in Isaiah 11 as "emblems" or figures of speech, standing for character traits in the souls of individuals.

In the years leading up to the 1827 Separation, Edward Hicks was one of the most outspoken critics of the Philadelphia elders and wealthy leaders. He was invited to join the supporters of Elias Hicks at the confrontation with leading elders in December 1822. He was unable to attend and wrote to a friend that he "did guess that his presence would 'stir up a greater degree of enmity' than Elias's."[26] In his *Memoirs* he frequently expressed severe criticism of the Orthodox leaders. We also find him later strongly opposing many Hicksite Friends who he felt went too far in rejecting the authority of the Bible or the saviorhood of Jesus, or whom he saw as too "political" in their opposition to slavery. He did, however, repeatedly recognize his harsh judgmentalism as a fault within himself. Edward Hicks died in 1849, at the age of sixty-nine.

As he read the Bible and tried to apply it to life situations, Edward Hicks seems to have been taking cues from a number of eighteenth-century Friends. On at least one occasion, he continued the practice of seeing the Bible as spelling out a succession of dispensations:

> Having given the views that I think have been given me of the perfection of the first covenant, including the dispensation of John the Baptist and the outward appearance of Jesus Christ, I now come to the Christian dispensation which is a higher step of the ladder that leads into the kingdom of heaven. A kingdom that is not of this world—a kingdom whose subjects never did nor never can fight with carnal weapons.[27]

In Edward Hicks' discourse based on Isaiah 11:6–9, he continued John Churchman's practice of "spiritualizing" the Bible, by applying historically oriented passages to the inward spiritual states of individuals.[28] Job Scott had referred to "the spiritual import, meaning, and mystery of many passages."[29] In an 1825 sermon in New York City, Edward Hicks used this principle in applying the parable of the prodigal son, who

> had spent his substance with harlots. And how many at the present day spend their substance with harlots, not merely in the sensual but in the spiritual meaning of the word. When harlot is spiritualized, it means cursed self. . . . How many spend their precious substance on harlots, for it is spent on themselves![30]

Edward Hicks several times fell into Samuel Fothergill's habit of using biblical texts in ways that were quite foreign to their original contexts:

> Then there were to be found walking *in the path of humble industry*, . . . such men as Samuel Bownas, John Richardson, John Woolman, James Simpson, John Churchman, and Elias Hicks, and many others that might be mentioned, . . . who, no doubt will shine forth in the brightness of the firmament as stars for ever and ever. *'But the fathers, where are they? and the prophets, do they live for ever?'* where are the bright talented youth of this day, the interesting children of Friends to be found? We fear not all walking *in the path of humble industry* as Christians.[31]

The prophet Zechariah had written:

> Be ye not as your fathers, unto whom the former prophets have cried, saying, Thus saith the LORD of hosts: Turn ye now from

your evil ways, and from your evil doings: but they did not hear, nor hearken unto me, saith the LORD. Your fathers, where are they? and the prophets, do they live for ever? (Zechariah 1:4–5 KJV).

Edward Hicks was using the quotation to emphasize how far his contemporaries had declined from the virtue of their ancestors, but Zechariah had used the words to show how the ancestors had turned away from the path of virtue and to urge his contemporaries *not* to follow the ways of their "fathers"!

> Friends have been rapidly declining from their first principles and practices. . . . Ever since the setting up of West Town Boarding School, in Pennsylvania, such schools as are recognized by our discipline have been neglected and are falling into decay, while the learning and wisdom of the world, which cherish pride and religious consequence, have divided in Jacob and scattered in Israel, to the everlasting disgrace and injury of many, causing the LORD's humble faithful servants secretly to cry in the mournful language of the prophet: "By whom shall Jacob arise, for he is small."[32]

He was quoting the prophet Amos:

> Thus hath the Lord GOD shewed unto me; and behold, he formed grasshoppers. . . . And it came to pass, that when they had made an end of eating the grass of the land, then I said, O Lord GOD, forgive, I beseech thee: by whom shall Jacob arise? for he is small. The LORD repented for this: It shall not be, saith the LORD. Thus hath the Lord GOD showed unto me: and, behold, the Lord GOD called to contend by fire, and it devoured the great deep, and did eat up a part. Then said I, O Lord GOD, cease, I beseech thee: by whom shall Jacob arise? For he is small. The LORD repented for this: This also shall not be, saith the Lord GOD. (Amos 7:1–6 KJV)

Amos was interceding for his people, pleading with God not to punish them. Edward Hicks was using the quotation to bemoan the small number of Friends who had remained faithful.

> Here the devil of intemperance comes in, and hurries them down the ladder to the devil of impatience, whose vindictive

> anger marshaling the malevolent passions—jealousy, envy, hatred, and revenge—produces quarrelling, fighting, and murder. The poor soul, now arrived at a perfect devilish state, lifts up its eyes in Hell, being in torment. When the SAVIOUR descended into and suffered for this state, He cried out, "My God, my God, why hast thou forsaken me?"[33]

In the biblical context, Christ's descent into hell took place after he died, not when he was on the cross, where he spoke these words.

> The dear young friends had just got nicely settled, and John had gone to market, when dear Sarah was taken with the cramp cholic, and died in about an hour, leaving a child fifteen or sixteen months old. The circumstances of her marriage and settlement, were so much like my dear S. P., that it called into action all my tenderest feelings, awakening the deepest sympathy for her poor afflicted father, who appears to be now trembling on the brink of the grace. I could only pour forth my tears and prayers in silence, fearing the "*cloven tongue as of fire,*" had been already sounding its bell unavailingly amongst them.[34]

The phrase, "cloven tongues like as of fire," was from Acts 2:3—the Pentecost event, when the apostles received power from the Holy Spirit and began their world-wide mission—hardly what Edward Hicks was trying to convey.

Edward Hicks clearly admired such eighteenth-century reformers as John Woolman and John Churchman and strove heartily to continue in their tradition. He readily followed reforming Friends—Churchman, Samuel Fothergill, Job Scott—in their ways of interpreting the Bible. But his deep-felt artistic gift impelled him forward on a path that was in tension with that tradition. Nothing in his background or experience made it possible for him to acknowledge his art as a ministry in the service of Christ and the people of God. Perhaps it was this inner stress and strain that found an outlet in his persistent testiness toward those Friends who did not fully hew to the tradition of the Quaker reformers.

John Wilbur

John Wilbur was born in 1774. His parents, Thomas and Mary Wilbur, were active members of the Society of Friends. He was born and lived his entire life in Hopkinton, Rhode Island, where he worked as a farmer and land surveyor. In 1793 he married a Connecticut Friend, Lydia Collins. He was a lifelong member of South Kingston Monthly Meeting in Rhode Island Quarterly Meeting and New England Yearly Meeting. He was recorded as a minister in 1812.

In 1824, while attending a meeting of ministers and elders in his own monthly meeting, he noted that

> I did in my measure feel thankful that we who constitute this meeting, have hitherto been preserved from the jar and commotion with which our Society is at this time shaken in several sections of the country, on account of unsoundness in doctrine in divers individuals.[35]

In October 1827, at the height of the Hicksite-Orthodox controversy, he was traveling among Friends in New York Yearly Meeting. At one place

> there appeared to be much unsoundness, or a want of faith in the outward coming of Christ, the Saviour of the world. . . . Very little can be done for those who are unsound in the Christian faith, unless there is some room yet left in their minds, or way is made by the power of Truth to enforce the doctrine most surely believed by us as a people; namely the necessity of the coming of our Lord and Saviour Jesus Christ, and of his offering up his precious life that we might be reconciled to God; for if this faith is wanting, . . . all is wanting, . . . there being, then, no foundation to build Christianity upon.[36]

John Wilbur was clearly in unity with his yearly meeting when it united in siding with the Orthodox party during the separation of 1827–28. He approved and was inspired by the actions of such Friends as Thomas Shillitoe, when they publicly confronted and denounced Elias Hicks. As he later wrote:

> Will any one among us now say, that no individual therefore had a right to gainsay the doctrine of Elias Hicks?
>
> And were Isaac Stephenson and Samuel Wood, while travelling with certificates in New England, chargeable with a breach

of order for exposing the doctrines of Elias Hicks, because the latter was at the same time travelling with a certificate to the westward? The same question might also well be asked with relation to George Withy and Thomas Shilletoe, and others, about the same time, for exposing the same doctrines, under the same circumstances.[37]

Wilbur's unity with and love for Shillitoe was well expressed in his reference to a night in 1832 during his visit to England: "I went to Tottenham, and spent the night with my dear, aged friend, Thomas Shillitoe."[38]

John Wilbur made a major trip in the ministry to the British Isles, arriving in England in August 1831, and finally leaving England for home in January 1833. As he traveled around, he became increasingly alarmed about developments among Friends. Many were joining with clergy and other non-Friends in Bible societies and associations; many were expressing religious beliefs that appeared to have more in common with contemporary evangelical Protestants than with the views of early Friends. He wrote

> that unbelief of either that part relating to what has been done for us without us, by Christ's outward coming and mediation, or in his second coming, without sin unto salvation, by his grace, spirit, and power in our hearts, to our practical guidance into all Truth—that an unbelief in either of these legitimate members of the Christian covenant, will frustrate our salvation.[39]

Wilbur found a number of Friends who shared his apprehensions. One who became a strong friend and supporter was George Crosfield. Late in 1832,

> having been met here by my dear friend, George Crosfield, we went with him to Liverpool, where Ann Jones also soon came; and she, with George and Margaret Crosfield, and Jonathan Flounders, went into an examination of a series of letters which I had written to George Crosfield on religious subjects; and it was their united opinion, that the state of things required the publication of such matter as is contained in these letters. . . . I left the disposal of them to George Crosfield and other friends, to do as they thought best with the letters.[40]

While awaiting final decision on the publication of these letters, John Wilbur had written to his wife:

> How much, or how great, is the impending danger, cannot well be determined now. . . .
>
> There are many here, and some among the foremost rank, who are disposed to think, that the writings of Robert Barclay and others among our ancient Friends, are incorrect, and do not hesitate in so saying; and further say, that the Scriptures are "the Word of God," and the first, if not the only rule of practice, as well as of faith; and recommend that ministers rely upon them more and more for a qualification to preach.[41]

George Crosfield promptly had the six letters by John Wilbur published. This small volume contains the fullest published account of Wilbur's religious views.

In dealing with the authority of scripture, Wilbur based his view squarely on that of Robert Barclay:

> Robert Barclay in his apology for the true Christian divinity, has . . . answered the great question, whether that principle which contains the light, grace, spirit, and faith of the gospel; or the Bible, is the first and best leader and controller of the Christian's life and practice; and he has fairly made the Bible to decide this question itself. None need do more than simply quote all the passages from the Scriptures which speak in favour of both these positions, and there will certainly be found a great preponderance in favour of the ground taken by our early friends, and taken also by the apostles, in following the directions of our Lord, as to the guidance of his spirit, and its operation upon men's hearts.[42]

If the Light or Spirit and then the scriptures hold first and second places in the hierarchy of authorities for Christian faith and practice, Wilbur placed the writings of the first Friends in third place:

> If we compare the Scriptures with the writings of our early friends, there will be nothing lost to the latter by placing the former above them, and in the higher sphere of that exalted rank, where they do deservedly and ever ought to stand, far above all modern writings. . . . For as the Scriptures being authentic and true, place themselves below Christ and his blessed Spirit, so the writings of our worthy predecessors being also true,

place themselves meekly and modestly, entirely below the holy Scriptures,—a correct position.[43]

Wilbur clearly saw the Bible as a source of doctrinal statements: "How needful it is to have a full belief in the doctrines of Scripture, and in every part of them."[44] He had listed seven propositions, and said of them: "Not one of these requisites, all of which are indispensable to our future well being, should be overlooked or excluded from the summary of our faith in the covenant of life and peace." He went on:

> To exemplify and demonstrate the foregoing positions, I would refer to the subjoined passages of Scripture, as being distinctly applicable to them, and which, collectively, would seem to constitute and include the whole covenant of life and salvation.[45]

At this point, he footnoted twenty-eight biblical passages as proof texts. It is clear that Wilbur, like the evangelically-oriented Friends whom he opposed, looked to the Bible as a source book, containing propositions from which Christian doctrines were to be deduced.

Wilbur began his second letter with a fascinating commentary on the fate of the angels who followed Satan or Lucifer in the primal rebellion against God's reign:

> If it be, as has been affirmed, that enmity took root in some of the heavenly company, and that they through pride were led into rebellion, and an attempt to set up and establish a kingdom for themselves in opposition to, and above the throne and kingdom of God; still we have no reason to believe that the needful and mighty act of God in expelling from the regions of light their arch leader with all his band, had, or could have, any effect as a reconciliation, or any tendency to remove the enmity, however humbling their defeat and condition. No, nor that it were possible for those who had been created free partakers with their blessed and eternal King in the riches of his glory, after such daring rebellion and attempted usurpation, could ever be restored to that glorious state which they had lost by their fall.[46]

He attempted to prove the impossibility of their restoration by appealing to two passages in the letter to the Hebrews:

> For it is impossible for those who were once enlightened, and have tasted of the heavenly gift, and were made partakers of

the Holy Ghost, and have tasted the good word of God, and the powers of the world to come, if they shall fall away, to renew them again unto repentance. HEB. vi. v. 4, 5 & 6.—also HEB. x. v. 26.[47]

In themselves and in their contexts, these passages were clearly directed not toward heavenly beings at the beginning of time, but toward the author's Christian contemporaries. A twentieth-century Friend, New Englander and biblical scholar Alexander Purdy, has recognized this point with especial poignancy: The author of Hebrews 6:4–6

> meant what he wrote; and that the impossibility of repentance applied to apostasy, the deliberate and willful denial of Christianity, rather than to sins of weakness and ignorance seems certain from the context. . . . The pastoral instinct is revealed in these sharp words. The author is deeply concerned about the readers. . . . The phrases heaped up in vss. 4–5 are intended to remind the readers of the richness and glory of their Christian experience.[48]

In this instance, Wilbur echoed the tendency of Samuel Fothergill and Edward Hicks to apply biblical passages to situations that were completely foreign to their original historical contexts.

In his second letter, Wilbur touched on the nature of Christ's atonement:

> This was therefore a sacrifice of a sweet smelling savour unto God, in which, and by which, he would blot out from his presence the transgression of every penitent sinner, and obtain a place and ground for him, whereon he would deign to meet him; and such too as would enable him to receive the divine grace, and prepare him for the guidance of the divine Spirit. . . .
>
> After the expiation of repented sins, He the Mediator of the whole glorious covenant of life and salvation, is to us a mediator still, keeping with us, and constantly teaching us the denying of all ungodliness.[49]
>
> If we do not by the power of the agency which God giveth us, work with him, and endeavour to keep his commandments, then the covenant to us is broken; yea, and *by us* is also broken.[50]
>
> In every covenant there is either a promise, an obligation, or a

> condition, between two at least; thus in that between God and us, after the first step which he himself has taken, to make way for all his promises, as well as even the application of the atonement, it is upon the condition of our obedience and fulfilment of our part of that covenant, which ensures to us an eternal inheritance.[51]

It is evident that initiating and maintaining the covenant between God and the obedient people of God was, for Wilbur, an important aspect of his understanding of Christ's work of atonement.

Wilbur reported in his *Journal* on a quarterly meeting that he attended in Norwich, England, during the final week of 1832. There, he lamented that

> some unsound doctrines appear to have crept in—such as . . . a trusting in a mere imputed righteousness for salvation, without regard to obedience, and those works which are wrought in God, through the constraining and sanctifying influence of his spirit.[52]

He was here opposing (with Robert Barclay) an important aspect of the satisfaction theory of the atonement.

In England, Wilbur was especially disturbed by the success of Joseph John Gurney in publishing books that contained doctrines that did not always agree with the writings of the earliest Friends. With a few other Friends, Wilbur confronted Gurney in London at the time of the 1832 Yearly Meeting, because "I believe him to be unsound in the doctrines of Friends."[53] Gurney sailed to America in 1837 for an extended journey in the ministry among Friends; Wilbur met with him again in Newport, Rhode Island, in June 1838. On both occasions Gurney defended and restated the positions that he had published. During Gurney's American tour, Wilbur repeatedly warned other Friends, through correspondence and in person, that Gurney was unfit to serve as a Friends minister because of the erroneous doctrines that he preached and published.

Wilbur based his case against Gurney on "the *soundness or unsoundness* of [his] doctrines."[54] He agreed with the evangelicals that sound Christian doctrine was essential; his difference was that the criterion for determining soundness of doctrine was consistency with "the writings of the first Friends. . . . Whosoever . . . deviated either in faith or practice, became subjects of dealing by the true intent of that discipline."[55] What Wilbur missed was that those early Quaker statements of faith were not creeds, which individual Friends would have had to subscribe to or face discipline.

By 1839, the leadership of New England Yearly Meeting had appointed a committee to stop Wilbur from continuing to criticize Gurney. The committee tried to persuade South Kingston Monthly Meeting to disown Wilbur. When this effort failed, the committee eventually persuaded Rhode Island Quarterly Meeting to dissolve South Kingston Monthly Meeting and to transfer its members to another Monthly Meeting, which then proceeded, in 1843, to disown Wilbur. Appeals from Wilbur and South Kingston Friends to the Yearly Meeting resulted in a separation in 1845. About five hundred Friends formed a yearly meeting, that supported Wilbur; about six thousand Friends became a Gurneyite Yearly Meeting.

Attempts by both New England bodies to be recognized by other yearly meetings met varying and only gradually developing responses. The Wilburite-Gurneyite split took place in Ohio Yearly Meeting in 1854. Philadelphia Yearly Meeting avoided a substantial separation only by the desperate decision in 1857 to discontinue the exchange of epistles with *all* other yearly meetings.

After 1845 Wilbur continued to travel in the ministry—mostly giving support to the scattered groups of Friends who stuck to the old, "conservative" Quaker doctrines. His wife died in 1852. In 1853 and 1854, he made a second trip to Great Britain, accompanied by one of his sons, Amos Wilbur. John Wilbur died in 1856. In 1859 his surviving children published his *Journal* with the official permission of the Wilburite New England Yearly Meeting.

Johnathan Dymond

I wrote an essay on the religious ethics of Jonathan Dymond in 1976. A brief summary of the essay was eventually published as part of my *Quaker Religious Thought* article on "Quaker Peace Witness."[56] What follows here is a lightly revised version of that essay.

Jonathan Dymond (1796–1828), Friend, linen-draper of Exeter, England, is best known as the author of two books. The first of these, *An Inquiry into the Accordancy of War with the Principles of Christianity*, was published in 1823. *Inquiry* is said to have been "immensely influential of the thinking of American pacifists throughout the whole nineteenth century."[57] Dymond's second work, *Essays on the Principles of Morality*, was published after his death. For many decades, Friends valued this book highly; well into the twentieth century, it was being used as a textbook in Friends schools, such as Westtown School in West Chester, Pennsylvania.

Today, Dymond seems almost unknown among Friends. Why should a body of writings, once so highly regarded, have fallen into such neglect? Perhaps an examination of the works themselves can provide us with some clues.

Dymond clearly stated his first, fundamental principle of morality: "The *communicated* will of God is the Final Standard of Right and Wrong."[58] On the question of how God's will is communicated, Dymond was equally explicit: "A Christian writer . . . is obliged, in conformity with the principles of his religion, to acknowledge the divine, and therefore the *supreme* authority of Scripture."[59] He recognized that this formal statement did not at once settle all moral problems: "The written expression of the Divine will does not contain, and no writings can contain, directions for our conduct in every circumstance of life."[60] In addition, the Bible does not contain a single, consistent system of ethics:

> One of the very interesting considerations which are presented to an enquirer in perusing the volume of Scripture, consists in the *variations* in its morality. There are three distinctly defined periods, in which the moral government and laws of the Deity assume, in some respects, a different character.[61]

When Dymond attempted to deal with these considerations, however, we begin to run into problems in interpreting his thought.

In his solution to the internal problem, the variations within the scriptures, Dymond followed a well-worn trail—the "dispensational" route—which we have already seen in the thought of Friends of earlier generations: William Penn, Ralph Sandiford, Job Scott, and Henry Tuke. God has had a different will for each of the three main periods, or dispensations, in biblical history. His commands to the patriarchs were the supreme authority, in their time. The Law of Moses was God's express will for the Jewish people—but only until the time of Christ. The New Testament alone expresses God's will for the third, Christian dispensation—for the period since the appearance of the Christ:

> None of the injunctions or permissions which formed a part of the former dispensations can be referred to as of authority to us, except so far as they are coincident with the Christian law. To our own Master we stand or fall; and our Master is Christ.[62]

At this point, Dymond seemed to allow a subordinate place for any Old Testament commands that do not clearly contradict "the general spirit"[63] of the New Testament. In another context, however, his rejection of Old Testament authority was far more sweeping:

> The manner in which the author of "truth" prefaced some of his most important precepts is much to our present purpose. "It hath been said by them of old time, an eye for an eye," &c. He then introduces his own precept with the contradistinguishing preface—"But *I* say unto you." This, therefore, appears to be a specific abrogation of the *authority* of the legal injunctions, and an introduction of another system. . . . The truth is, that the law was abolished because of its imperfections. . . .
>
> We therefore dismiss the dispensation of Moses from any participation in the argument.[64]

In practice, Dymond generally did dismiss the Law of Moses; he rarely appealed to the Old Testament in his detailed ethical arguments or in his specific applications of morality to particular situations and issues.

Instead, wherever the New Testament provided no relevant precept or principle, Dymond recognized "some subordinate authorities, to which . . . it is the will of God that we should refer."[65] In one listing of such subordinate rules or principles, he suggested: "'Sympathy' may be of use, and 'Nature' may be of use, and 'Self-love,' and 'Benevolence;' and to those who know what it means, 'Eternal fitnesses too.'"[66] Dymond paid particular attention to two important principles. One of these principles was "the law of nature, . . . the authority, in moral affairs, of what are called natural instincts and natural rights."[67] The other principle was utility: "We ought to pay regard to what is useful and beneficial,"[68] or to "the endeavor to produce the greatest sum of happiness."[69] He occasionally also used the term "expediency" as an equivalent to "utility," but most frequently he did so with a negative connotation, when he criticized moralists who let expediency overrule the dictates of the New Testament.

Among the interpretive problems that arise are these: Why should such principles as utility and the law of nature be preferred to the Old Testament as the authorities to be followed when the New Testament says nothing? And if utility, law of nature, sympathy, and benevolence are separate rules or principles, how much weight should be given to each? What is to be done if the implications of two or more of these principles conflict in a given situation? Clear answers to these questions are hard to find in Dymond's writings; indeed, I sometimes wonder if he was even aware that such problems exist.

Actually, Dymond recognized yet another way in which the will of God is communicated to humans. God's will is known not only through scripture and through such rational principles as utility and natural law; it is also communicated directly, immediately, to each individual:

> Every human being possesses, or is furnished with, moral knowledge and a moral law. . . .
>
> Whence then do they obtain it?—a question to which but one answer can be given; from the Creator himself. It appears therefore to be almost demonstratively shown, that God does communicate his will immediately to the minds of those who have no access to the external expression of it.[70]

This mode of learning God's will seems to be subordinate and secondary: "This direct communication may be limited, it may be incomplete, but some communication exists."[71] "We never affirm that the Deity communicates *all* his law to every man."[72] What is the nature of this immediate communication of God's will? It is clearly *not* the same thing as conscience: "Let us then, when we direct our serious enquiry to the immediate communication of the Divine will, carefully distinguish that communication from the dictates of the conscience. They are separate and distinct considerations."[73] Beyond this, Dymond did not go. What does this communication feel like? How is it recognized? No answers were given. In practice, this principle did not enter into the working out of Dymond's ethics. At the end of his chapter on the immediate communication of God's will, he admitted: "If, in conclusion, it should be asked, What assistance can be yielded, in the investigation of publicly authorized rules of virtue, by the discussions of the present chapter? we answer, Very little."[74] This "mode of moral guidance," indeed, "is little adapted to the formation of external rules,"[75] and must therefore be mostly ignored in a systematic study of the principles of morality. I wonder again: Is there never any conflict between God's direct revelations to individuals and the dictates of utility or of natural law—to say nothing of the New Testament itself? In case of such conflict, what then? Or if this direct communication provides so little substantive content for his study, why mention it at all?

Dymond was aware of some problems in interpreting the New Testament itself. For example: "We willingly *grant* that not all the precepts from the

Mount were designed to be literally obeyed in the intercourse of life."[76] How does one determine which of Christ's teachings are to be followed literally? A couple of examples may prove illuminating. In the case of Matthew 5:34, "Swear not at all," Dymond concluded: "We have plain emphatical prohibitions—prohibitions of which the distinctness is more fully proved the more they are investigated."[77] From "such distinctness of evidence as to the universality of the prohibition of oaths by Jesus Christ,"[78] Dymond drew the literal conclusion: No Christian should ever swear a judicial oath. In the case of Matthew 6:19, "Lay not up for yourselves treasures upon earth," on the other hand, Dymond rejected a literal application of the command. He admitted, "I once saw a book that endeavored to prove the unlawfulness of accumulating any property; upon the authority, primarily, of this last quoted precept." But the author of that unnamed book was among those who interpret "such precepts in a more literal sense than that to which they appear to have been designed to be applied."[79]

Why is the prohibition of oaths to be interpreted literally, but not the prohibition of the accumulation of property? The clearest reason for the latter is that "such rules are seldom mistaken in practice."[80] The common practice of Christians, in interpreting this saying, appears to be sufficient authority for rejecting its literal sense. But why does the same consideration not apply to the interpretation of Christ's prohibition of judicial oaths? Dymond recognized the issue, but argued here against the principle of common practice:

> Upon every subject of questionable rectitude that is sanctioned by habit and the usages of society, a person should place himself in the independent situation of an enquirer. He should not seek for arguments to defend an existing practice, but should simply enquire what our practice ought to be. One of the most powerful causes of the slow amendment of public institutions, consists in this circumstance, that most men endeavor rather to justify what exists than to consider whether it ought to exist or not. This cause operates upon the question of oaths. We therefore invite the reader . . . to know nothing of the customs of the present day; and to have no *desire* to justify them.[81]

The conclusion clearly followed: Christ meant the prohibition against oaths to be taken literally. The question remains: Why did this argument not apply equally to Christ's prohibition of laying up "treasures upon earth"?

In discussing another injunction from the Sermon on the Mount, "Resist not evil" (Matthew 5:39), Jonathan Dymond developed an extended hypothetical argument:

> Supposing again, the Christian Scriptures had said, *an army may fight in its own defence, but not for any other purpose*. We do not say that the exceptions to *this* rule would be so many as wholly to nullify the rule itself; but we say that whoever will attempt to apply it in practice, will find that he has a very wide range of justifiable warfare; a range that will embrace many more wars than moralists, laxer than we shall suppose him to be, are willing to defend. If an army may fight in defence of their own lives, they may and they must fight in defence of the lives of others: if they may fight in defence of the lives of others, they will fight in defence of their property: if in defence of property, they will fight in defence of political rights: if in defence of rights, they will fight in promotion of interests: if in promotion of interests, they will fight in promotion of their glory and their crimes. Now let any man of honesty look over the gradations by which we arrive at this climax, and I believe he will find that, *in practice*, no curb can be placed upon the conduct of an army until they reach it. There is, indeed, a wide distance between fighting in defence of life and fighting in furtherance of our crimes; but the steps which lead from one to the other will follow in inevitable succession.[82]

In the tract, however, Dymond added a footnote:

> The reader will not suppose that when we maintain that the temper and spirit of Christianity require us not to kill an assassin, we assert that *no resistance* ought to be made to him. Although every attempt to specify the precise nature and degree of lawful resistance would probably be in vain, yet we are ready to allow that some species of self-defence are lawful, and indeed obligatory. A man may expostulate with an assassin—he may disarm him—these, and many other similar things he may do, and in doing them he would, doubtless, . . . be performing an act of very great benevolence towards the aggressor.[83]

But once these first exceptions have been made to the simple, sweeping injunction, "resist not evil," why are we not already on the same type of slippery slope that Dymond so vividly denounced? Or, if it is possible and necessary to draw the line somewhere between disarming the assassin and killing him in self-defense, why is it not possible (logically or psychologically) to draw the line at some step between fighting in defense of life and fighting to promote our crimes?

Another surprising point is Dymond's optimism about the ease with which conclusions may be reached on matters of political morality:

> Having once established the maxim—which no reasonable man disputes—that the proper purpose of government is to secure the happiness of the community, very little is wanted in applying the principle to particular questions but honest conscientious thought.[84]

With similar sweeping confidence, he declared:

> The fundamental principles which are deducible from the law of nature and from Christianity, respecting political affairs, appear to be these:
>
> 1. Political Power is rightly *possessed* only when it is possessed by consent of the community;
>
> 2. It is rightly *exercised* only when it subserves the welfare of the community;
>
> 3. And only when it subserves this purpose, by *means* which the moral law permits.[85]

The process by which Dymond then proceeded to deduce the first of these principles is of interest:

> Perfect liberty is desirable if it were consistent with the greatest degree of happiness. But it is not. Men find that, by giving up a part of their liberty, they are more happy than by retaining, or attempting to retain, the whole. Government, whatever be its form, is the agent by which the *inexpedient* portion of individual liberty is taken away. Men institute government for their own advantage, and because they find they are more happy with it than without it. This is the sole reason, in principle.[86]

He had formally stated that the principles are deduced from natural law and from Christianity, but his actual argument used the principle of expediency or greatest happiness as its major premise. The argument also involved a major inductive generalization: "Men find that" government produces greater happiness than does anarchy. Dymond's evidence for this generalization is hard to find.

On a few questions, Dymond's arguments not only raise serious questions but even appear to contain serious inconsistencies. In one of these cases, Dymond appealed in one context to the "common consent of mankind" argument: "Some men say that the New Testament contains no prohibition of suicide. If this were true, it would avail nothing, because there are many things which it does not forbid, but which every one knows to be wicked."[87] A few pages further, however, he explicitly challenged "common consent" on the grounds that this appeal frequently tends to hide fallacies in moral reasoning:

> The reader may the more willingly enquire whether these propositions are true, because most of those who lay them down are at little pains to *prove* their truth. Men are extremely willing to acquiesce in it without proof, and writers and speakers think it unnecessary to adduce it. Thus perhaps it happens that fallacy is not detected because it is not sought.[88]

Again, as I have already noted, Dymond explicitly provided for situations not covered by the New Testament: These are precisely the situations in which he appealed to such principles as utility or the law of nature. It follows that any "argument from silence" of the New Testament would prove nothing. Yet at least once he leaned heavily on just such an argument from silence:

> Jesus Christ legislated for *man*—not for individuals only. . . . He legislated for *states*. In his moral law we discover no indications that states were exempted from its application, or that any rule which bound social did not bind political communities. If any exemption were designed, the *onus probandi* rests upon those who assert it: unless they can show that the Christian precepts are *not* intended to apply to nations, the conclusion must be admitted that they *are*.[89]

But Dymond himself had already supplied the burden of proof that he here demanded! Since the New Testament is silent on the question of whether states and nations are covered by its own precepts, "It is the Will of God that we should refer"[90] to one of the subordinate principles for the solution of this question. And it is indeed difficult to see how a general, universal, rational principle, such as utility or the law of nature, can ever refer the nation back again to the specific historical revelation of the New Testament.

Frequently throughout his *Essays on the Principles of Morality*, Dymond appealed to the principle of expediency or utility as a valid, if subordinate, principle of ethics. In contrast, in *An Inquiry into the Accordancy of War with the Principles of Christianity*, he explicitly rejected any appeal to this principle in moral decision-making: "Calculations of expediency, of 'particular and general consequences,' are not intrusted to us, for this most satisfactory reason—that we cannot make them."[91]

We run into a similar conflict of statements in dealing with the law of nature as a principle of morality. In *Inquiry*, Dymond pointedly denounced any appeal to this principle:

> I do not know what those persons mean, who say, that we are authorized to kill an assassin by *the law of nature*. Principles like this, heedlessly assumed, as of self-evident truth, are, I believe, often the starting-post of our errors, the point of divergency from rectitude. . . . Nature makes no laws. A law implies a legislator; and there is no legislator upon the principles of human duty, but God. If, by the "law of nature," is meant any thing of which the sanctions or obligations are *different* from those of revelation, it is obvious that we have set up a moral system of our own, and in opposition to that which has been established by Heaven. If we mean by the "law of nature," nothing but that which is *accordant* with revelation, to what purpose do we refer to it at all? I do not suppose that any sober moralist will statedly advance the laws of nature in opposition to the laws of God; but I think that to advance them *at all*—that to refer to *any* principle or law, in determination of our duty, irrespectively of the simple will of God, is always dangerous. . . . I believe that a reference to the laws of nature has seldom illustrated our duties, and never induced us to perform them; and that it has hitherto answered little other purpose than that of amusing the lovers of philosophical morality.[92]

In *Essays*, on the other hand,

> We conclude the general proposition is true—that a regard to the law of nature, in estimating human duty, is accordant with

the will of God. . . . If this authority were questioned, perhaps it might be said that the expression of the Divine will tacitly sanctions it, because that expression is addressed to us under the supposition that our constitution is such as it is; and because some of the Divine precepts appear to specify a point at which the authority of the law of nature stops. . . . The tendency of the law of nature is manifestly beneficial. No man questions that the "original impulses of our nature" tend powerfully to the well-being of the species.[93]

On the face of it, there seem to be many problems, anomalies, and inconsistencies in Dymond's reasoning. This may simply mean that the basic thrust of his thought can be found only by probing beneath the surface. Can we find in his writings any deeper, more general principles that provide the thread of consistency has thus far eluded us? Does he reveal, either in his basic theological position or in hints as to his own religious insights and experience, or else in any analysis of the underlying structure and dynamics of society, any clues that may help us to unify his thought into a complete and consistent position?

The nature of religious experience is, at most, incidental. Dymond vigorously objected to the practice of "narrating our own religious feelings."[94] In general, he showed an aversion to any form of "enthusiasm or fanaticism."[95] In any case, serious attention to specifically "religious" obligations is unnecessary, for *"the authority which imposes moral obligations and religious obligations is one and the same*—the will of God."[96]

Theologically, Dymond referred to God as man's "Creator" and "the universal Parent of mankind."[97] He is "an Omniscient Being, and who also is the Judge of mankind."[98] Jesus Christ is "our Saviour."[99] Dymond concluded his *Essays* with the ringing affirmation "that the true and safe foundation of our hope is in 'the redemption that is in Christ Jesus.'"[100]

I sense that these theological affirmations are merely formal and have little import for Dymond's ethics. He substantially confirmed this impression when he asserted "the unfitness of attempting to deduce human duties from the attributes of God. . . . The truth indeed is, that we do not accurately and distinctly know what the Divine attributes are."[101] Theology has little or nothing to contribute to Christian ethics; the source of morality is the sheer, even arbitrary, will of God: "Our exclusive business is to discover the actual present will of God, without enquiring why his will is such as it is, or why it has ever been different."[102] More precisely, the only relevant theological affirmation is that Jesus Christ is "our lawgiver."[103] What is of crucial importance is "that moral system which the Christian revelation institutes."[104]

Unsurprisingly, then, Dymond emphasized "those solemn, discriminative, and public declarations of Jesus Christ, which are contained in the 'sermon on the mount.'"[105] Yet Christian ethics is not simply a slavish, literal repetition of these sayings. The methods of literary criticism may appropriately be applied to these precepts:

> Another obviously legitimate ground of limiting the application of absolute precepts, is afforded us in just biblical criticism. . . . In deducing public rules as authoritative upon mankind, it is needful to take into account those considerations which criticism supplies. The construction of the original languages and their peculiar phraseology, the habits, manners, and prevailing opinions of the times, and the *circumstances* under which a precept was delivered, are evidently amongst these considerations. And literary criticism is so much the more needed, because the great majority of mankind have access to Scripture only through the medium of translations."[106]

One outcome of this emphasis is that we can expect to find in the New Testament not only specific rules for specific cases:

> There are numberless questions of duty which Christianity decides, yet respecting which, specifically, not a word is to be found in the New Testament. These questions are decided by general principles, which principles are distinctly laid down. These three words, "Love your enemies," are of greater practical application in the affairs of life, than twenty propositions which define exact duties in specific cases.[107]

In general, then, "Much may be learnt respecting human duty by a contemplation of the spirit and temper of Christianity as it was exhibited by its first teachers."[108] Besides these broad, sweeping statements, somewhat more specific guidelines are available for the interpretation and application of New Testament ethics:

> We have to refer—to the general tendency of the revelation; to the individual declarations of Jesus Christ; to his practice; to the sentiments and practices of his commissioned followers; to the

opinions . . . which were held by their immediate converts; and to some other species of Christian evidence.[109]

When applying New Testament morality to daily life, we do not need to concern ourselves with the possible inconvenient consequences of our actions: "What then is the principle for which we contend? *An unreasoning reliance upon Providence for defence, in all those cases in which we would violate His laws by defending ourselves*.[110] But Dymond himself did not simply rest on this "unreasoning reliance." The consequences of obedience to the law of Christ, he suggested, are likely to be quite consonant with rational calculations of utility:

> After all, the general experience is, that what is most expedient with respect to another world, is most expedient with respect to the present. . . . Perhaps in nineteen cases out of twenty, he best consults his present welfare, who endeavors to secure it in another world.[111]

In particular, the evidence is that quiet disobedience to unjust governments works:

> It is by no means certain that Christian opposition to misgovernment would be so ineffectual as is supposed. Nothing is so invincible as determinate non-compliance. He that resists by force, may be overcome by greater force; but nothing can overcome a calm and fixed determination not to obey.[112]

Dymond had equal confidence in the effectiveness of Christian renunciation of war and of armed defense:

> A *uniform, undeviating* regard to the peaceable obligations of Christianity, *becomes the safeguard of those who practise it*. . . . The evidence of experience is, that a people who habitually regard the obligations of Christianity in their conduct towards other men, and who steadfastly refuse, through whatever consequences, to engage in acts of hostility, *will experience protection in their peacefulness:* and it matters nothing to the argument, whether we refer that protection to the immediate agency of Providence, or to the influence of such conduct upon the minds of men.[113]

Christian principles will prevail, not only in the cases of individuals and of nations, but also in the long run of human history: "It is the will of God that war should eventually be abolished. . . . *Christianity will be the means of introducing this period of peace.*[114] Dymond's optimism was, in addition, rounded out by a typical nineteenth-century faith in progress:

> That there are indications of an advancement of the human species towards greater purity in principle and in practice cannot, I think, be disputed. There is a manifest advancement in intellectual concerns:—Science of almost every kind is extending her empire;—political institutions are becoming rapidly ameliorated;—and morality and religion, if their progress be less perceptible, are yet advancing with an onward pace.[115]

So far, this exposition of Dymond's understanding of God, humans, and society has produced little, if anything, to solve our problems. The inconsistencies and incompleteness, in his stated premises and in the structure of his arguments, are the heart of the problem. The more fundamental, ultimate grounds of his thought do not provide much help in resolving the problem. If I turn the focus to the *conclusions* of his arguments, however, the clue to his thought becomes startlingly evident. There is an obvious and thoroughgoing consistency to these conclusions: Uniformly, unvaryingly, on every issue with which he dealt, he ended up affirming and supporting the established beliefs and practices of the Society of Friends.

Everything falls into place, then, if we posit an unstated fundamental premise as underlying all of Dymond's ethical thought: The will of God is, indeed, the final standard of right and wrong, but the fundamental, authoritative source for our knowledge of God's will is the Quaker tradition. This basic starting point is, indeed, an unstated, suppressed premise. Dymond in numerous cases did appeal to the practices and experience of the Society of Friends, but always as illustrations of the behavior he recommended. He never explicitly appealed to Quaker practice as the authority or even as a reason for affirming certain forms of action or for rejecting others.

We can proceed a step further. The authority of the Quaker tradition, in Dymond's thought, was not simply that of the first generation of Quakerism—an authority to which Friends themselves have often appealed. For example, neither Fox, Barclay, nor any other British Friend of that generation totally and unconditionally condemned slaveholding, but for Dymond there was no doubt: "The Moral Law of God condemns the slave system. If, therefore, we are Christians, the question is not merely decided, but *confessedly* decided: and what more do we ask?"[116]

Again, Dymond's reference to the immediate communication of the will of God was, of course, necessary because the Quaker tradition required it. Yet Dymond did not follow Barclay in asserting that scripture "is not the primary adequate rule of faith and manners."[117] British Friends in Dymond's day were giving more and more emphasis to the supreme authority of scripture. By this time Friends rarely in practice expected to receive immediate inspiration on matters of basic moral behavior; these issues had long since been settled. The immediate revelation of God's will was customarily restricted to such specifically "religious" questions as whether to preach in meeting for worship at any given date and time, or whether to undertake a journey in the ministry. On the question of immediate divine revelation, then, as on the question of slavery, Dymond's conclusions affirmed not the positions of Fox and Barclay's generation, but the practices of the Quakers in Dymond's own time. These practices were, in effect, the end product of a cumulative development of Quaker tradition. We can therefore restate Dymond's basic, unstated premise as follows: The authoritative source for our knowledge of God's will is the *received tradition* of the Society of Friends.

Many of the problems in interpreting Dymond's thought are now resolved. On what principle do we decide between utility, the law of nature, and the Old Testament as a moral authority in any particular instance? On what principle do we choose between a literal and a figurative interpretation of a New Testament passage? When do we use arguments from silence, and when do we reject them? When do we unquestioningly accept a "common consent" argument, and when do we reject it? In all these cases, the answer is simple: That argument is used, which most readily produces a conclusion that accords with those practices enforced by the received Quaker tradition.

The inconsistencies between Dymond's *Inquiry* and his *Essays*, on the validity of ever appealing to such principles as expediency and the law of nature, can also be resolved. In *Inquiry*, which was written first, Dymond was dealing with only one problem area—that of war. Since many anti-pacifist arguments in that day were founded on these principles, the shortest way out was simply to reject them totally; a firm and uncompromising appeal to the New Testament was the clearest way to support the Quaker position. However, Dymond proceeded to deal with a much wider range of moral issues in *Essays*. In the process it became clear to him that the New Testament was simply silent on many issues on which the Quaker tradition had formulated firm positions, either explicitly or in implicit but actual practice. Some further principles had to be found that could be used to support the Quaker position in these areas. In many cases, utility and the law of nature turned out, after all, to be very useful principles to have around.

Careful study makes it clear that the long final chapter of Dymond's *Essays* was a revised and reworked version of his *Inquiry*. In this revision, he carefully omitted his earlier rejection of the principles of utility and natural law. By keeping these principles absolutely subordinate to the New Testament, he remained able to preserve his argument against the lawfulness of defensive war, and to refute such thinkers as Paley who on occasion subordinated New Testament precepts to considerations of expediency or utility.

In short, between the time of the writing of *Inquiry* and that of *Essays*, Dymond changed his mind about the validity of the principles of utility and natural law. I can safely say that *Essays* expressed his more fully considered views on these questions.

Why should Dymond suppress his real reason in presenting his arguments? Referring to himself as author of *Essays*, he affirmed:

> His motive is, to advocate truth without reference to its popularity; and his hope is, to promote by these feeble exertions, an approximation to that state of purity, which he believes it is the design of God shall eventually beautify and dignify the condition of mankind.[118]

He clearly believed that "that state of purity" was already embodied in the life and practice of the Society of Friends of his own time. But—despite the example of a few pioneers like Stephen Grellet—Quakerism as a whole was then not actively evangelistic or missionary in its emphasis. The fervent desire of George Fox's generation to convert all England to the true faith had long since died out. Organized foreign missionary work and the revival movement on the American frontier had not yet become part of the Quaker scene. Dymond himself was clearly repelled by religious enthusiasm and fanaticism; it would have been constitutionally impossible for him, as a traditional Quaker, to go for all-out proselyting of his fellow Christians. Yet he was deeply convinced that Quaker practices were truly reasonable, and he hoped, by appealing to the gentle voice of reason, to persuade other rational Christians to adopt the fruits of the Quaker faith, without forcing them to undergo the traumatic process of radical conversion to the roots of that faith.

Dymond's specific arguments, taken separately, were often incisive. But he lacked the overall perspective of the truly systematic thinker. He also lacked the perceptiveness of self-critical insight, which might have helped him to see the incompleteness and inconsistency in his arguments when they were brought together into a whole. In consequence, he was constantly, even if unconsciously, guilty of stacking the deck in his logical argumentation. Where his reading had made him aware of arguments that led to conclusions that diverged from Quaker practice, he was brilliant at developing trenchant refutations. Where such counterarguments had not previously been produced, he seemed often unaware that choosing a different course of argument, from among the premises and principles that he generally accepted as valid, might well have led to a different ethical conclusion.

Perhaps the body of Jonathan Dymond's work can serve us best as an object lesson: If we are truly concerned to recover and to reappropriate the insights of our Quaker tradition, we would be well advised to become aware of the pits into which we can fall if we are not totally honest and open, both to ourselves and to others, about the full meaning of this faith and tradition, including its deep Christian roots and its intermediate premises, as well as its ultimate radical consequences.

Lucretia Coffin Mott

Lucretia Coffin was born on the island of Nantucket, Massachusetts, in January 1793. Her parents, Thomas and Anna Coffin, were Friends. Thomas was captain of a whaling ship. In 1803, while his ship "was cruising for whales along the coast of South America, it was seized by a Spanish man-of-war, on the charge that it had violated neutrality. . . . They were hauled into the port of Valparaiso, Chile, and the ship impounded."[119] Thomas returned home by foot over the Andes to Brazil, and then as a ship's passenger back to the United States. He changed his career, became a merchant, and moved his family to Boston in 1804.

When Lucretia was thirteen, her parents sent her to a Quaker boarding school at Nine Partners, in New York state. James Mott, son of the school's superintendent, was a young teacher at the school. In 1808 fifteen-year-old Lucretia had completed all of the school's courses, and she stayed on as a teacher. After a year or so, it was clear that Lucretia and James were interested in marrying each other. Lucretia's parents had moved to Philadelphia,

Friends and the Bible: A Nineteenth-Century Sampler

where her father had opened a nearby factory. Lucretia came home to her parents and persuaded her father to take James as a business partner. In April 1811, Lucretia and James were married in the Friends meeting house at Second and Pine Streets in Philadelphia. From 1811 until 1857 Lucretia and James lived in Philadelphia. After 1857, they lived the rest of their lives in "a remodeled farmhouse in Chelten Hills, rolling farmland north of the city,"[120] which they named Roadside.

Between 1812 and 1828, Lucretia gave birth to four daughters and two sons. She was recorded as a minister in 1821. When the Great Separation took place in 1827 Lucretia and James chose to be Hicksites. "In May 1830 she was chosen as clerk of Philadelphia Women's Yearly Meeting."[121]

In August 1830, a young journalist, William Lloyd Garrison, was a dinner guest at the Motts' home. He was just coming to the conclusion that the only solution to the evils of slavery was the immediate abolition of all slaveholding. The Motts became long-time friends and supporters of Garrison. They became actively involved in the abolitionist movement. In 1833, Lucretia was a leader in the founding of the Philadelphia Female Anti-Slavery Society. Friends had long disapproved of working together with outside groups. Lucretia and James were working actively with "hireling" ministers from other denominations in their anti-slavery work. Many Friends looked with suspicion on these activities.

Late in 1839, the British and Foreign Anti-Slavery Society issued an invitation to a World Anti-Slavery Convention, to be held in London in June 1840. The Pennsylvania Anti-Slavery Society appointed Lucretia and James and four young women as its delegates to the world convention. The Motts spent about three months in England, Scotland, and Ireland, during which Lucretia kept a detailed diary; it was eventually published in 1952.[122]

The delegates knew before they left America that there would be strong opposition to the seating of women delegates at the convention. Some of the strongest opposition came from British Friends who were members of the British and Foreign Anti-Slavery Society:

> The British Friends had received an epistle from the Orthodox Friends in America warning them to be on their guard against the Motts. The letter, Lucretia subsequently learned, was written by Stephen Grellet, and was actually read in London Yearly Meeting. Although the London Friends feared her chiefly for her heresy, it seemed apparent that they were also determined to use

their not inconsiderable influence on the convention to prevent her from being seated.[123]

A week before the convention began, the Motts arrived in London and found lodgings at a comfortable rooming house, where a number of American delegates were already lodging, including "H. B. Stanton, & his nice Elizabeth."[124] Henry B. and Elizabeth Cady Stanton were not only there as delegates, they were also enjoying their honeymoon. On the opening day of the convention, the motion to admit women as members of the convention was soundly defeated. The women were given seats as observers "behind the bar." Five days later, when William Lloyd Garrison arrived, he refused to accept his seat at the convention and joined the women behind the bar.

A number of individual English and Irish Friends warmed up socially to the Motts. Samuel Gurney, a brother of Elizabeth Fry and Joseph John Gurney, at first failed to invite them to a party, but on a later occasion he entertained Lucretia and James and other American convention delegates. Fry was not won over. At Samuel Gurney's, "Elizabeth Cady Stanton . . . recalled, years later, that Fry had conspicuously avoided meeting Lucretia on this occasion, going indoors when she was out, and out when she was in."[125]

During their stay in England, Lucretia Mott and Elizabeth Cady Stanton became close friends, and they inspired each other to become active in fighting for women's rights in addition to their mutual commitment to abolishing slavery. They continued to correspond and talked about women's rights at Stanton's home near Boston whenever Mott came to that city for anti-slavery and other meetings. In the summer of 1848 Mott traveled to the Finger Lakes region in New York state to visit her sister, Martha Coffin Wright, who lived in Auburn, and Stanton, who had recently moved to Seneca Falls. Mott, Wright, Stanton, and two other women met for tea on July 13. After extended conversation, they composed a call to a women's rights convention, which they published the next day in a local newspaper. The convention was to meet in Seneca Falls on July 19–20. The five women met again on the 16th: "One of the group hit upon the idea of rewriting the Declaration of Independence as a way of encompassing their grievances and expressing the spirit of 1848: 'We hold these truths to be self-evident: that all men and women are created equal. . . .'"[126] A large crowd showed up for the convention. They adopted the prepared Declaration of Sentiments and a number of resolutions, including a call that women should secure the right to vote. At the close of the convention, "One hundred of the men and women present signed their names to the Declaration of Sentiments. As the most prominent person there, Lucretia was the first to sign."[127] The Seneca Falls Convention was the formal beginning of the women's suffrage movement in the United States.

In the years that followed, Lucretia Mott continued to be an active—and increasingly respected and admired—leader in the abolitionist and women's rights movements and among Hicksite Friends. She entertained a constant stream of visitors in her home, and she was actively involved in the founding of Swarthmore College, which opened in 1869. James died in 1868. Lucretia died in November, 1880.

Lucretia Mott was always bold and outspoken in her views. She highly valued reason; she could even urge: "Let us love that Divinity of Christ that is conformable to man's intelligence and reason."[128] She spoke of "the divine gift of reason with which man is so beautifully endowed."[129] She even implied that rationality was the essence of God's own nature and spirit: "Let us keep hold of the faith that is in accordance with reason and with the intelligent dictates of the pure spirit of God."[130]

Mott firmly believed in reason; she also believed that human history was a story of advance and progress: "There is not a more interesting object for the contemplation of the philosopher and the Christian—the lover of man, and the lover of God, than the law of progress—the advancement from knowledge to knowledge, from obedience to obedience."[131] Human society is progressing not only in knowledge, but also in morality:

> This law of progress is most emphatically marked in our day, in the great reformatory movements which have agitated the truth-loving and sincere hearted, engaged in the work of blessing man.[132]
>
> There is this continued advance toward perfection from age to age.[133]

The social reform movements that mark human progress have even resulted in improvements in theology and in interpreting the Bible.

> It is for the following generation to go on and make yet other advance steps. Such advances are beautiful when we come to look at them. Those of the past have given some Theologians noble

ideas; they have come to have more expanded views and to rejoice in the belief of the continued advance of humanity. How much better the Theology which has resulted from these great movements. They have led us to read our Bibles better.[134]

For Mott, to read the Bible or any other writings better meant using our intelligence and understanding when we read:

> If we attain to the State when we can say "Father forgive them, for they know not what they do"; we must come to understand that spirit, and by obedience be established in this high mountain of the Lord above the influence of sectarian feelings. We desire this attainment but in what manner shall we seek and how shall we find it? In no other way, than by aiming and arriving at the great truth that the highest righteousness is the true condition of man; exalting the standard of justice and mercy, truth and honesty. . . . If we read understandingly and intelligently the religious history of ages long past, [we] find this standard of truth set above all forms and ceremonies by the prophets and righteous servants of God, from generation to generation.[135]

She especially applied this standard of reading with intelligence to the study of the Bible: "The Bible, in the intelligent reading and growing intelligence with which it is pursued with proper discrimination, . . . had its uses. How many have found consolation in Scripture testimonials suited to their almost every state?"[136] She insisted that "Many do err not knowing the scriptures, or the truth—not reading intelligently, not understanding the truth aright."[137] Again, referring to the use of Bible passages to oppose women's rights, she said,

> It is of the greatest importance that religiously-minded women, those who have been accustomed to regard this volume as their rule of faith and practice, should be led to examine these Scriptures, and see whether these things are as our opponents claim. And if they will read that book intelligently, . . . with a reliance on their own judgment, they will discover that the Scriptures cannot be wielded against us.[138]

George Fox and Margaret Fell had read the Bible empathetically; Mott emphasized reading the Bible intelligently.

One result of Mott's attempt to read the Bible intelligently was that she came to distinguish between the timeless, divinely inspired quality of some parts of the Bible and the merely human, fallible origin of other parts:

> Free thinkers may . . . fail to award to the Scriptures all the beautiful and blessed instruction they contain. I have for some years accustomed myself to read and examine them, as nearly as I would any other book, as Early education and veneration would permit. I have now no difficulty in deciding upon the human and ignorant origin of such parts as conflict with the known and eternal laws of Deity in the Physical creation: be the claim to the miraculous ever so high, & the assumption of the Prophetic and God-inspired, ever so strong. Still less, if possible, do I waver then any violation of the Divine and Eternal law of right, such as murder in any of its forms, Slavery in any of its degrees, and Priestcraft in its various phases as palmed upon the religious world is declared to be "Thus saith the Lord". It is impossible by any Theological ingenuity to reconcile the moral code of the Old & New Testament, as proceeding from Him who is "without variableness or shadow of turning" Far safer, therefore is it, to admit *man* to be fallible than judge God to be changeable.[139]

In a letter to Irish Friend Richard Webb, Mott was commenting on some writings she had recently read:

> It is cause of rejoicing that Religious-minded persons dare to speak & write so plainly . . . —The criticisms are so just & the reasons so good, why they the Scriptures of the Jews should not be read indiscriminately in schools or in any elementary training. . . . And I . . . agree entirely with the reasons given for judging rightly of this Idol of Christendom—At the same time I love the Scriptures & can say with Theodore Parker: "You cannot open this book any where, but from between its oldest & newest leaves there issues forth truth—words that burn even now tho' they are 2 or 3000 yrs. old"—I may not have quoted it quite right from memory.[140]

She could also be critical of some of the widely-revered persons in the Bible: "It is evidence of the superstition of our age, that we can adhere to, Yea that, we can bow with profound veneration to the records of an Abraham, the sensualist Solomon, and the war-like David, inspired though they may have been."[141]

She could become most eloquent when contrasting the heights and the depths of biblical writings:

> None can revere more than I do, the truths of the Bible. I have read it perhaps as much as any one present, and, I trust, with profit. It has at times been more to me than my daily food. When an attempt was made some twenty years ago to engraft some church dogmas upon this society, claiming this book for authority, it led me to examine, and compare text with the content. In so doing I became so much interested that I scarcely noted the passage of time. Even to this day, when I open this volume, so familiar is almost every chapter that I can sometimes scarcely lay it aside from the interest I feel in its beautiful pages. But I should be recreant to principle, did I not say, the great error in Christendom is, in regarding these scriptures taken as a whole as the plenary inspiration of God, and their authority as supreme. . . . Well did that servant of God, Elias Hicks, warn the people against an undue veneration of the Bible, or of any human authority, any written record or outward testimony.[142]

I can hear, in Mott's questioning of the divine inspiration of portions of the Old Testament, echoes of the problems first raised by Abraham Shackleton and Hannah Barnard. Where their questioning was at times cautious and hesitant, hers was bold and even defiant. Mott did acknowledge the importance of Barnard in pioneering the trail that she was now traversing:

> This generation is indebted to . . . honorable men and women, not a few. Let me name Hannah Barnard who came forth amid the darkness and error that prevailed, and in this country as well as in England, bore a noble testimony to truth, as opposed to superstition and tradition. She exposed the benighted reliance on Jewish authority, which led the people to find sanction for war and other evils and abuses; rebuking them for their sin and great wrongs, sustained by an unwarrantable use of the Scriptures. Her name was cast out as evil and trampled upon by those high in authority, both in England and in this country.[143]
>
> Divers Quaker women since that time, have been eminent as preachers. Hannah Barnard of Hudson, a native of Nantucket, of the last century, was regarded one of the greatest ministers in the Society. She travelled in England, & was there *deposed* by

the ruling powers in the Society of course, for daring to express doubts of the Divine authority of the Jewish Wars—as well as more openly than Friends were wont, to deny the atonement & scheme of Salvation. She returned home to Hudson & was much respected thro' a long life for her good works.[144]

Mott did not simply use her own unaided reason in interpreting the Bible. She was also ready to make use of the results of the critical biblical scholarship that was beginning to flourish. In 1841, a year after her return from Great Britain and the World Anti-Slavery Convention, she was speaking out for the right of women to speak in public. She began by suggesting that some of Paul's advices were directed at particular local situations and were not meant to apply to the church throughout the ages:

> I am aware that the apostle Paul recommended to the women of Corinth, when they wanted information, to "ask their husbands at home." I am not disposed to deny, that under the circumstances of the case, he did it wisely. But do we find him saying, that they were not to preach or prophecy? So far from it, that he has expressly given them directions how to preach and prophecy. And what this preaching and prophesying were, is defined by the same apostle as "speaking unto *men* to edification, and exhortation, and comfort."[145]

She continued, in arguments that echo those of Margaret Fell, Robert Barclay, and Benjamin Lay, to appeal to Paul's "declaration to the Galatians, that, to as many of them as had put on Christ, there was neither Jew nor Greek, male nor female; and also in his expressions of gratitude to the women helpers in the gospel."[146] She was able to add one example not mentioned by those earlier Friends, from Romans 16:1:

> In the phrase in which "Phebe, the servant of the church," is mentioned, those who are familiar with the original have found, that the same word which is, in her case, translated *servant*, is, in the case of men, translated *minister*. And has not conscious evidence been afforded by this translation, of the priest-craft and monopoly of the pulpit, which have so long held women bound?[147]

Decades later, in the year before her death, "Lucretia Mott argued in 1879 that some parts of the Bible had now been 'set aside by competent authorities as spurious.'"[148]

Mott opposed a too-literal reading of the Bible. She referred to the language of mystery and to "spiritual language," which are characterized by metaphors, figures of speech, and parables:

> There is something said, to be sure, about the subjection to the husband, but it was also said that it was spoken in a mystery in reference to the Church, evidently not intending thereby to apply it literally. In the metaphors of that age you know there is great liberty taken on other subjects; why not on that?[149]

> There is a religious instinct in the constitution of man. . . . This has been likened, by various figures, emblems, parables, to things without us and around us. It has been variously interpreted, variously explained; for no nation has a spiritual language, exclusively such. We must therefore speak of our spiritual experiences in language having reference to spiritual things. And we find this has been the case, especially in the records of the Jews, the scriptures of Israel, and what are called "Christian scriptures." They abound in emblems and parables.[150]

Mott was sure that there are great truths to be found in the Hebrew and Christian scriptures—but not only in those writings:

> How many are the testimonies of these Scriptures which suit the state of those who are desirous for truth and righteousness to prevail on the earth, how beautiful is the testimony from the beginning to the end of the Scriptures, to the discriminating servant of the highest that is born to righteousness, truth, uprightness, justice and mercy, peace and universal love? . . . How satisfactory then are the corroborating testimonies of Scripture but not more so than the testimonies of many other servants of God. Why not regard all the testimonies of the good, as Scripture, recorded in every age and in every condition of life? These Scriptures are valuable because they bring together the testimonies of so many ages of the world, but are there not equal testimonies born to the truth that are not bound in this volume?[151]

For Mott, this was the highest, ultimate truth: "The true, eternal foundation, that thou do justly love mercy and walk humbly with thy God"[152]—words proclaimed by the prophet Micah.

Mott frequently reiterated that she rejected the idea of Christ's "vicarious atonement"; she referred to

> the erroneous views which prevail in Christendom, of the divinity of Christ, and the vicarious atonement. . . .When preachers for fear of losing their reputation in the religious world, speak of their faith in the Divinity of Christ, and the vicarious atonement, they are retarding Christian progress by their want of simplicity and frankness.[153]
>
> Faith in Christ has become so involved with a belief in human depravity, and a vicarious atonement, imputed sin and imputed righteousness.[154]

From the connection she made here between the atonement and imputed sin and righteousness, and the fact that she practically never used the noun "atonement" without the adjective "vicarious," it seems clear that what she was actually rejecting was the satisfaction or substitution theory of the atonement. She gives no evidence that she was even aware that any alternative view or theory of the atonement existed. But I do find her proclaiming that "Jesus . . . has astonished the world and brought a response from all mankind by the purity of his precepts, the excellence of his example"[155]— words that bring strikingly to mind the central thrust of the moral-influence view of the atonement.

Abraham Lawton

Abraham Lawton was born in England in 1800. From 1828 until his death in 1882, he held membership in a succession of Hicksite meetings, including Chester, Pennsylvania, and Wilmington, Delaware; monthly meetings in Philadelphia Yearly Meeting; and Coeymans and Hudson monthly meetings in New York Yearly Meeting. His residences in New York were all near the Hudson River, south of Albany. He was a farmer. In 1835 or shortly thereafter, he married Elizabeth Bancroft.

In the 1860s, Lawton, his brother-in-law Joseph Bancroft, and another Hicksite Friend "opened a meeting in Philadelphia that was open to all Friends. They seem to have seen it as a call to reunite all Friends."[156] In and around 1864 and 1865, he published a number of pamphlets in connection with this project. He gathered these pamphlets and a letter or two into a book that he published in Philadelphia in 1866, under the title *Some Testimonies of Truth Set Forth for the Healing of the Nations*.

Lawton's writings are crowded with biblical quotations, citations, and metaphors in a way that reminds me strongly of the writings of George Fox and Edward Burrough. In contrast to Fox and Burrough, I found it difficult in most instances to decipher just what Lawton was trying to get at—what points he was trying to make or to prove. It sometimes seemed that he was just pouring out a cascade of biblical pictures and metaphors:

> As Paul says, "Be ye transformed by the renewing of your mind that ye may prove what that good, and perfect, and acceptable will of God is," by which the church is sanctified and kept in the inheritance of the just, who are fed by the everlasting Gospel of peace, and have their feet prepared by it, to preach it, as they are called to publish their peace from the beauty of Mount Zion, the city of the saint's solemnity, and whose situation the Lord hath appointed for the joy of the whole earth; and that his name may go forth from that joy or consolation of Israel, by his covenant with the Jew inward, whose worship in spirit and in truth their father seeketh, and leadeth them into, to glorify them within, that put on God's strength, and riches, and rejoice in the marriage of the Lamb; because they dwell with him in his kingdom that is come on earth, that the tabernacle of God may be with men, as it is written "I will dwell with them;" and again, by his sure covenant, "I will be their God and they shall be to me a people;" in that day when "I will be merciful to their unrighteousness, and their sins and iniquities will I remember no more." Such overcomers shall all know the Lord by conversion from the tongue of the Egyptian sea, and men shall go over dry shod when they are saved from the tongues of the evil doers, that come from the elements that shake, rend and destroy man's comfort and peace, because they follow their own imaginations, and sow to the flesh, (and through the spirit they mortify not the deeds thereof;) and, as the Prophet said to such that were laden with iniquity, are "a seed of evil doers," that might learn knowledge by the ox, and the ass; and an acknowledgement of considered reverence, and turn from rebellion, and not trust in lying words, but thoroughly amend their ways and their doings, by putting away the evil thereof; and then he would cause them to dwell there.[157]

A favorite biblical metaphor of Lawton's was that of the rock. He wrote:

> O, look unto this great rock that hath such an Almighty shadow in a weary land, when a king does reign in righteousness, and his princes do rule in judgment; and a man shall be for a hiding place from the wind and a covert from the tempest; and (as a refreshing stream or) as rivers of water in a dry place, Is. xxxii. 1, 2.[158]

We can note how he has transposed the order of the actual KJV text of Isaiah 32:1–2: "Behold, a king shall reign in righteousness, and princes shall rule in judgment. And a man shall be as a hiding place from the wind, and a covert from the tempest; as rivers of water in a dry place, as the shadow of a great rock in a weary land."

In 1 Corinthians 10:4, Paul wrote: "And did all drink the same spiritual drink: for they drank of that spiritual Rock that followed them: and that Rock was Christ" (KJV). Paul was alluding to a couple of incidents in the story of the Israelites in their desert wandering, including Numbers 20:11 KJV: "And Moses lifted up his hand, and with his rod he smote the rock twice: and the water came out abundantly, and the congregation drank, and their beasts also." Lawton referred to these passages when he wrote: "Truth's Heavenly Father is honored, and does also honor those who honor the fountain from whence the living water gushes out, as he speaketh and men do live upon that spiritual rock; the fountain of life."[159]

He used the metaphor of the rock in other ways:

> Faith is substance, or the rock of God's spirit in union with men of a pure heart.[160]

> The truth is a great mystery, a great rock, and a great fortress, or a munition of defence to rely upon. God is that rock; his work is perfect, and he works not out of that strong tower of justice and judgment, where every man is safe in his redeeming name.[161]

In a very different context, Lawton quoted from the account of Paul's encounter with the risen Christ on the road to Damascus, Acts 9:4–5: "His Father, who said unto Saul, 'Why persecutest thou me?' Here Jesus appeared as Lord and Judge; and Saul fell at the words, 'I am Jesus whom thou persecutest: it is hard for thee to kick against the pricks.' "[162]

Lawton went on to combine the metaphors of Paul's kicking and of the rock in a surprisingly original but unbiblical way: "Kick not against Paul's rock."[163] We find this mixed metaphor again and again:

> Oh! that men would learn not to kick against the rock like Saul, who was a kicker and despiser thereof.[164]
>
> Whosoever strive to separate divine worship from imperative duty, kick against the Rock of Truth, and strive against their Maker's will.[165]
>
> Saul kicked against the immovable rock, and pierced his own soul; and being in the power of darkness, he knew not the voice of the rock of God.[166]
>
> Paul held the mystery of the faith as he learned faith, and was subdued by the rock so hard to kick against, and so piercing to Saul, the kicker, and the pretender to authority that never leads men to acknowledge the truth....
>
> Then kick not against Paul's rock, which he held the mystery of in Christ his rock.[167]
>
> Some friends after this world's friendship, kick hard against Paul's godly rock, that redeemed him from the commandments and traditions of men.[168]

In one of his pamphlets, I can observe the goal that Lawton was aiming to achieve in his biblical arguments. This pamphlet is "The Healing Virtue of the Plain Language Described."[169] Here he was using the Bible to argue for using the Quaker "plain language," including the refusal to swear judicial oaths.

Early in his argument, he affirmed,

> They who follow the light of life straight forward, have no condemnation; because they walk not after the flesh, but after the spirit; and are upright in their generation of good and just men, to whom there is no condemnation....
>
> The upright, straight road of duty and peace, is a safe path. ... If men sin and turn their faces from the light of life, and their backs to the truth, they should return, return straightly back, narrowly; ... so that there is none occasion of stumbling in them that follow the comforter, the light of life, and do not walk in

darkness, but will be saved from the power of Satan, by being transformed in person, and by speaking the truth in soberness, for the service of the Lord.[170]

We can see clear citations here of Romans 8:1: "There is therefore now no condemnation to them which are in Christ Jesus, who walk not after the flesh, but after the Spirit" (KJV), and of Psalm 112:2: "The generation of the upright shall be blessed" (KJV).

Lawton portrayed the man "whose goings are established in the Truth, that is equal on every side, because God's way is in him, and his righteousness upholds him, and his right hand of wisdom sustains him forevermore."[171] The underlying reference here was Isaiah 41:10: "I am thy God: I will strengthen thee; yea, I will help thee; yea, I will uphold thee with the right hand of my righteousness" (KJV). He went on:

> The word unchangeable yea, and nay, has power over every other word or words. Let the same sure rock remain your yea for testimony, and your nay be your nay truly, unchanged, by abiding in that shelter and fortress. Add nothing to the truth, and rob him not of anything; and the truth will remain entire, lacking nothing for your reward; and he will not forsake thee if thou dost not forsake truth, he will cover thee with his shield, and under his wings thou shall trust.[172]

The exact words "He will not forsake thee" are in Deuteronomy 4:31 KJV. Similar language can be found in Deuteronomy 31:6 and 1 Chronicles 28:20 KJV: "He will not fail thee, nor forsake thee;" Deuteronomy 31:8 KJV: "He will not fail thee, neither forsake thee;" Joshua 1:5 KJV: "I will not fail thee, nor forsake thee;" and Hebrews 13:5 KJV: "I will never leave thee, nor forsake thee."

Lawton continued his argument:

> Surely the holy nation does come, and may be beheld by the new man in the virtue of the king's reign, and through his righteous prince's rule; . . . and the stammering tongue shall be ready to speak plainly by virtue of the holy nation that speaketh the truth in righteousness, which is of the Lord, who leadeth his heritage; . . . and that justifies them by their words of truth, that are no more than that their yea is yea, and their nay is unchangeably nay, . . . and will not add to it or take from the Truth.[173]

I heard here sharp echoes of several biblical passages:

> A holy nation (1 Peter 2:9 KJV).
>
> He that walketh uprightly, and worketh righteousness, and speaketh the truth in his heart (Psalm 15:2 KJV).
>
> He that speaketh truth sheweth forth righteousness (Proverbs 12:17 KJV).

Lawton went on to insist:

> They may return, repent and live, by learning to do well; which is the only ground and pillar of Truth, by overcoming death through the daily death of the cross, to receive Christ's daily crown of life. . . . When men speak righteously, they also see righteously.[174]

This passage included allusions to 1 Corinthians 15:31: "I die daily" (KJV), and to Luke 9:23–24: "Let him deny himself, and take up his cross daily, and follow me. For whosoever will save his life shall lose it: but whosoever will lose his life for my sake, the same shall save it" (KJV).

At length in this argument we come across a remarkable passage that resounds with the language of the early Quaker Lamb's War:

> The Son of the living God . . . feeds all his flock in the throne of his father, and who builds them by his wisdom, to support one another, and to be a refreshing dew from the Lord one unto another, as he is their daily bread, and sure water, which is given them; and springs up within them unto eternal life; and which life sustains all men who do cast their burden upon the Lord for a shield and sure defence, by the sword of his mouth that men shall live by, in the testimony God dwells in, ministers in, feeds his flock in, and clothes all his children in.[175]

We find Lamb's War language again in the heading of another pamphlet that Lawton included in his book:

> *The song of a great and marvellous work for the cause of Justice and Truth in the earth; which the saints of God do sing in the spirit and in the understanding also; having the victory over the beast, his image, his mark, and the number of his name, which is the number of a man that is of the earth and earthy.*[176]

Lawton here tied the Lamb's War theme into a Christus Victor view of Christ's atonement, as clearly and firmly as George Fox had made that connection.

3
Friends, the Bible, and God: Holiness and Modernist Friends

In his book *The Transformation of American Quakerism*, Thomas Hamm vividly describes how two movements late in the nineteenth century made a drastic impact on the direction of American Quakerism, particularly Gurneyite Quakerism. These movements were the Holiness movement in the 1870s and 1880s and the modernist movement in the 1890s and the first decade of the twentieth century.

As Hamm told it:

> To understand the whirlwind that swept through the Gurneyite yearly meetings during the 1870s, one must look to a small group of ministers and the experience that they shared: an instantaneous, postconversion sanctification that they believed, freed them from any desire or propensity to sin and filled them with the power of the Holy Ghost. They found this teaching on

sanctification outside the society in the post-Civil War interdenominational holiness movement. . . .

Late in the 1860s the holiness movement attracted a number of young Friends, especially young ministers. . . . The holiness revival movement among Friends was from the beginning one of ministers, one that exalted ministerial standing and stressed its prerogatives.[1]

During the 1870s and 1880s, revival meetings became immensely popular in most Gurneyite yearly meetings and brought in thousands of new members. Many leading elders and other moderate Friends

acquiesced in the new growth and agreed with the notion of forming in each monthly meeting pastoral committees of elders, overseers, ministers, and other concerned members to see to the spiritual welfare of new Friends. The idea proved popular, . . . but revival Friends had come to their own solution, and on the pastoral question, as on so many others, they effectively outmaneuvered the moderates by introducing the one-person pastorate that the moderates dreaded.

The revival's commitment to pastors was inextricably linked to its view of the ministry. The revival centered on preaching, impossible without ministers. Furthermore, ministers were a divinely appointed class, "the noblest of the race, called of God to teach and lead the rest of us."[2]

Dougan Clark, Jr. was a prominent member of this group of Holiness ministers. He and Joseph H. Smith paid especial credit to David B. Updegraff of Ohio for bringing about the astonishing changes in the character of Gurneyite Quakerism:

Some of us, who had been reared in proximity to a fossilized and somewhat disintegrated Quakerism, would never have known what the real, living thing was, had it not been for the life and work of David Updegraff. Wherever he has been and has worked (together with a few other blessed men and women of like spirit) we find the Friends' church to be different from what it is in places that barred the door upon this humble but mighty servant of God. . . . Different in that exclusiveness has given way to evangelism; and where . . . they are now zealous and active for others' salvation. Different in that their abstinence from singing . . . has given way to the singing of Psalms and hymns and spiritual songs, as the Bible enjoins. Different, too, in that their prejudice against an "hireling ministry" and a pastoral oversight has so far yielded, that men called to this work are in some places receiving a measurable support to aid them in giving themselves wholly to it.³

When the first Quaker anti-slavery protest was issued in Germantown, Pennsylvania, in 1688, two of the three Friends who had joined Francis Daniel Pastorius in signing it were Dirck Op-den-Graeff and his brother, Abraham Op-den-Graeff. Abraham's great-great-great-grandson, David Brainerd Updegraff, was born in Mount Pleasant, Ohio, in 1830. Mount Pleasant was a small town not far from the Ohio River. His parents were Friends. His father, David Benjamin Updegraff, a businessman and farmer, was an elder in Short Creek Monthly Meeting in Mount Pleasant. His mother, "Rebecca Taylor Updegraff was a recorded Friends minister, born in Loudon County, Virginia. . . . She . . . began traveling in the ministry in 1826."⁴

David Brainerd Updegraff attended Haverford College near Philadelphia for one year, 1851–52. In September 1852, he married Rebecca Price; they had four children. He made his living as a businessman and farmer. In 1854, when the Wilburite-Gurneyite split occurred in Ohio Yearly Meeting, he went with the Wilburite faction. In 1860, David and Rebecca went through conversion experiences during a series of revival meetings at the Methodist church in Mount Pleasant. After that, they switched from the Wilburite to the Gurneyite Friends meeting in Mount Pleasant. Rebecca died in 1864, at the age of thirty-five.

In 1866 David Updegraff married Eliza Mitchell, a Presbyterian. David and Eliza had four children; she finally joined Friends in 1891. During the 1869 sessions of Ohio Yearly Meeting (Gurneyite), David was holding evening prayer and Bible study meetings in his home. John Inskip, "one of the originators of the Holiness camp meetings of the nineteenth century,"⁵ was staying in his home and talking about the Holiness movement. On that occasion, David had a dramatic and sudden experience of complete sanctification by the Holy Spirit. This was the key turning point in his life. He immediately began preaching the Holiness message in both Quaker and interdenominational gatherings. He was recorded as a minister in 1872.

Updegraff introduced many innovations at Friends revivals, or protracted meetings, which were considered by participants as new and controversial. . . . While other denominations may have considered Updegraff's methods merely flamboyant, to Friends they were shocking. Among his innovations which eventually became a permanent part of many worship meetings were singing, loud vocal public prayer, use of the altar for prayer, calling on people by name to testify, and public reading of the Bible.[6]

Like many other revivalist and Holiness preachers, his preaching was often intensely emotional in tone. The action that caused the greatest controversy among Gurneyite Friends, however, came when he asked a Baptist pastor in Philadelphia to baptize him in water, in 1882. After this he urged Friends meetings to include baptism and communion in their worship. At the 1885 sessions of Ohio Yearly Meeting, an attempt was made to require monthly meetings to remove ministers or elders from their status if they took part in or promoted the practice of these sacraments. The attempt was defeated. From then on, Ohio Yearly Meeting officially "tolerated" this departure from Quaker tradition.

Most other Gurneyite yearly meetings went on record as opposing the practices of baptism and communion. In an attempt to resolve the controversy, a conference of all Gurneyite yearly meetings met in Richmond, Indiana, in September 1887. David Updegraff was one of Ohio Yearly Meeting's delegates to that conference. The major action taken by that conference was the publication of a lengthy statement of Quaker faith and practice, which has become known as the Richmond Declaration of Faith. This Declaration included extended statements of the Quaker understanding that true baptism and communion were not "outward acts."

Most Gurneyite yearly meetings adopted the Richmond Declaration. Ohio Yearly Meeting did not. When Gurneyite yearly meetings organized themselves into the Five Years Meeting in 1902, Ohio Yearly Meeting did not join that body. Gradually, during the twentieth century, some other yearly meetings pulled out of the Five Years Meeting (later called Friends United Meeting) and eventually joined with Ohio into a body now known as Evangelical Friends Church International.

In the final years of his life, Updegraff was employed as pastor of his home meeting in Mount Pleasant, Ohio. He died in May 1894.

In 1892, Updegraff published a number of his sermons and addresses in a book with the title *Old Corn*. In 1895, Dougan Clark, Jr. and Joseph H. Smith published a biography, *David B. Updegraff and His Work*. In this book they included substantial extracts from his writings without specifying titles or page numbers for their sources.

In reference to 1 Corinthians 14:34–35, Updegraff wrote: "If Paul refers in this Scripture to the *same kind* of 'speaking' that he does in chapter 11 verse 5, then he most undoubtedly *contradicts* himself. But that is *impossible*. We must, therefore, *harmonize* these passages."[7] Why is it *impossible* for Paul to contradict himself? Updegraff must be making an unquestioning assumption that every statement in the Bible is literally true.

He made his view, that every word in the Bible must be literally true, quite clear in his polemic against historical and literary criticism of the Bible, which was becoming widely accepted in scholarly circles in the late nineteenth century:

> "What is meant by the phrase Higher Criticism?" It is generally understood to apply to a method of investigating the Bible just the same as any other book. That is, it takes nothing for granted. It ignores the testimony of the Bible concerning itself. Its claims of inspiration, authenticity, and infallibility are allowed only so far as established by the scientific, linguistic, and historical scholarship of men, mainly destitute of any spiritual intuitions whatever. Its first effect, therefore, is to disparage and discredit the Bible. . . . The *common people* of Christendom regard the Bible as the Word of God, . . . and rightfully resent any assumption of a possible mistake about its plenary and verbal inspiration.[8]

> Jesus Christ has better business for every one of His real followers, than to *debate* with an infidel crew that denies His very existence, and that of His word.[9]

> As for the Bible itself, we have no concern. It is not one book among many; it is *The Book*, God's own book, and it will stand as impregnable as Gibraltar, as it always has stood against the fires of criticism, the assaults of infidels, and the malice of devils. But our anxiety is for those who are being caught with the prevalent delusion, concerning the necessity of a *critical* 'systematic study of the Bible in order to be prepared for its defence.'[10]

We can get the flavor of Updegraff's use of scripture in his discussion of divine guidance:

> Let us now glance at some of the various methods of divine guidance.
>
> (1.) First, in the words of the text: "I will guide thee with mine eye." In the constant language of the New Testament this must be defined to mean the personal leadership of the Holy Spirit. To the fully consecrated and obedient child of God, the Holy Spirit is promised as an indwelling personality, to sanctify, enlighten, fill and govern the entire being. "He will burn up the chaff with unquenchable fire." "When he, the Spirit of truth is come, he will guide you into all truth." "And they were all filled with the Holy Ghost," and the promise is unto you and all that are afar off, even as many as the Lord our God shall call. "For it is God which worketh in you, to will and to do of his own good pleasure." We have only quoted a single text in proof of each of these special offices of the Spirit, while they could be multiplied indefinitely. But we need to emphasize the inseparable connection between these crowning characteristics of the full salvation of Jesus Christ. If the spirit governs or guides a man, that man must be filled with the Spirit; and if filled, sanctified; and if sanctified, "Christ must dwell in the heart by faith."[11]

He openly described his approach here as one of using proof texts. These texts prove their points, because the Bible has become for him a treasury of authoritative precepts, absolute in their validity.

He continued, piling text upon text to establish the genuineness of each mode of divine guidance that he listed:

> (2.) Again, the Spirit guides us by the written word. "Thou shalt guide me by thy counsel." The general principles, precepts, promises and commands of God's word are directions plainly written out for our guidance in all of the ordinary affairs of life. David says, "I will run the way of thy commandments, when thou shalt enlarge my heart." "Thy word have I hid in mine heart, that I might not sin against thee." "Through thy precepts I get understanding." "I esteem all thy precepts concerning all things to be right; and I hate every false way." "Order my steps in thy word." What folly it is for men to look for any direct revelation of God's

will who neglect obedience to that will as it is revealed in the Bible![12]

(3.) That the Spirit guides us through a sanctified judgment will need but little remark.

"The meek will he guide in judgment." "I pray that your love may abound more in knowledge and in all judgment." God will speak to us by influencing the action of the mind, and the judgment that has been enlightened and sanctified through the Spirit.[13]

(4.) The fourth method of guidance that we mention briefly, is by the ministry of others.

"Thou leddest thy people like a flock by the hand of Moses and Aaron" (Ps. 77:20). And numberless passages might be cited in connection with Caleb and Joshua and Samuel and others. The Lord sent Saul to Ananias to be told what he should do. In answer to prayer he sent Peter to Cornelius, and Philip to the Eunuch, who was trying to understand the Scriptures, but said, "How can I, except some man should guide me?" "And God hath set some in the church" for the edifying of the body of Christ. The "manifestation of the Spirit" to one is for the profit of all. "Strengthen ye the weak hands and confirm the feeble knees." "The things thou hast heard of me . . . commit thou to faithful men who shall be able to teach others also." When John says, "Ye need not that any man teach you," it is to fortify the believers against the teaching of men as *men* only, and not as true ministers of Christ. It was written "concerning them that seduce you" (1 John 2:27). For men to believe they have no further need of the teaching of true gospel ministry is to furnish the strongest proof of ignorance and fanaticism.[14]

It is worth noting a few specific quirks or problems in Updegraff's biblical arguments. After quoting Matthew 10:8 ("Freely ye have received, freely give"), he asked: "'Received' what? Manifestly the gospel of their salvation!" But why is this answer so "manifest"? He went on:

"Behold, I send you forth as sheep in the midst of wolves." Could they be Christ's "sheep" and yet "unconverted"? . . . "He that receiveth you receiveth me." Is it conceivable that such a complete identification with the Lord Jesus could be affirmed of the unconverted Jew?[15]

But this entire "proof" depends on his own assumption about the nature of Christians' spiritual development—that this consists primarily of two specific, distinct, datable experiences: conversion and sanctification. Indeed, Updegraff's whole effort, in this particular context, was to determine at just what point in their spiritual life the apostles experienced these two events:

> Let us, then, examine "whereunto they had attained" *before* the day of Pentecost, and whereunto they were advanced *at* the day of Pentecost. Or, to adopt the familiar language of the inquiry: (1) "When were the apostles converted?" and (2) "Did the apostles ever receive the second blessing?"
>
> (1.) It is necessary, first of all, to settle, if we can, upon the time when the apostles were "converted."[16]

Updegraff showed some confusion in regard to the covenant that God established with the Israelites in the time of Moses. He asked regarding that covenant:

> And how was this under the first covenant? How precious are the unfoldings of the designs of the "God of all grace." ... From this blood-sprinkled mercy seat henceforth "the Lord called unto Moses and spake unto him out of the tabernacle of the congregation," vindicating his name as "the Lord, the Lord God, merciful and gracious."[17]

But a couple of pages earlier, he had mentioned God's covenant with Abraham: "His 'covenant of promise' imposed no other conditions, made no other demands, but was one of unconditional grace. '*I* will show thee.' '*I* will make of thee a great nation.'" And then he went on to God's covenant through Moses, "about four hundred years later":

> This was a new covenant, not of grace, but of works, "the one from Mount Sinai which gendereth to bondage." One to which "all the people" became responsible, responding to God's demand to "obey my voice indeed, and keep my covenant," "all that the Lord hath spoken will we do."[18]

Was the covenant at Mount Sinai "the first covenant" or "a new covenant," a second covenant four hundred years after the first covenant with Abraham?

Like William Penn, Ralph Sandiford, and some other Friends, Updegraff espoused the idea that human history, under God, went through a sequence of dispensations—but with a significant change. Beginning with Penn, these Quakers affirmed that there were three dispensations:

1. The dispensation of angels, beginning with Abraham.
2. The dispensation of the Law, from Moses through John the Baptist.
3. The dispensation of Christ, the Son of God, beginning with Jesus.

The main difference in the dispensations is in the ethical behaviors that God required in each time period.

For Updegraff, the primary difference in the dispensations was that each was a "great era in the worship of God;"[19] they were "three distinct stages in the development of the divine mind and purposes as to man's redemption. . . . There was a marked difference in the internal life and experience of the worshipers in each, as well as in the external manifestations."[20]

He also made a significant shift in the time periods covered by the three dispensations: The first was "THE 'DISPENSATION OF THE FATHER,' during which, for fifteen hundred years, He accepted such outer court worship from loyal Israel"[21]—apparently beginning with Moses, and ending *before* John the Baptist. The second dispensation was

> a transition period, occupying a brief interval from the preaching of John to the day of Pentecost—a period in which men obtained "knowledge of salvation, by the remission of their sins," and came to know "after the flesh" the Lord Jesus, who was manifesting Himself. . . . This is accurately and properly called the DISPENSATION OF THE SON.[22]

Since Pentecost, according to Updegraff, we are in "the midst of the blessings and privileges of" the third dispensation:

> this the last and most glorious DISPENSATION OF THE HOLY GHOST. . . .
>
> Since Jesus was glorified and all the conditions of man's redemption completed, the Holy Spirit has come to effect in human consciousness all the promised results of this salvation, and so to fuse the thoughts of God with the mind of man that His will may be done from the heart, and that testimony for Christ

may possess an intensity of power, adequate to the increasing difficulties and exigencies of "the last days."[23]

I believe the chief thing Updegraff hoped to gain by proposing this revised dispensational theory was that it gave him a handle to argue against the traditionalized "ritualism" of Quietist Quakerism and to provide "liberty" to emphasize the more energetic and emotion-stirring practices of the revival movement, even within the Quaker context.

Another way in which Updegraff attacked traditional Quaker Quietism was to appeal behind it to the preaching and practice of the earliest Friends. I find at least one significant problem with this tactic. He insisted that

> George Fox . . . and his compeers discerned, with remarkable clearness, both the needs and the spirit of their time. And, inasmuch as they had come to an experimental knowledge of Christ enlightening and saving their own souls, they recommended a like experience to others, as a solution of the problems that troubled them; they then sought to unify and incorporate into a worshiping body those thus brought out of darkness into light. . . . Their success was remarkable, and the result was that the 'Friends' Church' became *the* sect of that age. . . .
>
> A 'personal *experience*' of the salvation they preached, was, of course, the primordial and fundamental fact. . . . The early preachers, as Fox, Howgill, Burrough, Naylor, have left on record plain and authentic evidence of this. They were witnesses unto a personal Christ, who had not only died for them, but lived to save them.[24]

My critique is that I have found no evidence that Fox and Burrough (at least) showed any interest in "soul saving," in individuals going to heaven or hell after death, or even in a "personal Christ." Their emphasis was—in the broadest sense—political: on the irruption of the reign of God into human history, and on the destined role of the church, the people of God, in that "Lamb's War."

Biographer Brent Bill has noted a weakness in the way that Updegraff thought about many issues:

> He appears to have been extremely well read. He seems not to have been very open-minded as a result of his reading; rather,

it would appear that he read with his mind on the defensive. His responses to controversial subjects indicate that he perceived everything in black and white, with no shades of gray.

In many areas, Bill noted, Updegraff would not necessarily avoid the issue, but "he saw only one true side—his side—and therefore, since his answers were the right answers, he was untroubled by any criticism of them."[25] Bill suggested that part of the problem was that he lived in a time when many others were similarly minded:

> Much of the problem in Updegraff's day was that people were so busy preparing their responses to each other that they seldom listened to what the other was saying. Updegraff . . . was, in fact, quite intolerant of others' positions, especially early in his ministry. Such intolerance naturally led to bitter feelings and misunderstandings.[26]

On the issue of women's ministry, in spite of his rigid literalism in reading the Bible, Updegraff was more successful than Joseph John Gurney in fitting his handbook approach to the Bible into the best of the ongoing Quaker tradition:

> We do more than claim Paul's exemption from the charge of *forbidding* the public ministry of women. We go farther and adduce I. Cor. 11:1–15, as positive evidence of his recognition and approval of such ministry. If we do not violate all common sense interpretation of scripture, we are compelled to understand Paul as recognizing both the *fact* and the *right* of Christian women to "pray" and to "prophesy" in the church.[27]

One reason for Updegraff's success was his deep involvement in the Holiness movement. For that movement, the account in Acts 2 of the gift of the Holy Spirit to the apostles was the key to their whole understanding of scripture. To Updegraff, that day was the beginning of the present dispensation. On the question of women's ministry, therefore, Acts 2:16–18 was necessarily the foundation text, to which all else must be harmonized:

> The day of Pentecost settled all questions of perplexity or prejudice on this matter, and the whole course of the present dispensation has confirmed the truth that in "Christ Jesus there is neither bond nor free, male nor female, but ye are all one in Christ Jesus." The Spirit was then given to male and female alike,

and Peter speaks of this as a special characteristic of the "last days;" and the writings of Paul abound in recognitions of "those *women which labored with me in the gospel,* with Clement also, and other of my fellow-laborers."[28]

Like Robert Barclay, Updegraff here made Galatians 3:28 a central text on this issue. And like Margaret Fell, he saw the importance of the examples set by women in proclaiming the gospel and exercising leadership in the early church:

> In tenderest language he [Paul] charges that the "beloved Persis," Tryphena, and Tryphosa, and others, be "saluted," and "greeted," and "helped." As for "Phebe, a *deaconess* (or preacher) of the church at Cenchrea," Paul gives her, as it were, a *carte blanche* to the church at Rome, both in respect to their love and their resources. "Assist her in *whatever business* she hath need of you," says the Apostle. Surely further proof is needless that Paul, and the whole Bible, for that matter, unmistakably and constantly teaches not only the *right* but the *duty* of women to prophesy, to teach, and to preach Jesus to the people, in the power of the Holy Ghost. May this be more than ever the day that David saw, when he said, "The Lord gave the word, and great was the company of *women* publishers."[29]

One factor that certainly moved Updegraff to argue so strongly in favor of women as ministers was the influence and example of his own mother. Rebecca Taylor Updegraff was a recorded Friends minister and an influential revival preacher:

> In all of these respects our sainted and queenly mother was to us as a model, and there was stamped upon our youthful mind the loftiest ideal of feminine grace and excellence, along with ministerial gifts of the highest order. For about fifty years Rebecca T. Updegraff preached the gospel of Jesus Christ, both at home and abroad, as constrained by the Holy Ghost. We never knew her to open her mouth, either in prayer or in ministry, without evidence that the Spirit accompanied her words, and many seals to her labors remain to this day. . . .
>
> Whenever we hear an imputation concerning the ministry of women, we instantly recall the memories and sweetness of our

mother's life. . . . The daughters of the Lord, upon whom He has poured out the spirit of prophecy, both in the present and in past days, have done their full share in extending the Kingdom of Christ. They are doing it yet, and their zealous labors for souls are abundantly owned of God. We remember with gratitude the names of a host of such, who have gone to their reward; and we would like to record the names of another multitude of holy women who are in the field and at the front to-day, with a Divine commission to rescue the perishing and edify the church. Many of them we enjoy the privilege of knowing personally and in gospel fellowship. . . . We want to cheer them on and encourage every heart. Would to God all the Lord's people were such as are these prophetesses![30]

David Updegraff made it quite clear that he rejected any "moral influence" theory of Christ's atonement:

There is a moral theory of the death of Christ that impeaches the divine truth about it. It is that His death is merely a manifestation of His love and sympathy proven by suffering, and designed to attract and instruct us by example, and thus "win our souls" to love God and man! Nothing can be more delusive than such a pseudo-Christianity, as this theory about the doctrine of atonement, which in fact subverts that doctrine. Such sublime self-denial may be lauded to the skies as transcending all other "sacrifices" ever made, and yet it makes nothing more of it than a sacrifice made to man, in order to draw out reciprocal love and joy!

In contrast to this view, Updegraff affirmed: "Christ 'hath given himself for us, an offering and a sacrifice to God,' rather than to man. A real satisfaction to divine justice, of infinite merit, and vindicating as well as satisfying every demand of law by bearing its penalty."[31] This passage suggests that he might hold to a satisfaction theory of the atonement. I found nowhere in *Old Corn* or the Clark-Smith biography that he spelled out his view of the atonement as fully and systematically as Joseph John Gurney had done, but I did find a number of passages that convince me that he did believe in some version of the "Latin" type of atonement theory—a satisfaction or substitution theory of the atonement:

The greatest difficulty of our day is to get men really convinced of sin. To feel that they are sinners and that there is an awful penalty attached to sin.... The Lord Jesus is an advocate who undertakes our case, not to get us out of the clutches of the law as innocent, not to secure our acquittal because of a flaw in the indictment, or to prove that we are not guilty, but He comes before the High Court of Heaven in behalf of clients who "confess their sins" and are willing to be estimated at their worst.... Our blessed Christ has paid all of our debt, even to the last farthing, and God will keep His promise to forgive. "He is faithful;" not only so, He is "just," and what has been paid by our surety will never be demanded of us as principals. Thus the atoning work of the Son of God avails as our trespass offering, and the blood of Jesus Christ cleanseth us from all committed sins.[32]

Christ died for the ungodly, and is "the justifier of him which believeth in Jesus." This is truly the substitutional, or vicarious aspect of the cross, in which Christ is, and must ever be alone.[33]

In the sacrificial offering of Jesus, there can be no other participant. *He trod the wine press alone!* The curse of the law was fulfilled upon Him. And the man that confesses his guilt, with faith in Jesus Christ as his substitute, has the "curse" of the law fulfilled on himself, in the person of that substitute.

Judicially, as well as spiritually dead, faith brings judicial life or justification, and to all such, there comes the regenerating and life-creating power of the Holy Spirit.[34]

Paul's doctrine of "the cross" is Christ dying for us, or as our substitute. "Bearing our sins in His own body on the tree." "Christ died for our sins." He bore the penalty due us. "It pleased the Lord to bruise him," and "the Lord hath laid on him the iniquity of us all." And it is equally true that Christ "offered himself without spot to God," and "hath given himself for us an offering to God." In thus dying for sins, Christ satisfies every judicial claim of the divine government, and makes it possible for God to continue to be just, and yet justify and acquit the vilest rebel that will truly repent and believe on Jesus Christ. Redemption through the blood of the cross and the necessity of the new birth is the grand canon of Christianity.[35]

Only the Latin type of atonement theory emphasizes the idea that the atonement is a legal, penal, or judicial transaction.

Dougan Clark was born in North Carolina in May 1828. His parents, Dougan and Asenath Clark, were both Quaker ministers. In 1835, they began to serve as the first superintendents of New Garden Boarding School, which later became Guilford College. Dougan Clark, the son, attended the Friends Boarding School in Providence, Rhode Island, and Haverford College. At Haverford he began a lifetime friendship with a fellow student, David Updegraff. In 1852, he graduated from Haverford College and married Sarah Bates. "In 1861, he received his degree of Doctor of Medicine from the University of Pennsylvania. . . . He practised the profession of medicine for a number of years."[36] He taught Greek and Latin at Earlham College from 1866 to 1876. Clark was recorded as a minister in 1869. He and David Updegraff began an extended visit to Great Britain, Ireland, and France in 1876. He wrote a number of books, many of them quite brief, and was a leading theologian of the Holiness movement among Friends.

In the 1880s, Clark was appointed as head of the newly established biblical department at Earlham College. In 1894, at the memorial service for Updegraff, "during the 1894 Gurneyite Ohio Yearly Meeting, Clark himself felt led to take on water baptism."[37] In Clark's own Indiana Yearly Meeting, this action could be met by revocation of his status as a recorded minister. The actual consequence was that Earlham College's "president managed it so that no students applied that fall for Dr. Clark's courses; and after waiting a week or so for students, Dr. Clark resigned."[38] "After his resignation . . . he preached occasionally but declining health made him withdraw from public service more and more."[39] He died in October 1896.

In his writings, Clark always referred back to the Bible as the primary authority for his views. He insisted that revelation, as we find it in the Bible, has not continued since the completion of the New Testament:

> The apostolic and prophetic gifts—as they were possessed by the writers of Holy Scripture—have ceased to exist in the Church. Since the Book of Revelation was written, no man has claimed, or could justly claim, that he was inspired in the same sense in which the writers of the Bible were inspired.[40]

He would certainly have rejected Lucretia Mott's suggestion that there are "equal testimonies born to the truth that are not bound in this volume [the Bible]."

The language that Clark used in showing how Christian theology and ethics are based on scripture is significant:

> No doctrine is binding upon you as an article of Christian faith; no precept is binding upon you as a duty of Christian morality, which is not either contained in the Holy Scriptures or "clearly inferrible therefrom."[41]

> Jesus gave the concise *germinal* principles of all gospel truth; and Paul *deduces* from these principles their logical consequences and develops them, under the inspiration of the Holy Spirit, into those wonderful epistles to the churches, which . . . form a large part both of the foundation and framework of every system of theological doctrine.[42]

> Science is a systematic presentation of truth. Theology is the most important of all sciences. . . . It is a systematic presentation of revealed truth. . . . The Theology of Entire Sanctification, therefore, is a systematic presentation of the doctrine of entire sanctification as derived from the written word of God.[43]

Here I see, in bold outline, clear statements of the "handbook" view of scriptural revelation. In this view, the Bible is a collection of divinely inspired propositions. These propositions are the premises from which all significant theological and ethical conclusions are to be logically deduced.

On the matter of interpreting New Testament passages regarding the ministry of women, Clark stood firmly with Updegraff in making Acts 2:16–18 and Galatians 3:28 the foundation texts:

> God gives to His Church, in every age, gifted men and women, whose calling and qualification are from the Holy Spirit, and who, under His guidance and direction, may "prophesy" or preach. . . .
>
> I use the phrase *men and women* advisedly, because, here again, the Church of Christ has been, and continues to be, quite too slow of heart to accept the fact that "there is neither Jew or Greek; there is neither male or female, but ye are all one in Christ Jesus." By so doing, she is evidently limiting the Holy One, who pours

out His Spirit upon daughters as well as sons, handmaidens as well as servants—that they may prophesy. I shall not argue the question, but simply express my firm belief that the authority of Holy Scripture, and the example of the early Church, recognize the ministry of women, and place it on precisely the same ground as that of men; and that is—the calling and qualification of the Spirit.[44]

In 1878 Clark wrote, "A one-man ministry is not taught in the Bible."[45] Thomas Hamm argued that "the first true pastorates" among Friends began that year; he noted that another early pastorate was that of "Dougan Clark, Jr., in Cleveland in 1882."[46] I found nowhere in his books that Clark mentioned or accounted for this change in his position!

In regard to the atonement, Clark wrote: "God . . . chose to accept the sacrifice of Christ in lieu of the penalty due to guilty man."[47] He went on to make it clear that he (and the students he was addressing) "adopt the propitiatory and substitutional theory of the Bible; a revelation, on the one hand, of the infinite justice of God, and on the other hand, of His infinite holiness."[48] In contrast, he wrote: "We . . . reject all uninspired theories of the atonement," significantly including in this category "the Satan theory, which maintains that Christ's death was a ransom paid to the devil to get man's soul out of his possession."[49] This understanding of the atonement as a ransom paid to Satan was held by a number of early church fathers; Gustaf Aulén has discussed it at some length as being the original form of the classical, Christus Victor view of the atonement.

Perhaps even more than Updegraff, Clark emphasized the idea that God's dealings with humanity underwent a series of changes or dispensations through history. In an original nuance, he suggested that we could speak of either three or four dispensations:

> By the term dispensation we understand the scheme or economy of grace, by which God ordains "principles, promises and rules" for the guidance and government of His people. We speak of the Patriarchal, the Mosaic and the Christian Dispensations as marking great eras in the history of God's dealings with men, and such an era, the most glorious of all, was inaugurated on the day of Pentecost, and will continue to the end of the age; namely, the Dispensation of the Spirit. . . .

> In the Dispensation of the Father—which includes both the Patriarchal and the Mosaic—the Father was specially employed. ... In the Dispensation of the Son—extending from the incarnation to Pentecost—the great work of human redemption, culminating in the death, resurrection and ascension of the Lord Jesus Christ, was accomplished. In the Dispensation of the Spirit, the Holy Ghost is at work in the great scheme of salvation as He never was before.[50]

For Clark it was clear that each successive dispensation marked a progress or advance over those prior: "As the Jewish dispensation was better than the Patriarchal, so the Holy Ghost dispensation is better than the Jewish." This dispensation was better or more glorious than its predecessors ones in clear, specific respects:

> Under this blessed dispensation of the Holy Ghost, believers in Jesus are raised to a higher plane of religious experience, and to more exalted privileges, and to more perfect liberty than ever was enjoyed before. More light to the understanding, more holiness to the heart, more peace and joy in believing, more power and efficiency for service, than God's people ever knew before—such are the grand privileges of the glorious dispensation of the blessed Holy Ghost, under which you and I, my dear reader, are permitted to live.[51]

Since Clark's approach to biblical interpretation was centered on drawing clear inferences from biblical propositions, he would have to be sure to begin with the plain, clear sense of the biblical texts he used. Yet, in at least a couple of instances, he allowed his own theological beliefs to influence his understanding of biblical texts. One such example involved the prophets Elijah and Elisha. Clark began by stating flatly: "Under the Jewish dispensation, prophets, priests, and kings were anointed with oil."[52] There is only one Old Testament verse that mentions a prophet, during the period of the Mosaic or "Jewish dispensation," being anointed by another human person: 1 Kings 19:16. Clark actually followed up his general statement about anointing with a quotation from 1 Kings 19:15–16:

> The Lord said unto Elijah in the "still small voice" upon the mount, "Go, return on thy way to the wilderness of Damascus: and when thou comest, anoint Hazael to be king over Syria, and Jehu the son of Nimshi shalt thou anoint to be king over Israel:

and Elisha the son of Shaphat, of Abel-meholah, shalt thou anoint to be prophet in thy room."[53]

A key point in Clark's argument was that it was unlikely that Hazael was actually literally anointed with oil. He based this conclusion on his theological belief that "the sacred oil was not to be poured upon any stranger. None but the true Israel were to be thus anointed."[54] (This belief could have been challenged by an appeal to Isaiah 45:1 KJV: "Thus saith the LORD to his anointed, to Cyrus," the emperor of Persia!) Clark then went on to argue, on the basis of this theological statement:

> If Hazael was really *anointed* to be king of Syria, of which we have no record, it is not likely that the holy anointing oil was used in his case. He was made king of Syria in order that through him the Lord might chastise his rebellious people of Israel for their sins. Most likely, therefore, the direction given to Elijah to "anoint" him king over Syria, was simply a symbolical prophecy that Hazael should be raised to the throne.[55]

It might have been more straightforward for Clark to have appealed to the actual account of the prophet Elisha's encounter with Hazael (2 Kings 8:7–15). In this account, there was no mention of an actual anointing; Elisha simply told Hazael: "The LORD hath shewed me that thou shalt be king over Syria" (2 Kings 8:13 KJV). The next day, Hazael assassinated the reigning king of Syria, "and Hazael reigned in his stead" (2 Kings 8:15 KJV). But in that case, Clark could hardly avoid the account of Elijah's first meeting with Elisha in 1 Kings 19:19–21. In that account, again, there is no mention of any literal anointing with oil; instead, while Elisha was plowing, "Elijah passed by him, and cast his mantle upon him" (1 Kings 19:19 KJV). If the anointing of Hazael was simply symbolical, the same could well be true of the "anointing" of Elisha—and we would be left with no actual examples of any Jewish prophet having been commissioned by being anointed with oil by another human being.

The case at hand is important because, in his dispensational analysis, Clark assigned high importance to the act of anointing:

> I suppose that no careful reader of the Bible can doubt that the anointing with oil, which is thus described and alluded to in many passages of the Old Testament, is emblematic of the Holy

Spirit, and His divine work in enduing and qualifying the believer for the position he is to occupy in the Church of Christ.[56]

Immediately after he proposed that the anointing of Hazael was "simply a symbolical prophecy," Clark drew this conclusion: "And so, under the gospel dispensation, the enduement of the Holy Spirit is only given to those who are converted to God. These are the true Israel, and upon these, and these only, is the Spirit poured out in His fullness."[57] But this conclusion is not based on a literal reading of 1 Kings 19:15–16. His original premise was, "None but the true Israel were to be thus anointed." Since, for Clark, anointing in the Jewish dispensation was functionally equivalent to the gift of the Holy Spirit in the present dispensation, his argument committed the fallacy of circular reasoning. He had begun it by assuming the truth of what he was trying to prove.

Another verse, that Clark twisted to fit his own theological agenda, was Genesis 6:3. He wrote:

> "And the Lord said, My Spirit shall not always strive with man."—Genesis vi 3.
>
> When the Lord Jehovah says, "My Spirit shall not always strive with man," He clearly intimates that His Spirit shall and does strive with every man *for a season*. Every individual has his day of grace, during which it is possible for him to yield to these blessed strivings, and to repent and be saved.[58]

More recent translations—the New Revised Standard Version and the Jewish Study Bible—state that the meaning of the Hebrew in this sentence is uncertain. If the meaning is uncertain, how can we draw any clear implications from these words? But even if we accept the King James translation as accurate, the context throws serious doubt on Clark's interpretation. The full verse in the King James Version reads: "And the Lord said, My spirit shall not always strive with man, for that he also is flesh: yet his days shall be a hundred and twenty years." The previous chapter contained the genealogy of men from Seth through Lamech, all but two of whom lived more than eight hundred years. The first seven verses of chapter 6 provide a brief segue into the story of Noah. The context makes it highly probable that this verse is God's statement that the physical life of human beings was going to be shortened to a maximum of 120 years. Only Clark's theological belief that the primary, perhaps the sole, role of the Holy Spirit has to do with leading individuals to repentance and empowering them to live sinless lives would give him any reason to introduce that particular work of God's Holy Spirit into this verse.

By the late nineteenth century, advances in historical and literary biblical criticism had become the most widespread bone of contention among interpreters of the Bible. Opponents of this biblical criticism insisted that it was impossible for there to be contradictions within the Bible. The Bible was inerrant or infallible; it could not even contain any errors of historical or scientific fact. Supporters of biblical criticism did not simply challenge the traditional authorship of biblical books; they were not surprised to find factual errors, inconsistencies, and even myths and legends in biblical writings.

Among Hicksite Friends, Lucretia Mott was in the radical vanguard; as early as the 1840s she welcomed the findings of critical biblical scholarship. Among Gurneyite Friends, on the other hand, radical Holiness preachers like David Updegraff insisted on the absolute authority and infallibility of the Bible and forthrightly rejected higher criticism. By the end of the 1870s, however, acceptance of biblical criticism and rejection of the book of Genesis as authoritative in scientific matters were finding their way into Gurneyite Quaker circles.

Dougan Clark, later to become a leader in the Holiness movement, attended the Friends School in Providence, Rhode Island, in the 1840s. A young Friend who attended the same school from 1879 to 1882 was inspired by long-time science teacher Thomas J. Battey:

> I first heard in his classes the astonishing fact that the world was not made in six days, six thousand odd years ago, but had a history of uncounted and uncountable years. He marshalled the evidence. . . . He laid before us the marvelous story of the evolution of the horse. He showed us the array of fossils. . . . He helped us to realize that the account in Genesis is a great poetic story through which some man in the primitive stages of human thought expressed the central truth of the ages that God is the Maker of all that is. This account, he made us feel, is not in terms of science, which was not born yet, but in terms of poetry and art and religion, which are as old as smiling and weeping. This beautiful sweep of inspired vision, he convinced us, offers no bar or hindrance to exact research and is not a substitute for a careful, reasoned, demonstrable method of divine creation.[59]

A Long Road

The student who later wrote these words was Rufus Jones.

Rufus M. Jones was born in 1863 in the village of South China, in south central Maine. His parents, Edwin and Mary Hoxie Jones, were Gurneyite Friends; his father was a farmer. Along with other close relatives who lived nearby, they were deeply religious Quakers. From this background, Rufus expressed the impact that Thomas Battey had on his religious faith:

> What all this meant to me, with my previous insular outlook and child-minded conceptions, can hardly be expressed. . . . I leaped forward to the new view and with it I won my spiritual freedom. I had grasped an Ariadne thread which was to be a constant and never failing clue. . . . Thomas Battey put the key into my hand which unlocked many doors, and he helped me to pass from a child's religion to that of a robust developing youth, and enabled me to cross this important bridge without any wreckage of faith.[60]

His final year at Providence Friends School was actually "a post-graduate year to pull up his Greek to meet college requirements."[61] Rufus Jones entered Haverford College in the fall of 1882. At Haverford, "From the very first one man towered above all others in importance in my new college life. That was Pliny Earle Chase, professor of philosophy."[62] In one of Chase's philosophy classes,

> Each member of the class was allowed to pick out one philosopher to read intensively and to report on at frequent intervals. I chose Ralph Waldo Emerson and the Transcendental School. The choice was more or less accidental, but it proved to be a very fortunate choice for me.[63]

Emerson had known some Friends, particularly in the anti-slavery movement. After hearing Lucretia Mott preach in Washington, D.C. in 1843, he "wrote his wife that 'it was like the rumble of an earthquake—the sensation that attended the speech and no man would have done so much and come away alive."[64] He was soon afterward a dinner guest at the Motts' home. When Lucretia Mott attended anti-slavery meetings in Boston in 1847, "The transcendentalists were interesting to her, although to her practical mind they were too sentimental and mystical. She liked Emerson as a friend but disagreed with some of his concepts."[65]

In his essays, Emerson mentioned George Fox several times, usually as one of a number of people who shared some important characteristic. In "Self-Reliance" he wrote:

> A man Caesar is born, and for ages after, we have a Roman Empire. Christ is born, and millions of minds so grow and cleave to his genius, that he is confounded with virtue and the possible of man. An institution is the lengthened shadow of one man; as, the Reformation, of Luther; Quakerism, of Fox; Methodism, of Wesley; Abolition, of Clarkson. Scipio, Milton called "the height of Rome;" and all history resolves itself very easily into the biography of a few stout and earnest persons.[66]

In "The Over-soul" Emerson referred to

> the opening of the religious sense in men, as if "blasted with excess of light." The trances of Socrates; the "union" of Plotinus; the vision of Porphyry; the conversion of Paul; the aurora of Behmen; the convulsions of George Fox and his Quakers; the illumination of Swedenborg; are of this kind.... Everywhere the history of religion betrays a tendency to enthusiasm.[67]

In his essay "Nature" he wrote:

> The poet, the prophet, has a higher value for what he utters than any hearer, and therefore it gets spoken. The strong, self-complacent Luther declares with an emphasis, not to be mistaken, that "God himself cannot do without wise men." Jacob Behmen and George Fox betray their egotism in the pertinacity of their controversial tracts, and James Naylor once suffered himself to be worshiped as the Christ. Each prophet comes presently to identify himself with his thought, and to esteem his hat and shoes sacred.[68]

The third lecture in Emerson's book *Representative Men* was titled "Swedenborg; or, the Mystic." In that lecture Emerson included George Fox in a listing of mystics:

> All religious history contains traces of the trance of saints,—... "the flight," Plotinus called it, "of the alone to the alone"; *Myesis*, the closing of the eyes,—whence our word, *Mystic*. The trances

of Socrates, Plotinus, Porphyry, Behmen, Bunyan, Fox, Pascal, Guyon, Swedenborg, will readily come to mind.[69]

Emerson used the word "mystic" on other occasions in this lecture. He referred to "Behmen, and all mystics."[70] He said of Plato, "This mystic is awful to Caesar."[71]

Rufus Jones powerfully portrayed the impact that these essays and other writings of Emerson made on his own thinking—especially on his understanding of what Quakerism was all about:

> Quite naturally I focused on the "Over-soul," "Nature," "Self-Reliance," "Spiritual Laws" and "Representative Men," as here I got the key to his philosophy. It was an epoch-making discovery. . . . Here I came upon my first specific interpretation of Mysticism, called by that name. . . . Emerson was in every sense far more a mystic than a philosopher. . . . I had now, too, for the first time really and truly discovered George Fox, and I was becoming conscious for the first time that mysticism lay at the heart of our Quaker religion, and that this was the *secret* of all my early religious life. It was peculiarly odd that I should owe to Emerson my awakening to the significance of George Fox. He had always been a household word, but I had quietly assumed that he was the peculiar possession of the small Quaker group to which we belonged and had no standing outside our limited Society. Here in Emerson I found him ranging in great company with the outstanding spiritual leaders of the race. I had thought he was a provincial, now I found that he was cosmopolitan. . . . It aroused my interest immensely and much has followed from that awakening.[72]

As I reflect on these words, I am surprised to discover a fresh sense of empathy or near sympathy with Jones. I once affirmed my agreement with the position

> that early Quakerism was not mysticism: Rufus Jones' interpretation of Quakerism, which did so much to revive and reshape a moribund Society of Friends earlier in this century, was mistaken in its central thesis; the very life of contemporary Quakerism is therefore founded on an egregious misunderstanding![73]

And I have not retracted this diagnosis. What I do recognize is a remarkable parallel between Rufus Jones's discovery early in life that the heart of early Quakerism was mysticism, and my own discovery in the first year of my retirement that the heart of early Quakerism was an empathetic approach to reading the Bible. In his reading of Emerson, Jones found George Fox "ranging in great company with the outstanding spiritual leaders of the race." He was still holding fast to this vision at the age of eighty-three when he delivered his lecture "The Great Succession of Torch Bearers." He listed some of these outstanding spiritual leaders or torch bearers: the fourteenth-century Friends of God (John Tauler, Rulman Merswin, Henry Suso); sixteenth-century spiritualist Anabaptists (Sebastian Franck, Hans Denck) and "greatest of all, the Silesian shoemaker, Jacob Boehme"[74]; and seventeenth-century Cambridge Platonist John Everard. I had found significant predecessors of Fox in the fourteenth-century Lollards and the sixteenth-century evangelical Anabaptists (Conrad Grebel, Menno Simons). Now, with my discovery of Fox's radical empathy with the people of the Bible, my vision of the great "communion of the saints" through the ages has expanded to see among his forebears the early Greek church fathers; the founders of the medieval *lectio divina* (Saint Benedict, Pope Gregory I); and Ignatius Loyola in the sixteenth century. And I see this great tradition renewed in the twentieth century in the Biblical Theology Movement (Karl Barth, Walther Eichrodt, Bernhard W. Anderson, G. Ernest Wright), and in the Black preachers cited by Peter Gomes—culminating in Martin Luther King, Jr. identifying with Moses: God "allowed me to go up to the mountain. And I've looked over. And I've seen the promised land. I may not get there with you" (April 3, 1968, speech in Memphis, Tennessee). On this I agree with Jones: Fox and the early Friends were indeed worthy participants in a great procession of Christian spiritual leaders and saints over many centuries.

Jones's senior year as a Haverford College student was 1884–1885. A young English Quaker scholar, J. Rendel Harris, had just joined the Haverford faculty as a full-time professor. At that time a friendship began, and it flourished to the point that Jones, in telling of a trip he made in 1897, could write: "I was fortunate, in a rare degree, to have as my companion of travel during the Swiss part of my holiday my old-time friend, J. Rendel Harris."[75]

Haverford students were required to write a graduating thesis as a requirement for a bachelor's degree. At the suggestion of his teacher and counselor, Pliny Chase, Jones chose "Mysticism and its Exponents" as the subject for his own graduating thesis. His reading for the thesis confirmed the insights he had discovered in reading Emerson, to the point that "I had here found the field of my life work. Hereafter all my reading and thinking and research work bore directly or indirectly on some phase of mysticism."[76] As his biographer has noted, however, "He had discovered the field that contained the treasure, but he had not yet seen how he was to go about digging for it. That would not come for several years."[77]

Jones's first book—*Eli and Sybil Jones: Their Life and Work*—a biography of his aunt and uncle, Friends' ministers and world travelers, was published in 1889. In that book he did not mention words like mystic, mystical, or mysticism. He even went to some lengths to distance himself from the thought of Emerson and other American Transcendentalists: "The difference between Transcendentalism and Quakerism has been thought slight; it is, however, immense."[78]

After graduating from Haverford in 1885, he taught for a year at Oakwood Seminary, a Quaker boarding school in Union Springs, New York, on Lake Cayuga. A fellow teacher at Oakwood was Sarah (Sallie) Coutant. In the summer of 1886, he received his MA from Haverford College, proposed marriage to Coutant, and sailed to Glasgow for a year of travel in Great Britain and Europe. While in England that year, Jones spent some time with William Charles Braithwaite, a member of a distinguished Quaker family who was the same age as Jones. This was the beginning of another close and productive friendship.

He returned to America in September 1887 and for the next two years was a teacher at the Friends school in Providence, Rhode Island. In July 1888, Rufus Jones and Sallie Coutant were married. From 1889 to 1893, he was principal of Oak Grove Seminary, a Quaker boarding school in Vassalboro, Maine. Rufus and Sallie had a son, Lowell Coutant Jones, born in January 1892.

In August 1893, the family moved to Haverford, Pennsylvania, where Rufus Jones became managing editor and publisher of *The Friends Review* (a Gurneyite Friends publication) and teacher of one course in philosophy at Haverford College. In some of the first issues of *The Friends Review*, that he edited,

> He set forth his ideas of salvation as a transformation of life rather than a theological transaction; of divine immanence; of the nature of the Inner Light; of truth as a personal experience

instead of a statement to which the mind gives assent; of the place of mysticism in the history of Christian thought.[79]

In July 1894, *The Friends Review* merged with *The Christian Worker* (which had been the publication for revivalist Friends within the Gurneyite branch). The merged paper was named *The American Friend*, with Jones as editor.

> Each issue contained two or three editorials by Rufus Jones. . . . Always the editor strove to find the fundamental thought and the basis of underlying unity, to place ideas in their historical perspective, to interpret Quakerism as George Fox conceived it, to persuade his readers that religious truth and scientific truth need not be enemies, that the Bible studied in the light of historical knowledge gained rather than lost in power and illumination.[80]

By 1896 that Jones was teaching courses in psychology and history, as well as philosophy, at Haverford College.

Caroline E. Stephen was born in England in 1835. Her parents were strong evangelical Anglicans. Her older brother, Leslie Stephen, was an Anglican clergyman who came to doubt his faith and eventually became a leading agnostic thinker. By the early 1870s, Caroline also recognized that she could no longer honestly affirm the theological statements that she was repeating in the Anglican liturgy. She was on the verge of becoming an agnostic herself when she attended a Friends meeting, where

> my whole soul was filled with the unutterable peace of the undisturbed opportunity for communion with God, with the sense that at last I had found a place where I might, without the faintest suspicion of insincerity, join with others in simply seeking His presence.[81]

She became a member of the Society of Friends. She never married, and for many years attended Cambridge Meeting. In 1890, she wrote a landmark book, *Quaker Strongholds*.

At that point in time, Jones was not yet actively promoting his belief that the heart of early Quakerism was mysticism. And yet we find Caroline Stephen writing in *Quaker Strongholds*: "Here we are confronted with the real 'peculiarity' of Quakerism—its relation to mysticism. There is no doubt that George Fox himself and the other fathers of the Society were of a strongly mystical turn of mind."[82] She did not state where or how she came to this conclusion, but I am left with the impression that she did not think she was introducing it as a radically new idea.

She went on to clarify that the early Friends

> were assuredly mystics in what I take to be the more accurate sense of that word—people, that is, with a vivid consciousness of the inwardness of the light of truth.
>
> Mysticism in this sense is a well-known phenomenon, of which a multitude of examples may be found in all religions.[83]

She provided her own list of important Christian mystics: "Thomas à Kempis, Jacob Boehme, Tauler, Fénelon, Madam Guyon, George Fox, William Law, St. Theresa, Molinos and others."[84]

Stephen insisted that

> also the idea of "substitution" as distinguished from actual experience of the transforming power of the righteousness of Christ, were vigorously rejected by the early Friends; and in this insistence upon the identity of righteousness with salvation lay, as I believe, the main secret of their strength.[85]

She recognized here not only that the first Friends rejected any substitutionary theory of the atonement, but that this rejection was of central importance.

Stephen also connected the Quaker conception of the Light within with a rejection of the idea that the Bible is literally infallible:

> Many of us have come to believe that one of the greatest hindrances to a real belief in or recognition of inspiration has been the exceedingly crude and mechanical conception of it as attributed to the letter of Scripture. From this hard and shallow way of thinking about inspiration, Friends have generally been preserved in proportion as they have held firmly the old Quaker doctrine of the inner light. . . . I believe the doctrine of Fox and Barclay (i.e., briefly, that the "Word of God" is Christ, not the Bible, and that the Scriptures are profitable in proportion as they are read in the same spirit which gave them forth) to have been a most valuable equipoise to the tendency of other Protestant sects to transfer the idea of infallibility from the Church to the Bible.

Nothing, I believe, can really teach us the nature and meaning of inspiration but personal experience of it.[86]

Caroline Stephen lived until 1909. Her second Quaker book, *Light Arising*, was published in 1908. This book included several articles which had previously been published in various periodicals. In two of these articles, she discussed at some length her understanding of the Quaker position on creeds. This discussion was clearly impacted by her own inability to continue to accept as true all of the creeds insisted on by the Church of England, her own heritage. In "The Quaker Tradition" she wrote:

> That the Voice of the Divine Teacher is to be heard "within," and that obedience to this inward teaching is all-sufficient, is no doubt as much a doctrine as any clause in the creeds; but it is a doctrine so all-embracing as to have a tendency to supersede creeds. . . .
>
> There is nothing in this article of belief to hinder soundness of doctrine; it hinders only the attempt to fix it in forms of words and to stamp these with finality and necessity. Friends certainly can never believe that all who do not "keep whole and undefiled the Catholic faith," *as defined in the Athanasian Creed*, "will perish everlastingly." But this does not involve the denial of a single article of that or any other creed. . . . Inward obedience may call upon us to accept the correction of our religious phraseology. In these days of shaking of all that can be shaken those may be thankful whose faith is not bound to any definite form of words.[87]

In "What Does Silence Mean?" she stated:

> Each separate article of every creed has been so vigorously and so publicly challenged and discussed that the undisturbed and unquestioning belief in any kind of orthodoxy can linger only in very sheltered spots. . . . A confession of ignorance is being extorted by sincerity from many who used, or whose parents used, to think that loyalty required from them the utmost positiveness of conviction.
>
> This state of affairs, whether good or bad, is too obvious to be disregarded. The Church of England with a very uncertain voice, and the Church of Rome more peremptorily, meet it by the demand for submission, and by the claim that the Church

is the Divinely appointed guardian of a body of truth, which Christians are no more free to dismember than to reject. Friends have always met it by the quiet confidence that (in the language of George Fox) "God is come to teach His people Himself"— and that there is "One who can speak to our condition," and Who, if we yield ourselves to His Spirit, will "lead us into all truth." The two methods are obviously incompatible.[88]

She concluded:

> If it be true, as I most earnestly believe, that our bond of union lies not at all in coincidence of mere opinion, but in the following of One Lord, must it not be our desire before all things to remove every stumbling-block or cause of offence from the path of those who are seeking light?[89]

In the final analysis, for Stephen the Quaker rejection of creeds rested on the conviction that verbal statements of faith are "mere opinion."

J. Rendel Harris was born in Plymouth, in Devonshire (southwestern England), in January 1852.

> He grew up in the Congregational Church, and later shared with his wife a religious conversion, which involved a very deep sense of dedication to God. They took part in . . . the Holiness Movement of the nineteenth century. In addition, Rendel Harris experienced what was called "the Second Blessing." . . .
>
> He joined Friends in Cambridge.[90]

He received his education at Cambridge University in England. After teaching at Cambridge for several years, he taught in the United States from 1882 to 1892, at Johns Hopkins University in Baltimore and at Haverford College. During his adult years, he spent as much time as he could in the Middle East, searching out and examining old manuscripts—mostly on biblical and grammatical themes. A favorite location was the ancient library at Saint Catherine's Monastery on Mount Sinai. In 1889–90, while on leave from Haverford, he purchased forty-seven medieval manuscripts (in Latin, Hebrew, Arabic, Syriac, Ethiopic, and Armenian languages). He donated these documents to Haverford College. In 1892, he returned to England to teach again at Cambridge University.

Harris was a very prolific writer. A significant book, first published in 1895, was *Union with God*, which consisted of a series of addresses he had previously delivered. Much of this book was devoted to biblical themes. In one address he insisted that inspiration was not identical with infallibility. Referring to primitive Christianity in a discussion of Paul's letters to the Corinthians, he wrote:

> The inspiration of the Church is a magnificent truth. . . . There is such a thing as primitive Christianity; but you will have to be careful where you look for it. You will not find it in the theory of the necessary infallibility of the teachers or the immaculateness of the people who were taught.[91]

Harris was an assured promoter of higher criticism—historical and literary criticism of the Bible. "Criticism is busied to determine truth and to recognise historical fact in literature. And do not be afraid of criticism. . . . You will dishonour Christ if you are afraid of criticism."[92]

Christian leaders traditionally believed that the gospel of Matthew had been written earlier than the gospels of Mark, Luke, and John. By the late nineteenth century, most critical scholars were convinced that this tradition was incorrect—that the gospel of Mark had been written first, and that the authors of Matthew and Luke had used Mark's gospel as a major source when they wrote their own gospels. Harris agreed with this critical view when he discussed the saying of Jesus:

> "Who is My mother? and who are My brethren? . . . Whosoever shall do the will of My Father in heaven, the same is My brother, and sister, and mother."
>
> You will find the passage in the Gospels at the following places: Matt. xii. 46–50; Mark iii. 31–35; Luke viii. 19–21. Of the three accounts, that in Mark is the best to study, because it is probably the most primitive form of the story.[93]

In his wholehearted support of historical and literary criticism of the Bible and his rejection of the infallibility of the words of scripture, Harris of course directly opposed positions taken by such Holiness Friends as David Updegraff and Dougan Clark. He also questioned the core belief of the Holiness movement—that the spiritual life of Christians centered in two specific acts of grace: first, conversion, and second, sanctification:

> I am afraid many people have been making a mistake. They have thought the proper thing to do was to try and get sinners clean first, and saints afterwards. But I very much question whether it is not exactly the opposite, and believe that the place to begin is the twenty-first chapter of the Apocalypse, where John says, "I saw a new Jerusalem" first, and afterwards goes on to say, "Behold, the tabernacle of God is with men."[94]

The Holiness preachers believed that conversion might well be the work of Jesus Christ in the heart of the believer, but they insisted that sanctification was specifically and exclusively the work of the Holy Spirit. Again we find that Harris proposed something very different. At the very least, we can be sanctified directly by Jesus Christ:

> We have this praying Christ.... We find, to our great satisfaction and delight, that He is very closely related to our spiritual advance in the prayers that He prayed, and that we can be sanctified by Jesus Christ's prayers, just in the same way as we are sanctified by a right belief in and an absolute devotion to His cross.[95]

Harris suggested that the Holy Spirit does work our sanctification, but that the Spirit does so through the intercessory work of Christ:

> We have, then, these prayers of Jesus.... They are connected, as I said, very closely with the subject of our sanctification. There is an intercessory Spirit abroad in the world, and there was an intercessory Spirit in the person of the Well-beloved.... What puts us right is the spreading out of the holy wings of Divine intercession over us, the love of God for the creature, the Spirit of God descending, and moving, and working, and pitying those of us who are out of the heavenly way; and so when our Lord came on earth He came with the wings of the creating Spirit, he came with wings of healing.[96]

In the nineteenth century, London Yearly Meeting was clearly aligned with the Gurneyite branch of American Quakerism. At the end of that century, two new, sharply contrasting movements appeared within Gurneyite Quakerism: the Holiness movement and the modernist movement. Three early exponents of modernist Quakerism were Rufus Jones, Caroline Stephen, and Rendel Harris. In their writings up to 1895, we can find two major themes that were central to Quaker modernism:

Friends, the Bible, and God: Holiness and Modernist Friends

1. A commitment to critical study of the Bible, with a particular expectation that the Bible cannot be taken as an infallible authority in such areas of knowledge as geology and biology or even on details of historical fact.

2. An identification of the heart of Quakerism—particularly in its first generation—with mysticism: a movement with a long and distinguished history.

A milepost in the rise of the modernist movement within Quakerism was a conference held in Manchester, England, in 1895. Quite a few younger Friends had been either inspired by the emerging biblical criticism or repelled by such evangelical doctrines as the substitutionary theory of the atonement, but they found little support or sympathy for their questionings within their meetings. The home mission committee of London Yearly Meeting wanted to not only prevent these young people from leaving, but also to make Quaker principles more widely known. In response to this concern, then, the yearly meeting had authorized the home mission committee to organize the Manchester Conference to discuss these issues.

Quaker historians with widely varying perspectives have recognized the enormous impact of the Manchester Conference. According to Martin Davie,

> Quakerism has sought to align itself with contemporary thought forms and to re-evaluate its relationship with its past. . . . The 1895 Manchester conference of the Society of Friends gave a new direction to the movement as the views traditionally held within the Society were gradually relinquished and more liberal ones were adopted.[97]

Rufus Jones claimed:

> The effect of this conference upon the attitude and outlook of the Society of Friends was far greater than any person realized at the time when the conference was being held. . . . It was a psychological moment, and the spiritual resultant was greater than the sum of its antecedents. The issue of the hour was squarely faced and the Society, in effect, had decided to go forward. It had showed its readiness to accept the sound conclusion of scientific and historical research, and to formulate its spiritual message,

and to carry out its social mission in vital correspondence with the advancing thought of the world around it.[98]

For Davie, nineteenth-century Quaker evangelicalism was in harmony with the original thrust and continuing tradition of Quakerism; the turn to liberalism or modernism in the late nineteenth and early twentieth centuries was the great deviation from the central message of Quakerism. For Jones, evangelicalism—especially as represented by the thought of Joseph John Gurney—was the great deviation, and Quaker modernism was a return to the essential message and values of the original Quaker movement.

More than a thousand Friends attended the Manchester Conference. No official actions or formal recommendations to the yearly meeting were made. A number of papers, written from a wide variety of theological perspectives, were read at the conference. The issues raised in the papers were discussed on the floor. The complete texts of these papers and transcripts of the discussions were published in 1896 in a one-volume *Report of the Proceedings* of the conference.[99]

A number of the papers read at the conference were presented by modernist Friends (many of them young—in their twenties and thirties). These papers included:

> W. C. Braithwaite, "Has Quakerism a Message for the World Today?"[100]
>
> John Wilhelm Rowntree, "Has Quakerism a Message for the World Today?"[101]
>
> Edward Grubb, "The Attitude of the Society of Friends towards Social Questions"[102]
>
> J. Rendel Harris, "The Attitude of the Society of Friends towards Modern Thought"[103]
>
> John William Graham, "The Attitude of the Society of Friends towards Modern Thought"[104]
>
> Richard H. Thomas, "The Vitalizing of our Meetings for Worship"[105]

Examples of modernist views on evolution, biblical criticism, and biblical infallibility can be found in quotations from the papers. Harris proclaimed: "It is certain that mankind has evolved out of lower forms of life,"[106] and, "The internal discords of all Scriptures, and of all explanations of Scriptures, ought to be enough to convince us that we have no infallibility in the house, not a drop!"[107] Graham affirmed:

> The claim for the mechanical infallibility of the Scriptures rests on less than any other great intellectual position known to me. It has nothing to rest on but the ill-informed views of the bishops of the early centuries, and against the dicta of those bishops Friends are in revolt on every kind of question.[108]

In the history of Quaker thought, the seed of the use of reason to criticize scripture had been sown by Samuel Fisher in the seventeenth century. The seed lay dormant for nearly a century and a half, until it was watered by Abraham Shackleton and Hannah Barnard. It was later fertilized by Lucretia Mott and other radical Hicksites. At the end of the nineteenth century, it finally came to full flower in the thinking of the new generation of modernist Friends.

These Friends were energized by the Manchester Conference. Their views had gained respectability, at least within London Yearly Meeting, and they were ready to spread their vision broadly. Their first major step was to form a committee to plan a summer school. Members of the committee included John Wilhelm Rowntree, J. Rendel Harris, Joshua Rowntree, and William Charles Braithwaite. The committee organized a two-week summer school, to be held at Scarborough in August 1897. Lectures and discussions were scheduled on a number of topics, with a strong emphasis on explaining and promoting biblical criticism.

From the time of the Manchester Conference, the accepted leader and spokesperson of the modernist Friends in Great Britain was John Wilhelm Rowntree. He had been born in September 1868 in the city of York, in northern England. John Wilhelm's parents, Joseph and Antoinette Rowntree, were Friends. Joseph's brother, Henry Rowntree, "had bought the cocoa business from the Tukes in 1862, and in 1869 asked Joseph to join him."[109] The business struggled during a depression in the 1870s. Henry's death in 1883 left Joseph in full charge of the business. In the 1880s, economic conditions improved, the company introduced new products, and the business grew rapidly.

As a schoolboy John Wilhelm Rowntree suffered from deafness, and his eyesight also began to deteriorate. When he graduated from secondary school in 1886, he began working in the family business and was soon taking on responsibility. At the age of twenty-one, he became a partner with his father. As a youth he went through a period of religious doubts: "The first doubt I ever felt . . . was a doubt of the miracle of the raising of Lazarus."[110] These doubts led him to a "brief, reluctant agnosticism."[111] Richard H. Thomas, a Friend from Baltimore, made a visit in the ministry to England in 1889 and 1890. Thomas joined faith with knowledge in his interpretation of Christianity; he was open to biblical criticism and considered work for social reforms as a way to help establish God's kingdom on earth. Rowntree later wrote that an address by Thomas "first enabled him to see Jesus Christ."[112]

Rowntree's hearing and eyesight became worse, and his physicians gave him dire prognoses: "Increasing blindness had been predicted in 1891, and three years later he was told on a visit to specialists that there could be no cure—he had in fact a life-threatening disease, . . . Retinitis pigmentosa."[113] "He went up to London to consult a specialist and was told that before he reached middle life he would be totally blind and deaf."[114] Retinitis pigmentosa is a name used today for a group of genetic disorders; in 1914, Dr. Charles Usher published a study of the combination of blindness and deafness in a variant of retinitis pigmentosa now known as Usher syndrome.

Rowntree emerged from these crises with an intense experience of God's love, a passionate love for the Christ of history, and a conviction that there was great work for young Friends to do in revitalizing Quakerism and its ministry. In July 1892, he married a fellow Quaker, Constance M. Naish. Over the next thirteen years, they had four daughters and one son. "Constance gave John much-needed love and support in the trials which life was to bring him and in the wider work to which he gave himself unstintingly."[115]

He spoke out at the yearly meetings in 1893 and 1894, urging that a place be found for young Friends in the work of the Society of Friends, even though many of them doubted evangelical doctrines that were then dominant in the yearly meeting. After his landmark address at the 1895 Manchester Conference, he was invited to speak at several quarterly meetings in 1896 and early 1897.

After the establishment of *The American Friend* in 1894, Rufus Jones promptly set out on a series of trips to get to know his constituency in many parts of the United States and Canada. Two influential Friends, backers of his editorial work, arranged for Jones to travel for two months in 1897 in England, Ireland, and the European continent. His time in England included attendance at London Yearly Meeting and visits to Friends in many places, including Oxford, Swarthmoor Hall, and "to Birmingham to visit the Cadburys, to see their famous chocolate works and the model town which they were building for their 2200 workers."[116] Then, "in the middle of June"[117] or "in July,"[118] "Rufus Jones and Rendel Harris went together to Switzerland on a walking trip. They planned their day's marches so as to arrive at Mürren on a week end, when they could meet a party of English Friends from York who were staying there."[119] That group included a number of members of the Rowntree family. The two days together, according to Rufus Jones, "proved to be one of the most eventful and important weekends of my life."[120]

Sunday morning began with a Quaker meeting in the hotel. While the rain came down, Jones and Rowntree spent hours talking together:

> Here began our immortal friendship. We spent an unforgettable Sunday together. Monday we climbed the Schilthorn—a ten thousand foot peak—and all the time we talked and talked of our future joint work for the Society of Friends. He was full of dawning ideas for his future work—though already so blind that we climbed the mountain arm in arm. . . . All the plans and all the dreams focussed upon the one purpose of preparing the Society of Friends for its mission in the modern world and for deepening the ministry in the meetings for worship. Two plans were settled between us during this visit: First, that I should write the History of Mysticism and work out the historical background of Quakerism down to the period of George Fox, and that he should write the History of the entire Quaker Movement, and secondly we proposed to meet each year of our lives either in England or America—a plan which we actually carried out.[121]

One circumstance that facilitated these annual meetings was that Rowntree located a specialist in Chicago to treat his increasing blindness. He combined consultations with this specialist with visits to Jones in Haverford.

When Rufus Jones left for England in May, his wife Sallie had been troubled by a lingering cough for several months. She planned to spend the summer in the Pennsylvania mountains in hopes of ridding herself of it, but the cough did not improve. When Rufus returned to New York in mid-July

1897, he received a frightening letter from Sallie. She had placed herself under the care of a lung specialist, Dr. Edward Trudeau, who insisted that she needed to go to his tuberculosis sanatorium in Saranac Lake, New York. One problem was how to care for young Lowell. Eventually Rufus took him home to Haverford and added childcare to his already busy life as an editor and a college professor. Sallie's illness progressed; in the fall of 1898, she moved from Saranac Lake to her father's home across the Hudson River from Poughkeepsie, New York. She died in January 1899, when Lowell was just seven years old. In the next few years, Rufus devoted his life to raising his young son.

The first two summer schools were held in England in August 1897 and in 1899. Rowntree had to retire from full-time work at the cocoa factory in 1899 because of his health and his increasing blindness; he remained on the board of directors of the firm. "Towards the end of 1899 he moved with his family to live in the village of Scalby, three miles north of Scarborough."[122] A third summer school was held at Haverford, Pennsylvania, in 1900; J. Rendel Harris and Rowntree were among the lecturers at that school.

Rowntree was feeling the need for a more substantial educational program than the summer schools. In an essay that he wrote in 1899, he "proposed that 'There should be established a PERMANENT Summer School, . . . a permanent Bible School, open to . . . persons of any age.'"[123]

In the summer of 1900, Rufus Jones became engaged to Ellen Wood. On a trip to Europe with her Quaker father and sister, she became ill with typhoid fever and died in Copenhagen in August. In September, visited a family of active Philadelphia Friends—Joel and Anna Cadbury and their six children. Their oldest child was Elizabeth Bartram Cadbury. Jones was about to leave for a year in Cambridge, Massachusetts; while he was there, he and Elizabeth carried on a lively correspondence. Jones was in graduate school during that academic year, studying philosophy at Harvard. One important influence at Harvard was a course taught by idealist philosopher Josiah Royce; Jones was impressed by "his profound treatment of mysticism as one of the major pathways to reality."[124] In February 1901, Jones accepted an offer to return to Haverford in the fall as a full-time professor of philosophy.

George and Richard Cadbury operated a cocoa and chocolate business, which had been founded by their father. They had opened a new factory in Bournville, just south of Birmingham, England, and built a town around the factory to provide low-cost housing for their employees. George purchased a mansion, Woodbrooke, in Selly Oak, not far south of Bournville, and lived there for a number of years. Eventually the family moved to another home, and they rented Woodbrooke out. In May 1901, George wrote a letter to a Quaker periodical, in which he proposed "a College for instruction in our own special views as Friends and in Biblical literature, accommodating 100 young men and women."[125]

In June 1901, Jones received his M.A. from Harvard. That summer he sailed with his son Lowell to England. They stayed at the home of John Wilhelm and Constance Rowntree in Scalby, and Rufus lectured at the five-week summer school (August and early September) in nearby Scarborough. Rufus and John Wilhelm spent much of their time "talking over their life-work together for a joint interpretation of mysticism and Quakerism."[126]

Back home in September, Rufus Jones took up his new teaching duties at Haverford. In November 1901, he and Elizabeth Cadbury announced their engagement.

> John Wilhelm [Rowntree] visited Manor House, the home of George and Elizabeth Cadbury in Birmingham, in January 1902. 'He and George have a great talk in the library', wrote Elizabeth in her diary. He met several local Friends, and then the Cadburys offered their former home, Woodbrooke, for use as a college.[127]

Henry Lloyd Wilson, a leading Friend in London Yearly Meeting, was ready to leave on a trip to America; John Wilhelm Rowntree wrote a letter and asked this Friend to deliver it to Rufus Jones in Haverford. In that letter, he invited Jones to become the first principal of the new college to be founded at Woodbrooke.

On March 11, 1902, Rufus Jones married Elizabeth Cadbury in the Twelfth Street meeting house in Philadelphia. In the summer of 1902, the two of them went to England to discuss the Woodbrooke position with George Cadbury and Rowntree. Jones spent two more months considering the offer. Much later he wrote: "It proved to be one of the two or three most difficult decisions I have ever made."[128] In early November, he made the decision to stay on at Haverford.

In December, George Cadbury offered the Woodbrooke post to J. Rendel Harris, who had just been appointed to a teaching position in theology at

Leiden University in the Netherlands. Harris promptly accepted, instead, the position as first director of studies at Woodbrooke.

J. Rendel Harris served as director of studies at Woodbrooke from 1903 to 1915. He was succeeded in that position by H. G. Wood. From 1918 to 1926, Harris was curator of manuscripts at the prestigious John Rylands Library in Manchester. He lived until March 1941.

On July 11, 1903, Rufus and Elizabeth Jones sailed to England for the opening of Woodbrooke. On their arrival in England eight days later, they learned that Rufus's eleven-year-old son Lowell had died on July 16 from a sudden illness. The opening summer school at Woodbrooke began July 23. Rufus delivered a series of lectures during the first two weeks of the summer school. The first full term at Woodbrooke opened on October 3. Mary Hoxie Jones, the only child of Rufus and Elizabeth, was born in 1904.

Early in 1905, John Wilhelm Rowntree decided to go to America for further treatments from his eye doctor in Chicago. He and Constance left England on the *Caronia* on February 25. When Rufus Jones met the ship in New York, John Wilhelm was seriously ill with pneumonia, and Jones rushed him to a hospital, where he died a few days later on March 9. John Wilhelm "was buried in the Friends Burial Ground at Haverford. . . . The funeral brought together many Friends of both branches of the Society, whose divisions he had so longed in his life to see healed."[129]

John Wilhelm Rowntree did not write any full-length books. Quite a few of his spoken addresses and written essays have been collected and published in several volumes, most of them posthumously. From these we can glean a few quotations that sharply illustrate his thinking in regard to mysticism, biblical interpretation, and the atonement.

In an essay on William Law, Rowntree wrote: "Like the true Quaker, Law was a mystic; that is, he regarded religion more as a matter of inward illumination than as a matter of outward form."[130] We see here his agreement with Rufus Jones in their understanding of the central thrust of Quakerism.

Rowntree was especially enthusiastic about the present and potential gains from biblical criticism:

> As yet but few understand how great a work Biblical scholarship is accomplishing. The place, even in comparative religion, of the prophets of the eighth century, B.C., the significance of

> their message, not only in the revised historical setting which has been given to it, but in relation to the principles which govern the conduct and relationships of modern individuals and nations, receives scant appreciation. Yet we shall scarcely exceed the truth in asserting that the critics have discovered the prophets, setting them forward for the first time in their true light.
>
> At least, it is certain that they have freed Christian ethics from Old Testament bondage, by compelling attention to the fallacy of verbal inspiration, and disclosing the internal evidence of a moral development, within the limits of the Old Testament itself.[131]

He went on to hint that biblical criticism will lead to the discovery of fresh new ways of understanding and interpreting our heritage:

> The work of criticism and of re-examination is, indeed, the re-conquest as a living possession of that which, accepted merely as an hereditary bequest, must remain an impotent gift. In the Society of Friends, . . . it may well be that in essence the testimonies will remain, but we shall gain at least the living expression of what we have made our own.[132]

Rowntree's thoughts on the atonement are particularly intriguing: "The love of Jesus is a love we can identify in human experience,—and remember Jesus is the Gospel. Then how does this affect the doctrine of the Atonement? We shall soon discover if we turn to the story of the Prodigal Son."[133] Key points in this discovery cropped up in the following pages:

> In this parable, we have the basis of the moral theory of the Atonement. . . . Forgiveness [is] the entrance into the peace of the Father's home. The condition of forgiveness is penitence—a condition involving primarily an inward fact and change, and there is absolutely no other condition whatever. . . . The sense of pardon actually . . . means a sense of harmony between the human soul and God. . . . Forgiveness does not imply a change in God but a change in man. . . . There is no question of a legal transaction. We are not here in the law courts, but in the region of moral realities. . . .
>
> Alienation from God is the punishment of sin, and alienation from God is hell. . . .

> The condition of penitence carries with it ... the necessity for the destruction of the power of sin, and as God's punishments are remedial, not vindictive, the very fact of penitence blots out the past. With penitence the first object of God's love Has Been ATTAINED, the sinner has been placed in the right attitude towards Him, his latent powers of good have been liberated, and are free to grow heavenward.[134]

I see here a clear rejection of the forensic basis of the satisfaction and substitutionary theories of the atonement and a hint of a Christus Victor view. If Rowntree thus far was in line with George Fox's own thought, the difference was that he had a far more optimistic view of the fundamental goodness of human nature than Fox had. Fox's ultimate optimism rested not upon human goodness but upon the love and power of God.

At his death, Rowntree had barely begun his part in the major writing project he and Rufus Jones had envisioned: the history of the entire Quaker movement.

> John had for some time been assembling the materials for his research and had amassed a considerable library of Quaker books. ...
>
> He shared the first-fruits of his labour at a Summer School at Kirkbymoorside, arranged for local Friends by Pickering and Hull Monthly Meeting (22nd–28th September 1904), when he gave three lectures on The Rise of Quakerism in Yorkshire.[135]

These lectures were later published in his *Essays and Addresses*.[136]

The original plan had been for Jones "to write a preliminary volume or volumes tracing the course of mystical movements and the place of Quakerism in the stream of mystical thought."[137]

In September 1905, Jones met with a small group of English Friends "in John Wilhelm's unique library at Scalby, to plan, if possible, for the continuation of the work which death had so sadly interrupted."[138] The outline for the project was agreed on:

> The plan called for a series of volumes, each with an introduction relating it to the whole study. . . . Authors were tentatively assigned to different volumes, and Rufus Jones was to be editor of the whole as well as to write several of the volumes himself. The

first volume, which was to be his, should set forth "the historical development of inward and spiritual Christianity as in contrast to the ecclesiastical and ritualistic types," William Charles Braithwaite was to write on the formative periods of Quakerism. The Rowntree Trust would supply funds for research, travel, secretarial help and books, as well as underwriting the expenses of publication.[139]

With the outline settled, work on the project went forward in earnest. As it developed, Jones shared the authorship of the volume on *The Quakers in the American Colonies* with two American Friends, Isaac Sharpless and Amelia M. Gummere. Jones also wrote the introductions to William Charles Braithwaite's two volumes on seventeenth-century Quakerism; his name is thus prominently associated with every one of the seven volumes in the completed series. Sixteen years brought the work to completion; the final volumes were published in 1921. The seven volumes make up the Rowntree Series, a monumental and well-researched accomplishment that still stands as the definitive history of Quakerism, subject only to the corrections that continuing research bring to light.

In the third book of his autobiographical series, Jones noted that some Friends had criticized him for neglecting Christ's atonement in his *American Friend* editorials. He responded:

> I was perfectly familiar with the slow development of these atonement ideas in the history of religious thought. I knew what Tertullian, Augustine, Anselm, Luther, Calvin, Wesley, and the long line of others, had contributed to the formulation of the Plan of Salvation. . . . I knew how sacred it had become, in fact, how essential for what these persons meant by "salvation."[140]

Most of the authors Jones listed were proponents of the Latin view of the atonement. The Latin theories are often classified as forensic theories because they are rooted in the language of law courts. Jones insisted, in contrast: "What was needed most of all was a fresh and deeper interpretation of *salvation* itself as 'a process of life' rather than as a 'transaction,' or as a legal, 'forensic' affair."[141] As he went on to develop his thought about "*a religion of life* as distinguished from a doctrinal religion,"[142] he slid away from consideration of the atonement as the question, what was it that Christ accomplished?

Jones showed more clearly the connection between Christ and the atonement in his earlier book, *The Double Search*. He began by defining the double search as "atonement—God's search for us—and prayer—our search for him."[143] He turned his attention first to atonement, and at the end to prayer. He began by touching on the "moral influence" view of the atonement: "Jesus that is called the Christ . . . is the pattern in the mount, . . . which has drawn the individual and the race steadily up to their higher destiny."[144] But he did not stop there: "This pattern-aspect of the Christ life is only one aspect, and we must not raise it out of due balance and perspective. *Christ is God humanly revealed.*"[145] For Jones, the Quaker position insists on continuity between the historical Christ and the inward Christ: "With perfect fitness, then, we speak of the inward Presence as the spiritual Christ. It is the continuation of the same revelation which was made under the 'Syrian blue.'"[146] At this point we see how Jones echoed and developed John Wilhelm Rowntree's insights:

> The Spirit of God identifies itself with the human me into which it enters and *whose life it becomes*. . . . A sort of metamorphosis, a transubstantiation, if the word may be permitted, takes place in the human being. Having been carnal it has become spiritual.[147]

Jones objected to theories of the atonement that "treat sin not as a fact of experience, but as the result of an ancestral fall, which piled up an infinite debt against the race."[148] He insisted, rather, that

> sin is no abstract dogma. It is not a debt which somebody can pay and so wash off the slate. Sin is a fact within our lives. It is a condition of heart and will. . . .
>
> The two fundamental aspects of sin, then, are (1) its inward moral effect upon the soul, its enslaving power over the sinner, and (2) its tendency to open a chasm between God and man.[149]

Like Rowntree, Jones appealed to the parable of the prodigal son:

> Christ . . . reveals God as a Father whose very inherent nature is love and tenderness and forgiveness. . . .
>
> But that is not all. Love always involves vicarious suffering. . . .
>
> The principle of vicarious suffering . . . appears at every scale of life, heightening as we go up. . . . It was a central truth of Christ's revelation that this principle does not stop with man; it

goes on up to the top of the spiritual scale. It finds its complete and final expression in God Himself. . . . The cross is the answer. . . .

What man hoped to do, but could not, . . . God Himself has done. He has reached across the chasm, taking on Himself the sacrifice and cost.[150]

Rowntree had written that the forgiveness wrought by the atonement "means a sense of the harmony between the human soul and God."[151] Jones expanded and deepened this thought:

Salvation . . . must be by a positive winning of the will. A dynamic faith in the man, must cooperate with that energy from God. . . .

The Redeemer suffers, but He does not suffer in our stead—He suffers in our behalf. . . . He makes his appeal of love to us to share His life as He shares ours. . . .

In the future the atonement . . . will come to express, as it did in the apostolic days, the identification of God with us in the person of Christ, and the identification, by the power of His love, of ourselves with Him.[152]

Jones has portrayed a poignant and appealing model of God's atonement, culminating in a divine-human union. This model does not seem to match any of Gustaf Aulén's three atonement types. However, Presbyterian theologian Gregory Anderson Love has modified and expanded Aulén's typology by proposing a variety of atonement models. One of these models is *"the enlightenment model of salvation,"* which is centered in "the belief that mystical experiences are powerful in leading to the transformed cognition which emancipates."[153] In this model, "All of these mystical encounters describe one experience: the transcendence of the self into the whole of reality, a whole composed of distinction-in-unity."[154] Jones's view of the atonement fits easily into Love's enlightenment model.

Love stated that Jesus is not "essential to an experience of salvation in the enlightenment model,"[155] even though "his role in salvation is not insignificant. . . . The cross has saving power through its symbolism. . . . The resurrection symbolically allows Jesus to play his role as catalyst for new insight for those living today."[156] Clearly, Jones showed deep and abiding love for Jesus of Nazareth and for what Jesus revealed to us about the nature and character of God. But, like Love, I see that Jones's metamorphosis and mutual identification between ourselves and God could readily take place even without specific action in history by Jesus Christ.

Rufus Jones became a widely honored leader among American Friends. He played major roles in the founding and early leadership of the American Friends Service Committee, the Friends World Committee for Consultation, and the Wider Quaker Fellowship. He died in June 1948 and was buried in a corner of the Haverford Meeting graveyard near his old friend, John Wilhelm Rowntree.

Luke Woodard

Luke Woodard was born on a farm near New Garden, in Wayne County, Indiana, in March 1832. His parents, Cader and Rachel Woodard, were Orthodox Friends. Luke's mother died when he was nine years old. In the spring of 1853, he married a Friend, Elvira Townsend. They had three children. During the early years of their marriage, first Elvira and then Luke had specific conversion experiences. Luke reported: "It was not long after my conversion that I first spoke in a public meeting. . . . My gift in the ministry was officially acknowledged by my Monthly Meeting at New Garden, Indiana, in Second month, 1862."[157]

Luke Woodard's experience of "entire sanctification" or "entire consecration" came at a meeting of ministers in Adrian, Michigan, in the autumn of 1871.[158] During the 1870s, he traveled widely through the United States and Canada, actively engaging in evangelistic work and speaking at revival meetings. Many of these meetings were in New York and Indiana.

Luke Woodard served as pastor in a number of Friends churches in the 1870s and 1880s. Most of these pastorates were brief—a few months each. He was pastor in Glens Falls, New York, for three years, beginning in October 1884. Later he served as pastor of the Friends Meeting in Muncie, Indiana, from 1891 to 1895. Luke and Elvira traveled in Great Britain and Ireland for a little over a year in 1895 and 1896, carrying traveling minutes endorsed by Indiana Yearly Meeting of Ministry and Elders. He described his work on this journey: "My mission over there was to preach the Gospel, not to introduce American methods of conducting meetings."[159] He did not mention the 1895 Manchester Conference, which took place midway through his and his wife's time in Great Britain.

During his long life, Luke Woodard wrote a number of books in a variety of genres, ranging from autobiography and travelogue to poetry to theology. He died in 1925.

Woodard provided a definition of revelation in his book *What Is Truth?* After listing a number of "doctrinal elements of Christianity," he continued: "The making known these truths and others related to them is revelation."[160] This definition echoed Joseph John Gurney's statement that a major goal of revelation was to unfold doctrines. As with Gurney, the consequence of this definition is that Woodard would also look on the Bible as a handbook, providing cognitive information from which he could deduce doctrinal conclusions.

Along with Gurney, David Updegraff, and Dougan Clark, we find Woodard also using William Penn's idea of biblical revelation taking place through a series of dispensations:

> That dispensation which preceded the ushering-in of Christianity, and by means of which the world was to some extent prepared to receive it, was not only prophetical, it was also typical.[161]

> This was unmistakably taught by the Levitical dispensation whose priesthood, sacrifices, and various rites, were a shadow of good things to come.[162]

> The Holy Spirit . . . was in the beginning; . . . The Holy Ghost spake by the mouth of David; and holy men of God spake as they were moved by the Holy Ghost. But in a sense not intermittent, a more bounteous effusion and power-enduing fulness, as had not been realized in the old dispensation, the "pouring out" was reserved till after Christ had ascended, as witnessed on the day of Pentecost.[163]

> The Mosaic dispensation as instituted at Sinai was a theocracy. It was changed in the time of Samuel to a kind of monarchical theocracy, which continued until Nebuchadnezzar, when the government passed out of the hands of God's chosen people, and "the times of the Gentiles" set in, which will continue "till

the times of the Gentiles be fulfilled," and the Lord Jesus takes over the government, when . . . He shall reign forever and ever.[164]

Unlike with Updegraff and Clark, I did not find that Woodard spelled out any clear or precise scheme or series of dispensations in biblical revelation.

The latter part of the nineteenth century saw the rise of a movement among evangelicals known as dispensationalism. The dispensationalists and the Quaker Holiness preachers shared a common theological view known as premillenialism. Premillenialism was based on a conviction that symbolic figures in the book of Revelation could be construed as a literal historical prediction that Christ will return to earth and reign for a thousand years before the final arrival of the kingdom of heaven. But there were also significant differences. A crucial aspect of dispensationalist belief was that the Jewish people, the nation of Israel, will play a central role in the process of history leading up to the return of Christ. I find no reference to this theme in the writings of Updegraff, Clark, and Woodard. They were primarily interested in the concept of dispensations as a tool for interpreting the past and the present of the people of God, but not the future course of history.

Like his fellow Quaker Holiness preachers, Updegraff and Clark, Woodard argued clearly in favor of women acting as ministers. Referring clearly to Mary Magdalene, he wrote:

> That woman was the first Christ-commissioned messenger of the glad tidings of the resurrection of the Lord! Is not this suggestive of woman's mission? Does it look as if the Lord intended to place upon her the ban of perpetual silence in reference to the gospel of the blessed God?[165]

Here at least, Woodard did not restrict himself to logical deduction from propositional statements in the Bible, but appealed to the living example of a biblical person. It is remarkable that he followed Benjamin Lay in grounding his argument on the person of Mary Magdalene.

In his books, Woodard devoted considerable attention to the subject of Christ's atonement. In *The Morning Star*, originally published in 1875, he developed his thought on the atonement in a chapter titled "The Death of Christ."[166] Early in the chapter, he wrote of the "doctrine of redemption by substitution. . . . *Christ dies by divine appointment for the redemption of a fallen world!*"[167] A few pages later, he referred to "a scriptural truth, viz: That

Christ, in his death, was substituted in the place of sinners, bearing their sins and dying *for* them."[168] He went on to spell out in some detail:

> Properly understood, there can be no objection to the doctrine of satisfaction. The sufferings of Christ are an offering both satisfactory and honorable to God—constituting a *ground upon which* God can pardon the breaches of his righteous law, and yet maintain its honor: can be both just and merciful—condemn the transgression and acquit the transgressor. But this is all conditional. The penalty of the law is not set aside in our case except as we embrace by a willing, hearty, and active faith, the terms of offered mercy. The gracious promises of God can not be construed to encourage sin; and though satisfaction for our sins is secured to us when we repent and turn to God, claiming pardon for the sake of his Son, still we are taught in the most impressive manner, that God can never be satisfied *with sin*, or *with us in our sins*. Let us never lose sight of this, when speaking of imputed righteousness, justification by faith, or satisfaction.[169]

Near the end of the chapter, he summed matters up:

> In the death of Christ, as the mighty *center* of God's amazing plan of mercy, there is a fitness commensurate with its own proportions.
>
> Doomed as we are to taste the penalty of sin . . . ; what a hallowed companionship is that we enjoy in the Man of Sorrows. . . .
>
> In the death of Christ is the highest conceivable exhibition of God's love.[170]

We find in this chapter that Woodard's Holiness theology was based on a view of the atonement that used much of the language of the forensic theories: "substitution," "satisfaction," "imputed righteousness," "penalty of sin."

In *What Is Truth?*, published in 1901, Woodard's longest and culminating chapter bore the title "The Atonement."[171] Early in that chapter, he reviewed several "theories quite opposite between those who have written with a view to explaining the exact nature of this mediatorial work." Among these "opposite" theories, he included: "Some of the Christian fathers regarded the sufferings and death of Christ as a ransom price paid to the devil," and, "Another view of the atonement . . . is known as the *moral influence theory*."[172]

In opposition to these views, Luke Woodard insisted: "What we maintain as the true, Scriptural view, on the other hand, shows God's grace and righteousness as existing, and proceeding in perfect harmony." According to this view, Christ was "our substitute." The atonement was "a deliverance effected by the substitutionary Sacrifice of Christ, who suffered, the just for the unjust, that He might bring us to God." Again, "The penitent and yet believing sinner is freely forgiven, and has peace with God: the impenitent is under, and in that condition must ever remain under condemnation. The wrath of God abideth upon him."[173]

A central assumption in Woodard's theory is that, under God's righteousness or justice, there is a severe penalty for sin:

> When grace becomes triumphant through our Lord Jesus Christ, it is not that the sanction and authority of divine law are weakened, or that the righteous Law-giver has become in the slightest degree indifferent to its requirements. Before the penalty can be removed, the offence must be pardoned. Before this pardon can be granted there must not only be repentance, but reliance upon One who has suffered the penalty in our stead: That penalty was *death*. Christ met it for us. He, by the grace of God, tasted death for every man. The Lord laid on Him the iniquity of us all. He suffered, for sins, the just for the unjust, that He might bring us to God.[174]

Woodard summarized this point: "Christ . . . suffered the penalty which we deserved." He characterized the result of this act as "a positive imputation of the merit of Christ to the believer, whose faith is counted for righteousness."[175] He added a characteristic Holiness-theology point:

> This is satisfaction in its two-fold aspect as it relates to what Christ has done for us, and to the resultant work in those who believe in Him. He has wrought in us that which was well-pleasing in His sight. If we call this imputed righteousness, we see in it something beyond a bare reckoning, a transference of merit; it is as well, impartation, a transfusion. He becomes our life. We are made partakers of the divine nature.[176]

We see in this chapter, as well as in the one written twenty-six years earlier, a clear statement of a forensic theory of the atonement—a theory to which Woodard could attach both terms: "substitution" and "satisfaction."

Woodard's forensic view of the atonement showed up more briefly in other contexts. In a chapter on "Humanity of Christ," he wrote: "Christ takes our place as our substitute, and becomes our surety before the law. *We have broken the law.* In pity for us, he interposes himself; and upon him, the willing substitute, the law visits its unrelenting fury."[177] In "Christ our Righteousness," he insisted: "As we are really unjust, it is plain that God can not account us just intrinsically; and if he declares us so, it must, in part, be imputatively; not on our own account, but on the account of another."[178]

In *A Panorama of Wonders*, published in 1921, he affirmed as a fact "that Christ being our substitute, died on our account, was made sin for us, suffered the just for the unjust." He added, in the same paragraph, "Crucifixion . . . is both experimental and judicial."[179]

I have elsewhere stated as one reason for rejecting forensic theories of the atonement:

> They begin with the premise that God's justice must be satisfied. But their model of justice is retributive justice, . . . which aims to punish individuals who have hurt other people. . . .
>
> Forensic theories fail the ethical test in their underlying premises. J. Denny Weaver insightfully summed this up: "Satisfaction atonement is based on an intrinsically violent assumption—restoring justice means punishment."[180]

It would appear that Woodard was attempting to deflect similar criticism when he wrote in his chapter on the atonement:

> The offering made by Christ on the cross did not effect, and was not designed to effect, any change in the nature of God. It was to make possible our forgiveness. It was a provision of grace on the part of the righteous Law-giver to show forth His righteousness, as well as His forbearance and mercy, not in the condemnation, but in the pardon of the transgressor. . . . The death of Christ was not to appease anger, but to meet the demands of His holiness. It was not to satisfy retributive justice, but public justice. The sinner therefore who accepts Christ, his propitiation, will be dealt with very differently from the one who does not accept

Him. God, being perfectly holy cannot feel indifferent toward sin. His unalterable holiness places Him in uncompromising opposition to all unrighteousness.[181]

The immediate problem is that Woodard made no attempt to define "public justice" or to clarify how it differs from retributive justice.

And, indeed, four pages later, Woodard admitted that retributive justice was the underlying issue that required atonement:

> The term *"Satisfaction"* is often employed by writers on this great theme of the atonement. Properly used and understood, there can be no objection to its use. It applies to the mediatorial work of our Saviour by which the righteous demands of the government of God, and the need of a revolted race are provided for. A work with which God is satisfied, well pleased; and by the term we mean such act or acts, as accomplished all the moral purposes which, to the infinite wisdom of God, appeared fit and necessary, and which must otherwise have been accomplished by the exercise of retributive justice upon transgressors in their own persons.[182]

Woodard did at this point add a clarifying footnote:

> There are two ways of satisfying governmental requirements. First, by obedience; or where that has not been rendered, by the payment of that which the law attaches as a penalty for its violation. . . . If the guilty one pays the penalty, we call it suffering retributive justice; if another, in no way involved in the transgression, pays it, we call it suffering in the place of another, to satisfy the ends of public justice.[183]

But this clarification still left retributive justice in place as the ultimate underlying problem or premise. We are left with the problem so insightfully formulated by Abraham Shackleton: "The character of the unchangeable God." The God of the forensic theories of the atonement is, at best, ambivalent: both punishing and merciful.

Toward the end of his chapter on the atonement, Woodard brought forth some powerful images as he turned his focus to the resurrection of Jesus Christ: "Through death He destroyed him that had the power of death, that is the devil."[184] And in the final words of the chapter, he brought us to "that cross on which Christ vanquished all the hosts of darkness, and bruised Satan utterly under His feet."[185] These are the words and the images, not of the satisfaction/substitution theories, but of the Christus Victor view of the atonement—and of George Fox. We must remember that by the nineteenth and early twentieth centuries, the memory of these alternatives to the forensic and moral influence theories had practically disappeared from the Christian dialogue. I am not surprised that Woodard failed to see any discrepancy. Even as late as the 1980s, a careful Quaker scholar could argue that the Latin forensic theories and the classical Christus Victor view "do not necessarily conflict with one another, because they are doing completely different things."[186] Only in the twenty-first century have atonement scholars like J. Denny Weaver and R. Larry Shelton brought forth fully-developed theories based on, or consistent with, the classical Christus Victor view of the atonement and made it clear that their theories "do indeed conflict with the forensic or Latin theories of the atonement."[187] We can hardly fault Woodard, therefore, for failing to recognize this inconsistency in his atonement imagery and language.

In his autobiography, Woodard stated:

> I regard Quakerism, rightly understood and wisely applied, as the truest expression of primitive Christianity, with which it is my privilege to be acquainted. It is a significant fact that every advanced step that has marked the history of other religious denominations, since the days of George Fox, has been in the direction of the position he and his coadjutors occupied.

He expressed "the conviction that our early Friends were guided by the Holy Spirit, and that the principles which they enunciated were sound."[188]

Three decades earlier he had lamented one exception to these general statements of praise for early Friends:

> I will mention a work entitled "Sandy Foundation Shaken," by William Penn. While this renowned author, in other writings of his, shows himself to be orthodox, and fully accepts the doctrine of the divinity and atonement of Christ, still, I can not but regard the work referred to as seriously defective, and consider it very unfortunate, both for the reputation of the author and that of the Society to which he belonged, that the work was ever made public.[189]

The exact point of Woodard's objection to William Penn's essay is a bit puzzling. Penn summarized the issues he argued against in the subtitle of *Sandy Foundation Shaken*:

> *Those so generally believed and applauded Doctrines, Of One God subsisting in three distinct and separate Persons; The Impossibility of God's pardoning Sinners, without a plenary Satisfaction; The Justification of impure persons, by an imputative Righteousness, Refuted.*[190]

Penn further clarified the first of these doctrines that he rejected: "the trinity of separate persons, in the unity of essence."[191]

Woodard inserted his footnote as an illustration of a remark in his chapter on the humanity of Christ:

> It is to be feared that in some cases the earnest advocate* of what, to every Christian believer, is a most glorious truth—the *unity* of the Godhead—has not guarded with sufficient care another point equally precious, viz: that the one God has revealed himself in the threefold character of Father, Son, and Holy Ghost, and that while these are not three *separate and distinct persons*, yet each holds a distinct office in the work of human redemption, and to each belongs the attribute of personality, and should be severally and equally regarded as God.[192]

Woodard *agreed* here with Penn's first objection, and since he did not himself use the term *trinity* when writing about God as Father, Son, and Holy Ghost, it is hard to see what his objection to Penn was on this point.

Woodard clearly disagreed with Penn on the need for satisfaction of God's justice and on justification as involving imputed righteousness. His footnote might have been more appropriate in his discussion of the atonement in his chapter on the death of Christ. But his suggestion that Penn's work was damaging to the reputation of the Society of Friends implied that *Sandy Foundation Shaken* stated views that were contrary to the thought of other Quaker leaders, such as George Fox and Robert Barclay. The exact opposite is actually the case: Penn was here expanding and developing ideas that we can also find in the writings of Fox and Barclay. For instance, on "trinity" and "three persons," Fox was prone to arguments such as these:

> As for the word trinity, and three persons, we have not read it in the Bible, but in the common-prayer-book, or mass-book, which

the pope was the author of. But as for unity we own it, and Christ being the brightness of the Father's glory, and the express image of his substance (of the Father) we own.[193]

Ye professors, who have given new names to the Father, the Word, and the Holy Ghost, (as Trinity, and three distinct persons,) and say the scripture is your rule for your doctrine, but there is no such rule in the scripture, to call them by these new names, which the apostle that gave forth the scripture, doth not give them: and because we do not call the Father, and the Word, and the Holy Ghost by your new names, therefore do you falsely say, that the Quakers deny Father, Son, and Holy Ghost.[194]

On atonement theory, Barclay clearly rejected the concept of imputed righteousness. When writing about the work of Christ, Fox and Barclay did not use terms such as *substitution, satisfaction,* and the *penalty of sin.* Indeed, it is "virtually impossible to find anything in Fox's writings that reflects the 'satisfaction' theory of the atonement."[195] When Woodard's comments on the soundness of the principles of early Friends and the unfortunate impact of *Sandy Foundation Shaken* on the reputation of the early Society of Friends are brought together, they leave me with a clear sense that he assumed most early Quaker leaders promoted a forensic theory of the atonement—an assumption that turns out to have been seriously mistaken.

In one instance when Woodard was developing biblical support for his views on the atonement, he used questionable practice in his interpretation of a biblical passage. Writing specifically on the righteousness of God, he accurately quoted the King James Version text of Paul's letter to the Philippians 3:8–9, and then continued: "Of another place he says of this righteousness of God—it is '*unto* [imputed to] all, and *upon* [imparted to] all them that believe.' See Phil. iii: 8,9, and Rom. iii: 22."[196] On the face of it, Woodard appears to have been reading key points of nineteenth-century Quaker Holiness movement theology into the fact that there were two prepositions in parallel in this verse.

When I began to check out various translations of Romans 3:22, the plot thickened. Modern translations tended to show only one preposition in this context. Even my modern Greek New Testament had only one preposition. I turned to Quaker New Testament scholar Paul Anderson for help: The King James Version was the translation of a text based on several Greek manuscripts that had been written in the twelfth century. In more recent centuries, textual scholars have gained access to many earlier manuscripts—including two important fourth-century Greek manuscripts that only became fully available in the nineteenth century (Codex Vaticanus and Codex Sinaiticus). And most earlier manuscripts, including Vaticanus and Sinaiticus, lack the Greek words that are translated "and upon all" in the King James Version of Romans 3:22. Presumably, Woodard was not aware of the more recent work in textual scholarship, which would have rendered his efforts completely futile in this instance.

Edward Grubb

Edward Grubb was born in October 1854, near Sudbury, in East Anglia, England. His parents, Jonathan and Elizabeth Grubb, were Friends. Jonathan, was actively engaged in pastoral work and evangelical preaching, sometimes to large crowds. Edward studied at two Friends boarding schools, Sidcot and Bootham, and then at Flounders Institute, a teachers' training center adjoining Ackworth Friends School in Yorkshire. He went on to study at London University, where he passed BA examinations in 1872 and 1876, and received an MA degree in 1879.

"In August, 1877, Edward Grubb and Emma M. Horsnaill were married at the Friends Meeting House at Braintree,"[197] Emma's hometown. Edward and Emma had six children, one of whom lived only three months. For nearly three decades, Edward worked as a teacher. He taught at Bootham Friends School from 1872 to 1876, and then as a private tutor in Westbury-on-Trym (near Bristol) until 1879. From 1879 until 1901, the Grubb family lived first in York, then in Scarborough, and then in Southport. In each of these locations, his teaching positions were part-time jobs, and he worked in two or more schools at a time.

Following his student days, Edward Grubb went through an extended period of intellectual doubt about the evangelical faith in which he had grown up, as he searched for a satisfying and nourishing Christian faith. During his Scarborough years, "He was . . . helped and stimulated by his association with John Wilhelm Rowntree of York. . . . Together and independently, they held numerous meetings for young Friends, particularly in the north of England."[198] He wrote articles in the *Friend* in which he sharply criticized the substitutionary view of the atonement. In spite of the controversy resulted, Grubb was recorded as a minister toward the end of his time in Scarborough. "He appreciated the honour, not so much for his own sake, though it was an encouragement to him, but principally as an evidence that a more enlightened attitude to theological questions was becoming accepted by Friends."[199] In 1895, just after the move from Scarborough to Southport, he read a paper on "Social Questions" at the Manchester Conference. From this time on, he was active in religious education work among Friends, organizing summer schools, lecturing widely throughout the country, and supporting and developing Woodbrooke's programs.

In 1901, Grubb made a major change in career. He accepted two part-time positions: as editor of a monthly publication, the *British Friend*, and as secretary of the Howard Association, "whose objects were the welfare of prisoners and the promotion of better prison conditions."[200] The Grubb family moved to a house in Croydon, outside of London.

In late 1900 and early 1901, Grubb made a trip to visit Friends in the eastern United States, and later traveled again to America in 1904, 1907, and 1919. In 1905, he resigned from his position with the Howard Association. The *British Friend* ceased publication in 1913.

During World War I, the No-Conscription Fellowship was founded in Great Britain "when, in 1915, it became evident that the Government intended to introduce a Conscription Bill."[201] Grubb agreed to serve as treasurer of the Fellowship.

> In the summer of 1916, . . . along with the other members of the No-Conscription Fellowship Committee, he was prosecuted for issuing a leaflet calling for the repeal of the Military Service Act. . . . The appearance of the elderly, white-haired, gracious figure of Edward Grubb among the young defendants and his clear testimony to his faith in the power of Christian love to overcome evil, and to the un-Christian character of wars, added weight and dignity to the proceedings. . . .
>
> The verdict upheld the case of the prosecution and the defendants were each fined £110, with the alternative of two months' imprisonment. . . . All the defendants, except Edward Grubb and the Rev. Leyton Richards, who were persuaded to allow their fines to be paid for them, went to prison.[202]

In December 1920, Edward and Emma Grubb moved to a house in

Letchworth, Hertfordshire. During the years in Letchworth, "His time was increasingly devoted to writing, gardening, . . . and the religious and other activities of the town."[203] "One Friend said of him that 'he was a prophet and saint in a straw hat who smoked and fished.'"[204] Edward Grubb died in January 1939, and Emma's death followed nine weeks later.

Edward Grubb wrote a considerable number of books on religious topics, such as Quakerism, biblical criticism, and Christian thought. In an early work, *The Personality of God*, he summarized his understanding of the nature and significance of revelation:

> The personal touch of God upon us, bringing with it the assurance of reality, is what we mean by Revelation. Revelation is a primary and fundamental experience. . . . It is deeper than all creeds, or opinions, or conclusions reached by argument.[205]

In his chapter "Creeds and Salvation," he spelled out his thinking on why he, as a Friend, did not accept the necessity for creeds:

> To thousands in the early Church salvation came as a life of freedom, hope and love,—a consciousness of personal sonship with God. . . . Only later did they begin to reflect upon the meaning of His life and death, and, when they did so, they did not all explain it in identical terms. . . . Such theologies were not essential. What was essential was the new life that had come to them, the new relation to God and men. This present and living experience was what for them constituted salvation. . . .
>
> Salvation from sin does not depend upon theology, but upon a personal relation to God, into which we are brought through a right relation (conscious or unconscious) to Jesus Christ. Theology is merely the rationalising of such experience, by a process of later reflection. . . . It is not meant, of course, that all theologies are equally sound or unsound: the rational grounding, ordering, and harmonising of religious beliefs is essential, if Christian faith is to maintain itself in the face of criticism. But a theology that will stand criticism is not necessary for the experience of salvation; and it is perfectly possible for us to have Christian fellowship with those whose lives manifest a measure of the experience, but who do not express their beliefs according

to our own standards. . . . We should be earnestly desirous to learn from them as well as to teach.

Christianity is not a system of "doctrines," Divinely revealed to men once for all in a series of propositions which we must accept under pain of eternal ruin. It is a life and an experience into which we grow by the surrender of our lives to the rule of Jesus Christ.[206]

Grubb was convinced of the need to use the tools of historical and literary criticism (higher criticism) in order to properly understand and interpret the Bible:

Since the real meaning of the Bible is of far more consequence to our spiritual and moral life than is the case with any other literature, it is all the more important that critical methods should be properly applied to it by persons who have the requisite knowledge and ability. For it is only as we have some real information about the purpose of the writer, and what he was trying to say, that we can rightly interpret his meaning; and this involves inquiry into the date at which he wrote and the circumstances with which he was faced.[207]

He was aware of objections raised by opponents of higher criticism: for instance, "That Criticism is the use of human Reason alone, and that the Bible can only be understood and appreciated by the light of the Holy Spirit." He granted the truth of this claim, but insisted that

it misconceives the issue. Criticism *is* the use of Reason, but it is only by the use of Reason that facts can be discovered and established as true. It is mere confusion of thought to say, as I have heard it said, that the light of the Spirit, without any use of Reason, will convince anyone that all traditional beliefs about the Bible are true—as that Moses wrote the whole Pentateuch, that the "beloved disciple" of the fourth Gospel was John, the son of Zebedee, and so on. It is perfectly true that we must have our Reason enlightened by the Spirit if we are to appreciate the *meaning and worth* of the facts, and to reach a true and vital understanding of what we read. . . . But, speaking broadly, the facts can only be established, so that every reasonable mind must accept them, by critical processes.[208]

As he developed his thoughts on biblical criticism and biblical study, Grubb made a point that had long been neglected among Quakers who wrote about the Bible:

> The science of Biblical exegesis is the endeavour to discover, with all the light that textual and historical study can supply, what the writers of the Bible had in their minds and wished to express; and to put ourselves at their point of view so that we may be able sympathetically to explain their meaning.[209]

> For the interpretation of the Bible, it is essential that we should be so far in sympathy with the writers as to understand, from some measure of our own experience, what they are driving at. ... The great declaration that "God is Love" has meaning for us just in so far as we know by experience what "love" is.[210]

He reached the conclusion that

> the Authority of the Bible, granted a measure of this personal knowledge of God, will be to us no theory reached by painful and sophistical argument, but a living reality, felt and accepted, because we have come for ourselves into an experience akin to that of prophets, psalmists and apostles, and understand by spiritual sympathy something of the truths they struggled to express.[211]

In Grubb's call for sympathy with the biblical writers, we find nearly a century and a half later an echo of John Woolman's deep sense of "near sympathy" with the prophets and other people in the Bible—and perhaps an even fainter reflection of that vibrant empathy that ran so deeply through the writings of George Fox, Margaret Fell, and Edward Burrough.

Sympathy, for Grubb, was a means that we make use of as we strive to apprehend the nature of the Bible's authority for us. "By Authority," he suggested, "we mean power to give us trustworthy guidance in our problems of truth and duty."[212] His ultimate affirmation was: "We need, finally, the Authority of the Spirit in our own souls if we are truly to understand Him, or the Scriptures that testify of Him. ... Deep below all outward authority is the inward authority of the Spirit."[213] On this point it seems clear that Grubb intended to be faithful to Robert Barclay's position on the authority of the Bible and of the Holy Spirit.

Grubb insisted that we cannot find in the Bible "a final and infallible standard of truth and duty. The Bible is indeed full of God; . . . but it is not infallible. It is . . . man's record of the great process by which God has specially revealed Himself to men."[214] Making a different approach to this point, he noted that

> the Inspiration of the Bible . . . *is* a matter of degree. There is not the same degree, or even kind, of inspiration in the genealogies of the sons of Jacob in I Chron. as there is in the story of Elijah's flight to Horeb (I Kings xix.); nor in the appeals for vengeance on enemies in some of the Psalms as there is in the cry for pardon and purity in Psalm li., or the restful confidence in the heavenly Shepherd expressed in Psalm xxiii. . . . The church and its members have always recognised that not all parts of the Bible are equally "profitable for instruction in righteousness." The very gradual process of Divine revelation, and with it the varying degrees of inspiration that have accompanied its different stages, are things that must be recognised if we are to have any real understanding of the Bible.[215]

Process and *progress* are key terms in Grubb's understanding of the nature of biblical revelation:

> The Bible is a record of life and growth. Its watchword is progress, its goal is in the future. . . . There is in it no static perfection, but the dynamic of a living process. It culminates in Jesus Christ; but its glance is still forward, for His Kingdom is not yet established in the earth. The Bible is the inspiration for the progress that is yet to be. It is, and must ever be, the text-book of the Christian life, and for the world-wide mission of the Christian Church.[216]

> We trace the growing and deepening convictions of inspired seers and teachers, and read them in the light of the revelation brought by Jesus Christ Himself, which answers to the deepest demands of our own reason and conscience."[217]

Grubb rejoiced "that this great process of progressive revelation, culminating in Jesus Christ, is recorded in the pages of Scripture as nowhere else in the world's literature."[218] Grubb's faith in progress was a typical expression of modernist Christian thought in the late nineteenth and early twentieth centuries.

Grubb was true to the example of John Woolman and the anti-slavery pioneers in giving biblical principles a central place in our quest for guidance on social questions:

> The modern study of the Bible recognises that there is in the New Testament no explicit condemnation either of slavery or war. But it points to the great principle of the worth of each human soul in the sight of God, and of the consequent brotherhood of all men as sons of a common Father. . . . What Jesus did was to sow the seeds of a principle that would in time, if men learnt it and were faithful to it, bring slavery to an end without any social convulsion.
>
> So in regard to war. It is the principle of human brotherhood that is laid down, and men are left to discover for themselves its application to the actual circumstances in which they find themselves. . . . We cannot use the Authority of the Bible without the vigorous use of our own reason and conscience; and the best light we have is gradually convincing the world that it is Christ's principles alone that can save it from utter destruction.
>
> The case is similar when we turn to the Bible for guidance on the great questions of social reconstruction. No definite instructions are to be found as to the form that a Christian society must take. . . . Jesus had delivered no commands on the matter; He had given them the principle of love and brotherhood, and left them to find out how to apply it.[219]

Grubb summed up his understanding of how biblical principles are to be applied:

> The appeal to the Authority of the Bible must be made, not mechanically, but with the use of reason and insight to discover the highest principles of life that have been revealed to men; and we must find out for ourselves how they are to be used. . . . The principle of spiritual equality in the Kingdom is clearly recognised; favoured classes are unknown. Greatness in the Kingdom is greatness of service, not ability to make other men serve. It is such principles we can learn from the Bible, and it is for us to discover how they are to be applied.[220]

It is interesting to compare the basic principles Grubb found in the Bible with Woolman's listing. We see here in Grubb's list human worth, brotherhood, love, spiritual equality, and service. Woolman named love, justice, and universality as biblical principles, and added liberty as a "natural right."

Grubb's book *What is Quakerism?* was first published in 1917. According to his biographer, this book "has since almost become a Quaker classic."[221] In the final chapter of the book, he issued a call:

> It is not enough to talk superficially about the Inward Light, or the Brotherhood of men. We ought to have these great intuitions vitally related in our minds to the other truths we hold—on the one hand to the fundamental Christian doctrines of Incarnation and Atonement, and on the other to the facts disclosed by scientific and historical study. We need a doctrine of God that is large enough and strong enough to bring together belief in Evolution, belief in Redemption, belief in God's personal revelation to each human soul, and belief in the spiritual bonds that hold humanity together.[222]

He presumably still had these thoughts in mind when he later wrote a chapter on "Evolution and Redemption" in his book *Christianity as Truth*.[223] In that chapter he wrote:

> The means whereby God works Redemption through Christ is the whole of what Christ was and did. Visibly, to the careful student of history, his coming into this world, his life of love, his obedience even to death, his victorious resurrection, changed the face of human life, bringing to men new possibilities of recovery from sin, of development of the best that was in them, in happy fellowship with God and one another. But it is in the Cross that the Christian has always found the centre and climax of the revelation of Divine love.[224]

In the paragraph leading up to these words, I discovered some remarkable foreshadowings of theological ideas that were yet to come to fruition:

> The Christian Redemption can only operate as man's will responds to the love of God as revealed in Jesus Christ. The awakening soul . . . follows the path of Jesus to the Cross, and finds that there are no depths of suffering and humiliation to which that Divine love will not stoop in its conflict with human sin; seeking victory not by force but by love to the uttermost. He goes

on to the Resurrection, and gains from it the assurance that the victory was really won; that the way of the Cross was no delusion, but that the inmost heart of the universe supported and affirmed it—proving that God's own way of conquering evil is that of gentleness and love.[225]

Gustaf Aulén's *Christus Victor* lectures, which proposed that some ancient views of the atonement actually affirmed God's victory through Christ over the forces of evil, were not delivered or published until 1930. Hugh Barbour's and Canby Jones's rediscovery of the Lamb's War theme in early Quaker thought did not come until the 1960s. Denny Weaver did not publish his "narrative Christus Victor" theory, with its emphasis on the nonviolent character of God's atonement through Christ, until the twenty-first century. Yet here, in Grubb's writing, were all of these ideas in germ. Of course, they had already been present in the Bible—for those, like Grubb, who had eyes to see.

Apart from this moment of insight, Grubb's understanding of the atonement moved in a different direction. In *What is Quakerism?*, he began with his understanding of the early Quaker position:

> What Atonement meant to the early Friends . . . was the Reconciliation of man to God. . . . Atonement for them was an *inward* work, a real change in man, or it was nothing.
>
> The Reconciliation of man to God, the winning of his will by sacrificial love, carries with it the opening of his inward eyes to *see* that of which he was but dimly conscious, or not conscious at all.[226]

Edward Grubb's 1922 work, *The Meaning of the Cross*, was devoted entirely to the question of what is the nature of the atonement, of the work that was accomplished by God in the person of Christ, and in particular in Christ's death on the cross. He surveyed various theories of the atonement that have been extant in the history of Christian thought.

Grubb strongly disapproved of the substitutionary theory of the atonement:

> The doctrine of Substitution has become, for many earnest minds, simply incredible.[227]
>
> Our thought of Salvation has deepened. We feel that the main

thing is not to escape from punishment, even in the next world, but *to escape from sin* and to be able to live rightly in this world.[228]

Prophecy culminates in the ideal of the suffering Servant of Jehovah. . . . [In] the last three verses of Isa. liii. . . . we cannot be at all sure what exactly was originally written. But if it was anything like the present Hebrew text, the Servant's "soul" (or life) is said to have been made "an offering for sin." . . . This great prophecy does not, any more than do the Jewish sacrifices, teach vicarious *punishment*. What it does teach is vicarious and redemptive *suffering*, like that of Jeremiah and other prophets. . . .

Vicarious suffering is woven deeply into the fabric of human life, and often it is, or may be redemptive.[229]

The upshot of Paul's thoughts about the redeeming significance of the death of Christ is, then, that he died as our representative (not as our substitute), in order that we might die with him (to sin), and live with him (to righteousness).[230]

Grubb was likewise extremely critical of the early Christian ransom theory of the atonement:

The Ransom theory goes to pieces on the idea of a *transaction* between God and the Devil, which is a bit of speculative mythology without any basis in experience; and also on that of a *trick* practised on Satan by the Father, which is unworthy of the character of God as revealed by Christ.[231]

Grubb looked more favorably on the subjective or moral influence theory of the atonement, first proposed by Peter Abelard—especially on the way this view was formulated by the nineteenth-century American preacher-theologian, Horace Bushnell:

Horace Bushnell (1802–1876) . . . wrote an important book on *Vicarious Sacrifice*, which contains perhaps the best modern presentation of the Abelardian view of the Atonement. He says that . . . it is in Christ that God's moral power operates for men—in all that he was, did, felt, and suffered. What he especially reveals to us is that there is a *human side* in God: he awakens our sense of the personal relation to God which sin has outraged, and at the same time draws out our confidence in Him. He proves by his death that *God suffers* for human sin. . . .

The sacrificial symbols in the Bible Bushnell regards as ways of adumbrating the truth of Divine self-sacrifice.[232]

Grubb especially appreciated that

Bushnell has, in my judgment, found a valuable clue to the use of sacrificial terms, and to the hold they have had, and still have, over many minds. True forgiveness, the restoration of right relations between those who have become estranged from one another, is a difficult and costly thing. In the case of sin against God the obstacle and difficulty that has to be overcome is not on God's side, but on ours; the language of sacrifice is in part an adaptation to the wrong ideas of God engendered in men's minds by their experience of alienation from Him. As such it may have had, and may still have, an important place in assuring people who wrongly thought of God as hostile to them that He is not really so. . . . Our thanks are due to Bushnell for helping to clear a real difficulty out of the way.[233]

Grubb concluded *The Meaning of the Cross* by outlining his own views on the atonement:

Look at the Atonement first as *the gift of God*. We need a gift that will in some way actually take away our *sin*, with its inevitable alienation of our souls from God and His peace. The Cross is the supreme manifestation that God does take it away; that He forgives it by bearing and enduring it Himself. . . .

The wrong that has been done *hurts*, and it costs much to restore the relation of love and fellowship. . . . Even if (an imperfect figure) it is compared to a debt, he who remits a debt takes the cost on himself. . . .

Human forgiveness, Jesus taught, is, so far as it goes, a true picture of the Divine. The father of the prodigal had been bearing the sin of his scapegrace son all the years he had been away from home. The Cross reveals to us supremely what the sin of mankind, including *our* sin, has always meant to the eternal heart of love: how it has hurt, how that Divine Love has always been bearing it, mourning over it, seeking to overcome it.[234]

In these words I see a clear reflection of Bushnell's ideas that sin involves a personal relationship between humans and God and that God suffers for human sin. In his continuing thought, Grubb emphasized subjective aspects of the atonement:

> Think of Atonement as *man's offering of himself to God*. . . . The Cross tenders our hearts and opens our eyes, because it reveals the love that sin outrages; and when we really *see* we are brought down in shame and humiliation. . . . *Our will must be won*, and this is the essence of Atonement.[235]

> When once we *see* the Cross, we start life afresh—the life of self-forgetful service of God and man.[236]

Grubb's position fits clearly into the subjective or moral influence type of atonement theory.

A major point of contention between the Holiness and modernist movements among Friends had to do with historical and literary criticism (higher criticism) of the Bible. This disagreement was representative of the conflict between the fundamentalist and modernist movements that divided most Christian denominations. One major question within this debate centered on the authorship of a number of Old Testament books. We can see a striking example of this difference in the writings of two Friends. On the one hand, in *What Is Truth?* Luke Woodard wrote:

> A more recent school of Higher Critics, headed by such men as Willhausen and Kuenan, have appeared on the field, assailing the Old Testament with very similar methods to those employed by their predecessors in their attacks on the New Testament. By these critics the Mosaic authorship of the Pentateuch is denied; they declare that "the accounts of creation were simply transcribed, or evolved, from a mass of myths and legends, largely derived by the Hebrews from their ancient relations with Chaldea, rewrought in a monotheistic sense, imperfectly welded together, and then thrown into the sacred books which we have inherited. The account of man's physical origin in Genesis, is expressed in the simple terms of prehistoric legend, and unscientific, poetic description," and "modern science, in substituting the reign of law for the reign of caprice, the idea of evolution for that of creation, has added, and is steadily adding, a new revelation divinely

inspired." They maintain that the book of Job is unhistorical; the story of Jonah is fictitious; a large part of the book of Isaiah was not written by that prophet, and that the book of Daniel was a forgery of some unknown author of far later date. The genuineness of other books of the Old Testament is also denied, or called in question.

There are different methods of answering these arguments of the Higher Critics.

. . . I will . . . take up that [line of defense] which is the most simple, . . . and yet, as it seems to me, the most convincing of all. It is that which plants itself upon the doctrine of the Deity of Jesus Christ, and the doctrine of Inspiration. . . . Numerous quotations from, and references to the various books of the Old Testament are found in the Gospel, the Acts, and the Epistles. Both Christ and His apostles put their endorsement upon them with an express or implied acknowledgment of their divine origin, and their ultimate authority. With them the Scripture "could not be broken." All parties agree that our Lord ascribed the Pentateuch to Moses. Now admitting that Jesus Christ is God, it follows that his teaching is infallible, and that the New Testament is His word. The unanswerable argument against "the theory which denies that the Old Testament history is trustwort[h]y, is, *that Jesus and the whole New Testament teach, in multiplied instances, and in unmistakable terms, that the Old Testament is true history, a correct record, whose supreme and responsible author is God.*" The authority of our Lord is the principal factor in the discussion; and what Christian will not . . . prefer disbelieving the theories of the Higher Critics, to believing the fallibility of the knowledge of our adorable, divine Saviour. There was wisdom in His speech, and there was wisdom as well, in His silence. Never man spake like this Man. When He spoke, it was only truth, for He was full of grace and truth. He came into the world to bear witness unto the truth. Where He is silent, His reserve could not arise from ignorance. To charge Him with fallibility, is nothing short of a blow directed against His Deity. To own His infallibility, is to acknowledge the authority of His apostles and the divine authority, and the authenticity of Moses and the prophets and the Psalms; the trustworthiness of the very portions rejected by the Higher Critics, as Hebrew legends, rabbinical tales and heathen myths, namely: the account of the flood, the overthrow of Sodom, the story of Jonah, and the book of Daniel the prophet, since He places His endorsement upon these very portions.[237]

On the other hand, in *Authority in Religion*, Grubb tackled this argument head-on:

> Criticism is simply the application to the Bible of common-sense methods of study—the same, precisely, that have to be used in the case of any ancient literature whatever. . . . Textual Criticism inevitably leads up to what is unfortunately known as "Higher" Criticism—the purpose of which is to ascertain as nearly as possible when and by whom a book or a passage was written, and what were the circumstances that called it forth—that we may be able to place it properly, to appreciate the intention of the writer, and to judge how far he was well-informed. . . .
>
> Such study, carried on with the desire, not to "pull the Bible to pieces," but to understand what it really teaches, has convinced nearly all serious students in the present day that many traditional views concerning the date and authorship of Biblical books are not correct. It enables us, for example, to state with very strong probability that the "Book of Isaiah" was not all written by the prophet and statesman of the days of Hezekiah, about 700 B.C., but includes prophecies by various writers extending over a period of some 300 years. It leads us to the belief that many of the beautiful Psalms attributed to David (about 1000 B.C.) were really written long after his time. In the case of the New Testament, while at present it supports the traditional view that the third Gospel and the Book of Acts were written by Luke the companion of Paul, it makes it very hard to believe that the Pastoral Epistles were really the work of Paul, and as certain as any such judgment can be that the Epistle to the Hebrews was not.[238]

The Bible contains a great deal of matter that does not carry its own evidence of inspiration; and yet we are told that the whole of it is inspired. There is a real sense in which we can rightly hold this to be so. What we have to lay hold of is a thread that runs all through it. . . . That thread is to be found in the conviction, with which the open-minded study of the Bible leaves us, that it is the record of *a great Divine process* by which the minds and souls of a portion of the human race were gradually prepared to receive a fuller manifestation of God—a process which culminated in the person and work of Jesus Christ. The Bible is man's record of this gradual process of revelation, it is not the revelation itself. We cannot find in it a final and infallible standard of truth or duty.... We cannot use it *mechanically*, when we seek in it guidance on our problems, as though all parts of it were on one level of Divine infallibility.[239]

The books of the Bible are human documents, each of which has had its human history.... Religious experience and insight is, indeed, an indispensable qualification for a sympathetic understanding and exposition of what the Biblical writers had to say; but, taken alone, it cannot possibly inform us how far their words have been correctly transmitted, when they lived, what were their circumstances and their modes of thought, whether their writings are to be understood as history, or parable, or poetry, or what degree of credence is to be attached to their statements of fact. For all these things we must use our independent powers of enquiry and historical and literary judgment, and we must use them unhampered by conceptions of authority. The truth, and nothing else, must be both goal and guide.

There are some who fancy that this labour may be spared by an appeal to the authority of Jesus Christ.... The Protestant ... often quotes His recorded utterances in regard to Noah, Jonah, Isaiah, or Daniel—or His apparent recognition of the Davidic authorship of a certain psalm (Mark xii. 36)—as settling, without labour of historical investigation, any question that might arise about them.... The argument is that since Jesus was Divine He must have known all about these matters, and therefore enquiry is superfluous and even impious; it implies doubt or disbelief in His Divine knowledge....

The question ... of His use of the Old Testament is serious, because His authority is often appealed to in order to maintain positions that free investigation has rendered untenable. It is strange that Christians who are really loyal to their Master can put Him into such a place of danger; it can only be because they do not know, and are unwilling to ask or to face, what the evidence really is. To say that, if Jesus Christ is Divine and therefore trustworthy, Moses must have written the Pentateuch and David the 110th Psalm, is to put Him at the mercy of the first critic who shows the contrary. And this contrary has, by cumulative evidence, been raised to such a degree of probability as to have convinced nearly everyone whose mind is open to the facts.240

If criticism shows us that some of the statements attributed to Jesus, and which He probably really made, are unbelievable, what becomes of His authority? Does it not lead to a direct denial of His Divine nature? Is not Christian faith attacked at its very heart? To answer such questions requires a book rather than a few paragraphs; here we can do no more than suggest the lines on which, it is believed, a satisfying answer may be sought. After all that can be shaken by criticism has been put on one side, the unbiased study of the New Testament seems to leave us face to face with two unshakeable facts:

(1) The real though sinless humanity of Jesus.

(2) The fact that His followers, including those who had known Him as a friend and companion, began to speak of Him in terms of worship, as Lord and Saviour.241

The Incarnation involved God's self-limitation or self-sacrifice, yet without making Him any less than God. He who "was rich yet for our sakes became poor" (2 Cor. viii. 9); though equality with God was within His reach, He refused it, and "emptied himself, taking on him the nature of a slave" (Phil. ii. 6, 7). This "Kenosis," which must be recognised by anyone who takes the Incarnation seriously, we can best think of on ethical lines, as essentially the same in nature as the self-sacrifice (which is also self-realisation) involved in all true love and loving service. . . .

If such thoughts are in the direction of the truth, then the authority of Christ as the eternal Word or Son of God is no other than the authority of God Himself, and is therefore final and absolute. But it is not *outward* authority. To find a final outward authority in Jesus Christ, we should have to attribute

Divine infallibility to every word He is reported to have spoken in the body, and to every thought that passed through His human mind. And this we cannot do without denying at once the imperfections of the record and the reality of the Incarnation. If Jesus Christ was truly man, then His thoughts in the flesh were compassed with limitation. A real man is one who learns, who grows, in mind as well as in body. An omniscient baby would not be a human child. Yet, if Jesus was not omniscient in His cradle, at what point did He become so?

The Christian belief is that the Son of God, for our redemption from sin, submitted Himself to become one of ourselves. He became, as the author of Hebrews says, our brother, "made in all things like unto his brethren" (Heb. ii. 17): a real man, a real Jew, fulfilling indeed the highest of His people's yearnings, yet sharing their limitations. He seems to have known nothing of Greek literature and philosophy, or of Roman Law; poetry and art and science were beyond His ken. But He was steeped, apparently from early youth, in His nation's sacred literature; and, while transcending immeasurably the religious ideas of His time, He spoke, and doubtless thought, according to the fashion of His day. The scheme of the universe to which His people held, He held also. To teach them a better astronomy was no part of the work He had come to do; and literary and historical criticism lay equally outside His sphere. He took as He found them the prevalent ideas about the authorship of Old Testament books; to have done otherwise would have hindered His purpose of revealing the Father and winning men from sin into the life of God. The more clearly we discern His purpose, and the more firmly we hold to it, the more unfettered will be our freedom of enquiry into matters of history.[242]

I have not found any evidence that Grubb had read *What Is Truth?* by Woodard. Both Friends presented points of view that were widespread within their respective movements. Woodard, indeed, articulated some objections to the "kenosis" theory in his book *A Panorama of Wonders*, published in 1921, twenty years after *What Is Truth?* and three years before Grubb's *Authority in Religion*:

Thus the higher critics assail the omniscience and infallibility of our Lord. Under the term "Kenosis," (from the Greek kenos, empty), they teach that He so emptied Himself of Divine knowledge, that He was fallible, liable to err as other men. They cite such passages as, "Jesus increased in wisdom and stature, and in favour with God and man." (Luke 2:52) They seem to overlook the fact that this was spoken of His childhood, and that He did not enter upon His public ministry until, as a man, He had attained His majority, at the age of thirty, and until after His baptism with the Holy Ghost, and God had proclaimed His sanction: "This is My beloved Son, in Whom I am well pleased."

The text, however, which is the principal support of their theory, is Mark 13:32: "Of that day and that hour knoweth no man, no, not the angels in heaven, neither the Son, but the Father." To take this as a proof that there were other things He did not know is wholly gratuitous conjecture. . . . We may safely accept any statement made by our Lord as true: if this applies to the one thing He said He did not know, why not apply it to His utterances when He speaks as one who professes to know?[243]

Woodard failed to deal with other texts that the kenosis theorists relied on, such as: "He had to become like his brothers and sisters in every respect, so that he might be a merciful and faithful high priest in the service of God" (Hebrews 2:17). Why should "every respect" not include the finite, limited, culture-bound extent of our knowledge?

Even though Woodard failed to derail the kenotic theory of Christ's incarnation, a careful theologian, D. M. Baillie, has shown that "there seem to be insuperable objections"[244] to this theory. For instance, if the eternal Word of God, who "himself is before all things, and in him all things hold together" (Colossians 1:17), "laid aside His distinctively divine attributes (omnipotence, omniscience, omnipresence) and lived for a period on earth within the limitations of humanity,"[245] we are faced with

> the simple question asked by the late Archbishop of Canterbury [William Temple] in objection to the Kenotic Theory. "What was happening," he asked, "to the rest of the universe during the period of our Lord's earthly life? To say that the Infant Jesus was from His cradle exercising providential care over it all is certainly monstrous; but to deny this, and yet to say that the Creative Word was so self-emptied as to have no being except in the Infant Jesus,

is to assert that for a certain period the history of the world was let loose from the control of the Creative Word."[246]

We must note, however, that Baillie raised these objections to the Kenotic theory only after he had established firmly "that Jesus' knowledge was essentially the limited knowledge of a man. . . . Theology has come to acknowledge unreservedly the human limitation of our Lord's knowledge."[247] It turns out that Edward Grubb would have been on stronger ground if he had bypassed the idea of God's self-limitation or kenosis and simply appealed to the ancient Christian claim that Jesus Christ was "truly God and truly man," in order to affirm the limitations to Jesus' knowledge and thus leave room for historical criticism to question the traditional views about the authorship of Old Testament writings.

Elbert Russell

In 1894 Holiness Quaker minister Dougan Clark had resigned from the Bible department at Earlham College because of the controversy aroused by his action of accepting water baptism. The president of Earlham left the position unfilled for a year, and then made the surprising move of appointing a young recent Earlham graduate who had almost no training in Bible or religious studies, Elbert Russell, to take charge of the Bible department. Russell later surmised that the president may have been attempting to avoid serious controversy by making such an appointment:

> To emphasize scholarship or to depart in any marked way from the vocabulary or emphasis of Evangelical theology would bring down upon the department the vigorous hostility of the fundamentalist leaders, such as David Updegraff, Walter and Emma Malone, Esther Tuttle Pritchard, Luke Woodard, and John Henry Douglas. If I had gone to any good theological school, I would have imbibed pretty certainly views which they would have regarded as heretical.[248]

The appointment was a gamble, which might have worked. As Russell stated it: "I did not seriously begin to question my inherited 'fundamentalist' theology until several years later," even though he was already repelled by "the dogmatism and intolerant spirit of many of the Holiness groups."[249] The ultimate outcome, however, was that over the next two decades while Russell taught there, the conflict between the Holiness and modernist movements in Quakerism came to focus on the Bible department at Earlham.

Elbert Russell was born in August 1871 on a farm two miles from Friendsville, in eastern Tennessee. His parents, William Russell and Eliza (Sanders) Russell, were Friends. William was a recorded minister, who "was away from home occasionally, holding revival meetings." Eliza and William Russell "died early in 1879 within two months of each other."[250] William Russell's father, Josiah Russell, was in Friendsville when his son died. He took his grandchildren (Elbert and his two sisters, Eva and Ruth) back to his home in West Newton, Indiana, a few miles from Indianapolis. The three children spent the rest of their childhood as part of a Quaker family in their grandparents' home.

Elbert Russell began his student years at Earlham College in the fall of 1890. He graduated in 1894 and stayed on at Earlham for another year, during which he took graduate-level courses in German and was in charge of the men's dormitory.

Russell tied his 1895 decision to accept the position to teach religion at Earlham to his and Lieuetta Cox's decision that their marriage would take place in August of that year. Cox, a Methodist girl from West Newton, became a Friend two years later. In due course they had two children, Josiah, born in September 1900, and Marcia, born in March 1903.

Russell's views on religion and the Bible began to change and mature:

> During my later student days and early teaching years at Earlham I read a number of books which thoroughly emancipated me from Biblical literalism. . . . My emancipation from the idea that the Bible must be historically accurate came more slowly, but I came finally to recognize that the Bible was valuable as a guide in religion, not a text book of science or history or an encyclopedia of religious knowledge. It was a great relief to be able to face the world seeking truth without . . . fear that some new discovery or theory would make Christian faith impossible or render the Bible valueless.[251]

A major event in Russell's life was "the visit of John Wilhelm Rowntree of England to America in 1898–1900 [that] was in many respects epoch-making in my religious thinking." Russell gladly accepted Rowntree's offer to donate religious books to the Earlham College library, "to be selected by himself and Rufus Jones."[252] These books included a two-volume commentary on the book of Isaiah by George Adam Smith; "The works of G. A. Smith on the prophets proved extraordinarily stimulating to me. I shared my discovery of *Isaiah* with my senior Bible Class."[253] Among other things, Smith presented extensive and cogent arguments that a major portion of the book of Isaiah, beginning with chapter 40, was written not by Isaiah himself but by a prophet in Babylon, during the Exile nearly two centuries later, whom Smith called Second Isaiah.

Russell reported:

> During the calendar years 1899–1900 . . . the inevitable conflict between the older evangelical leaders and the newer liberalism came to an open conflict in which I was inevitably involved. Very prominent among the older leaders were John Henry Douglas, Luke Woodard, and Nathan and Esther Frame. . . . Esther Tuttle Pritchard . . . shared the inevitable doctrinal intolerance of Evangelicalism. As my influence grew and my own liberalism became clearer and more pronounced, the latent antagonism of these leaders came into the open.[254]

In June 1900 Russell spoke on two subjects at the summer school at Haverford College. He was particularly stimulated by some of the other scholars at the summer school, including Rufus Jones and J. Rendel Harris. "The school . . . was a turning point in my career, . . . in that it revealed so clearly the deficiencies in my preparation for my work at Earlham that I resolved the following year to devote myself to further study."[255]

In 1900 Russell had some rather testy interviews with Esther Tuttle Pritchard at the summer Bible Institute at Earlham and with John Henry Douglas at Western Yearly Meeting in the fall. Pritchard "thought my questioning the historicity of parts of the Pentateuch tantamount to denial of its truth."[256]

In 1901 Russell turned in his resignation from Earlham, so that he could undertake graduate study at the University of Chicago Divinity School. Earlham's president "suggested that I apply for a leave of absence instead of resigning. I told him that I . . . would prefer to resign. If it seemed desirable for me to return when I had finished my studies, that could be a matter for negotiation at the time."[257] Two years later, he had completed all of the requirements for a doctoral degree at Chicago except for the writing of a dissertation. He expressed to the new president of Earlham his willingness to return to the college, if he could have full academic freedom to express his views in his teaching. After an interview with a committee of the college's trustees, he was reappointed to the Earlham faculty.

Between 1905 and 1907, Russell had personal discussions and a long correspondence with William P. Pinkham, editor of the newly established publication *The Evangelical Friend*. Pinkham charged that Friends "colleges were centers of unbelief and atheism, and that the professors were undermining Christianity and turning the youth away from Christian faith."[258] He later criticized Russell for not believing in the devil as a distinct personal being.

In 1909 Russell published a book, *Jesus of Nazareth in the Light of Today*. In this book he set forth his method and assumptions:

> The twentieth century man, who is in harmony with the historical and scientific spirit, who thinks in terms of the evolutionary philosophy, who presupposes commonly accepted results of the historical and literary criticism of the Bible, especially of the Gospels—what shall he think of Jesus of Nazareth? Let us attempt to form an estimate of his character and importance as a force in history in the same spirit and by the same methods by which we would attempt to estimate the significance of any other historical personage, such as Napoleon or Hannibal, Buddha or Mohammed."[259]

That would have been enough to send his critics up in flame—no matter that he concluded his book by confirming the uniqueness and divinity of Christ.

In 1909 was one of a number of Friends who organized a new West Richmond Monthly Meeting, which met at first in the Earlham College auditorium. That meeting later bought a property a couple of blocks from the college campus. Russell continued to actively press for a close relationship between the monthly meeting and the college that would involve the building of a meeting house on the campus.

Russell related that

> soon after 1911 agitation was begun by some members of the Board against my teaching. . . . Some of the Board were uneasy

about a course in the social applications of Christianity which I had recently introduced and which seemed too radical or socialistic in its tendency.

In 1912 he received an inquiry about becoming pastor of a Friends church, at a salary higher than he was receiving at Earlham. He went to the president of the college, "inquiring whether my status in the college was such that I had better consider the offer."[260] The president assured Russell that his position was secure, and arranged to match the salary proposed by the Friends church.

By 1915, however, "The question of the relation of the college to the Society [of Friends] came to a head over the question of building a meeting house on the campus and continuing and enlarging the working arrangement between West Richmond meeting and the college."[261] Russell also believed that other changes in college policy were having the effect of undermining his position as college pastor and head of the Bible department. He therefore resigned from the faculty of Earlham College, without knowing where he might go next.

Before the end of the academic year, some Friends in Baltimore arranged for him to teach and continue his graduate studies at Johns Hopkins University. He would also serve as an unpaid "resident minister" at Eutaw Street Meeting in Baltimore.

In his book *Jesus of Nazareth in the Light of Today*, Russell wrote:

> Jesus sought to become king of men, without robe or crown, throne or scepter, by the sheer force of his personality, by the convincing power of his teaching and the winning power of his love. By such means would he win his kingdom and on such a basis let it rest. . . . Against the world's hoary bulwarks of evil he set the blazing passion of his cross, and having seen the flame kindle in his disciples, he went his way sure that he had overcome the world. He planted his kingdom as seed and leaven in the hearts of men, confident of the vital power of its truth and love to grow and fructify in the soil of humanity, assured that it would permeate and transform the world. The power of an idea, or a resolution, or a passion to make history and to change and determine destiny is a commonplace of our thinking to-day, but with Jesus it was the daring of genius, the insight of inspiration.[262]

He was not in that context discussing the nature of Christ's atonement, but I find in these words a significant foreshadowing of some thoughts of Denny Weaver and Larry Shelton in their works on the atonement:

> The teaching and acts of Jesus pose the reign of God in conflict with the powers that oppose it. When Jesus was executed, the powers of evil enjoyed a momentary triumph—Jesus' very existence is removed. However, God raised Jesus from death, thereby revealing the reign of God as the ultimate power in the cosmos.[263]

> In the New Testament, the atonement of Christ serves a mediatorial role in initiating and maintaining God's new covenant with all humanity. . . . The covenant theme establishes the Christian community in the history of the people of God.[264]

I believe Russell's thoughts would fit well into a theory of the atonement that uses biblical theology themes (reign of God, mighty acts of God) as a framework to bring together Weaver's narrative, Christus Victor theory, and Shelton's covenant theory of the atonement.

In 1916, young Friends of Philadelphia Yearly Meeting asked Russell to deliver the first of an annual series, the William Penn Lectures. In this lecture, *The Christian Life*, he more explicitly addressed the question of Christ's atonement. He began:

> The other point has to do with the intensifying of this personal power thru the self-sacrifice of Jesus. A person's moral influence is usually in proportion to his ultimatum to the world when it would turn him from his purpose. His ideals gain power not only by their truth but by his sincerity. Other things being equal, convictions are contagious in proportion to men's willingness to suffer for them. More than anything else, voluntary suffering for the good of others makes personality dynamic and fruitful.[265]

He illustrated this point by citing William Lloyd Garrison, Paul, Tolstoy, and Socrates as examples. His ultimate example was Jesus:

> His love for his people was not limited by any consideration for himself. . . . Only by being lifted up on the cross could his life find power to draw all men to himself. His self-denying love thru the dynamic leverage of the cross, touches, redeems and transforms

men's lives, so that an ever-widening stream of righteousness and love has flowed from it thru the centuries. He became not only in his words and character the embodied and dynamic Truth of the Christian life, but his divine love, focussed in the might of the cross opens the Way of Life to those his spirit reaches.[266]

Like Edward Grubb, Russell clearly subscribed to the subjective, moral influence view of the atonement—even as each of them had his moment of insight that reached forward to something much deeper.

Russell's graduate studies at Johns Hopkins were primarily devoted to Hebrew and other Semitic languages. By 1917, he and his advisor were running into difficulties in agreeing on a project for his PhD dissertation. Meanwhile, some Hicksite Friends in the Philadelphia area had founded the Woolman School, somewhat on the lines of Woodbrooke in England. The school was reorganized in 1917 under a board of trustees from both the Hicksite and Orthodox branches of Friends. The trustees invited Russell to become director of Woolman School. He accepted the offer, and he and Lieuetta moved to Swarthmore in June 1917.

In late 1918 he wrote to the dean of the University of Chicago to inquire about the possibility of his finishing up his doctorate there. His studies at Johns Hopkins were accepted for credit toward a Chicago degree. He spent a few months organizing the material that he had prepared in 1903 for a New Testament dissertation and made a trip to Chicago in May and June 1919. At the end of that stay, he received his PhD from the University of Chicago.

In the summer of 1920, Elbert and his son Josiah sailed to England for the first All Friends Conference.

By 1926,

> It became more and more evident that there was no future for Woolman School under the old plan and the existing conditions. It had, however, aroused a greater interest in religious education among Friends and prepared the way for Pendle Hill, which finally inherited the good will, library, and other properties of the School.[267]

That spring Elbert Russell was offered a position as professor of biblical instruction at the newly established School of Religion (later to become the Divinity School) at Duke University in Durham, North Carolina. The School of Religion was founded and supported by the Southern Methodist Church, but had no problem with having a Quaker on its faculty. Elbert, Lieuetta, and Marcia moved to Durham in September 1926. In 1928, Elbert was appointed to the position of dean of Duke Divinity School.

In 1942 he published *The History of Quakerism*. I still recommend this book as the best available single-volume history of Quakerism.

He was dean of the Divinity School at Duke until he retired from that position in 1941. He then taught four more years at Duke, followed by one year at Guilford College, the Friends college in Greensboro, North Carolina. In 1946, Elbert and Lieuetta moved to St. Petersburg, Florida, where he died in September 1951. Elbert's autobiography covered his life through his retirement as dean of Duke Divinity School. His son, Josiah, added a brief account of the final ten years of Elbert's life.

4

Friends and the Bible: Quaker Bible Scholars

J. Rendel Harris

Martin Davie emphasized that modernist thought in early twentieth-century Quakerism was neither based on original thinking nor intrinsic to Quakerism. He provided some evidence for asserting "the paucity and derivative nature of Quaker theological scholarship at that time."[1] He overlooked the fact that the evangelical Quakerism that it was replacing had itself been largely influenced by the thought of the Wesleyan and Holiness movements. He also failed to note the immense impact that Quaker modernism has made in the wider Christian world. For instance, influential thinkers such as preachers Harry Emerson Fosdick and Howard Thurman, philosopher Charles Hartshorne, and novelist Theodore Dreiser have publicly acknowledged their own debts to Rufus Jones.

More specifically, Davie correctly noted "that Liberal Quakers were enthusiastic about the results of Biblical criticism." In this regard, he again insisted on "the dependence of Liberal Quakerism upon outside scholarship."[2] He failed to point out, however, that one of the early leaders of

Quaker modernism, J. Rendel Harris, was in his own right a prolific and highly original Bible scholar. The amazing fact is that since Harris's day a surprising number of Friends—especially considering the tiny percentage of Christians who are Friends—have become solid and influential Bible scholars, and that some of these have succeeded in contributing distinctively Quaker perspectives to the community of biblical scholarship.

In the areas of biblical criticism and early Christian studies, Harris wrote a vast number of books and articles. In an attempt to identify the thread of his research, I have worked through his books listed in the bibliography. Some of these books call for slow and mindful reading, as they are filled with quotations from ancient writers in the original Latin, Greek, and Syriac; sometimes these quotations are placed alongside each other in parallel columns. And yet we find Harris lamenting his own limitations. He mentioned that the commentary of Ephrem Syrus had long been available only in an Armenian translation, and that it was "unfortunate . . . that so many persons (myself amongst their number) are ignorant of Armenian."[3] This commentary had more recently become available in two copies of a Latin translation, which did not agree in all details. Critical work toward determining the original wording was needed: "I am sorry that my ignorance of Armenian does not permit me to undertake this correction."[4] He had to take a detour: "My researches in another direction have been very fruitful."[5] His detour was to try to reconstruct Ephrem's original Syriac words from later commentaries on his work and on the *Diatessaron* in the Syriac language.

Even though many of Harris's writings dealt with early Christian writings outside of the New Testament, they frequently had an impact on New Testament studies. For instance, some nineteenth-century critics had argued that the gospels and other New Testament books were not written until the second or even third century CE. Harris argued that his study of Tatian's *Diatessaron* (an early harmony of the four gospels) provided strong evidence that the gospels and other books of the New Testament were written much earlier. From his detailed examination of Tatian's work he concluded that

> the existence of Tatian's Harmony is momentous evidence for
>
> (i) the antiquity of the four gospels,
>
> (ii) of the Acts of the Apostles,
>
> (iii) of the first Epistle to the Corinthians,
>
> and perhaps of some other portions of the New Testament.[6]

Harris thus made an important contribution to the present-day consensus among scholars that the gospels and Acts were indeed written in the first century CE.

Scholars vary widely in their attempts to understand and interpret the theology of the gospel of John. Many believe that the writer of the gospel is concerned to address Greek-speaking readers in terms that they would have understood from Greek philosophy, or even as having been influenced by Greek philosophy, directly or indirectly, through the Jewish philosopher Philo who had tried to harmonize the Jewish scriptures with Greek philosophy. Others have claimed that the gospel was built primarily on Jewish religious thought, and some have seen the gospel as addressing both Jewish and Greek themes. This dialogue has often focused on the opening words of the gospel of John: "In the beginning was the Word [Greek *logos*], and the Word was with God [*pros ton theon*], and the Word was God" (John 1:1).

On this issue, Harris came down clearly on the side of those who saw the gospel of John as based on Jewish thought. In regard to *pros ton theon*, he argued: "We are dealing with what is called 'Translation Greek' or 'Semitic Greek.' The Marcan and Johannine uses are one and the same."[7] In regard to *logos*, his first step was to state:

> The *Book of Testimonies*, then, shows clearly that the doctrine that
>
> Christ is the Word of God
>
> reposes on an earlier doctrine that
>
> Christ is the Wisdom of God.[8]

The gospel of John says of the Word (*logos*): "All things came into being through him" (John 1:3). In Colossians, Paul had written of Christ, the Son of God: "In him all things in heaven and on earth were created . . . all things have been created through him and for him" (Colossians 1:16). Harris saw a connection with the eighth chapter of Proverbs, in which Wisdom said: When [God] established the heavens, I was there, . . . when he marked out the foundations of the earth, then I was beside him, like a master worker (Proverbs 8:27, 29–30).

The idea of Wisdom being involved with God in the Creation is echoed by two books in the Apocrypha: Wisdom of Solomon (The Book of Wisdom) and Wisdom of Jesus, the Son of Sirach (Ecclesiasticus). Proverbs and these two books belong to a genre commonly known as wisdom literature; Harris used the term *sapiential* books. He concluded his argument: "The key to the language of the Johannine Prologue and to St Paul's language in the Epistle to the Colossians lies in the Sapiential tradition, and not in the reaction from Plato or Philo or Heraclitus [an early Greek philosopher]."[9]

But what is the *Book of Testimonies* that Harris mentioned?

In 1893, Harris published a book about an early Christian writing, the gospel of Peter. Portions of that gospel had recently been discovered by French archaeologists in Egypt. Harris gave reasons to show that "the Gospel of Peter is . . . a product of the second century."[10] Toward the end of his book, he addressed the question of possible literary sources that the author of that gospel might have copied or borrowed from, and he surmised: "There is another possible source that suggests itself: a comparison of the text of Peter with the writings of Justin Martyr (a second-century Christian writer) will betray one or two very remarkable coincidences."[11] After detailing these similarities, he concluded:

> I think the real explanation of these coincidences is that both Justin and Peter had a little text-book of fulfilled prophecies, to be used in discussions with Jews. . . . The early Christian writers were very keen in reading the New Testament into the Old and the Old into the New. They found New Testament interpretations where we should never see anything of the kind."[12]

In 1901, Harris published an article in which he examined an eighth- or ninth-century Arabic manuscript from the collection at Saint Catherine's Monastery on Mount Sinai. It was written as a Christian tract in opposition to the Muslim religion, and included "the discussion of a string of texts which evidently belong to collections of *Testimonia*."[13] He continued: "The value, then, of the tract consists in the fact that it is a survival of anti-Judaic literature. Such literature began early in the Christian Church, in the nature of the case, and it lasted late; . . . it contains many forms of theological statement and many biblical quotations."[14] Harris deduced that many early Christian writers had been copying biblical quotations from a document or succession of documents that he called "collections of *Testimonia*." No such document has actually been discovered; Harris proposed its existence as a theory to explain the similarities among the Old Testament quotations in various Christian writings. He gave an example of one of these puzzling similarities in his 1901 article, when he wrote regarding the author of the anti-Muslim Arabic tract (I presume that the bracketed reference to Malachi 3:1 was inserted by Harris):

> In introducing one of his prophetic testimonies, he says:
>
>> God said by the tongue of Isaiah the prophet about the Christ and about John the son of Zacharia: I will send my messenger, etc. [Mal. iii. 1].
>
> Here the substitution of Isaiah for Malachi is an error of a type which is very common in collections of *Testimonia*, where the names attached to the extracts are frequently affected by original blunders as well as by faults of transcription; but since the same error is found in Mark i. 2, we have no need to go beyond the gospels for the explanation. Still the suggestion will present itself as to whether, after all, the original cause of the error may not lie in a false ascription in some collection of Testimonies, both as regards the Arabic writer and the Gospel of Mark.[15]

In 1905 Harris published an article, "Spoken by Jeremy the Prophet," in which

> I was able . . . to work out at some length the problem of the false ascription in the Gospel of Matthew (xxvii.9) of a series of prophecies which were supposed to refer to Judas the traitor, and were definitely ascribed to Jeremiah. . . .
>
> The controversy is, of course, as to how the Evangelist, supposed inerrant, could have ascribed to Jeremiah a prophecy of which the nearest parallel is in Zechariah (Zech. xi. 12) (though even in the supposed parallel the agreement between the book and its quotation is not very obvious).[16]

The passage referred to in Matthew is:

> Then was fulfilled what had been spoken through the prophet Jeremiah, "And they took the thirty pieces of silver, the price of the one on whom a price had been set, on whom some of the people of Israel had set a price, and they gave them for the potter's field, as the Lord commanded me" (Matthew 27:9–10).

More than forty years later, Sherman E. Johnson neatly summarized, in *The Interpreter's Bible*, the oddity of this quotation from "Jeremiah": "The passage is not from *Jeremiah*, but is a free paraphrase of Zech. 11:13, with some slight reminiscence of Jer. 18:2–3; 32:6–15."[17] Zechariah 11:13 reads: "Then the LORD said to me, 'Throw it into the treasury'—this lordly price at which I was valued by them. So I took the thirty shekels of silver and threw them into the treasury in the house of the LORD." In Jeremiah 18:1–3, we read: "The word that came to Jeremiah from the LORD: 'Come, go down to the potter's house, and there I will let you hear my words.' So I went down to the potter's house." In Jeremiah 32, in response to "the word of the LORD," which "came to me. . . . I bought the field at Anathoth from my cousin" (vv. 6, 9). None of these passages are in the form of predictions of future events; each of them is a report of actions that had previously been taken by the respective prophet. And even though Zechariah's phrase, "threw them into the treasury in the house of the LORD," does not appear in the quoted prophecy in Matthew 27:9–10, it is matched by the action of Judas as reported in the account of the events that fulfilled that prophecy (vv. 3, 5).

In this same 1905 article, Harris stated that

> it has been my habit, for some time past, to warn my students . . . that there are two lost documents of the early Christian propaganda, . . . the traces of which are to be found constantly in the first period of the literature of the Church. Of these the first is the *Collection of the Sayings of Jesus*, the second is the *Book of Testimonies* from the Old Testament. The first of these underlies the Gospels, and is especially an instrument for the conversion of the Gentiles: the second is an instrument for the refutation of the Jews.[18]

I presume that the *Collection of the Sayings of Jesus* is the hypothetical document, commonly today called Q, that most twentieth-century critical scholars look on as the source for many sayings of Jesus that are found in the Gospels of Matthew and Luke, but not in Mark. The *Book of Testimonies* is essentially what Harris was calling "collections of *Testimonia*" in his 1901 article. He indicated that, in early Christian writings, "the existence of centos from the Scriptures, combining passages in a set order and with substantially the same variations and connecting links, will often betray the use of the lost little book of which we are speaking."[19]

In particular, Harris made the suggestion

> that the Gospel of Matthew has been using a *Book of Testimonies*, in which the history and tragic end of Judas was explained as a

fulfilment of ancient prophecy, and that the mistake which has vexed so many righteous souls was not necessarily even an original one in the Gospel, but one which either existed in the *Book of Testimonies*, or was accidentally made by the Evangelist in using such a book.[20]

He summed up his argument:

It really seems as if Matthew had used, from his little text-book, first a sentence from Zechariah, and second, one from Jeremiah. . . .

My suggestion, then, is that the printed Greek text of Matthew is correct, but that it depends upon a lost collection of *Testimonies*.

From this, Harris drew this significant conclusion: "One part of the lesson would appear to be that the *Book of Testimonies* is older than much of the New Testament literature."[21]

In a 1907 article, Harris examined a recently discovered writing by a well-known, second-century Christian writer named Irenaeus, *On the Apostolic Preaching*. He referred in this article to "the collection of prophetic passages which I have shown to be current in the early Church, whose original title seems to have been *Testimonies against the Jews*."[22] The conclusion that he drew from this examination was that "there is no doubt that nearly the whole of the treatise of Irenaeus on the *Apostolical Preaching* is a commentary on a collection of Testimonies."[23]

In 1916, Harris published *Testimonies*, Part I. In this book he presented his theory of the existence of an ancient *Book of Testimonies* and laid out a great deal of evidence on which he based the theory. He incorporated his 1901, 1905, and 1907 articles into this book as individual chapters. He wrote in this book:

It is becoming increasingly clear that the *Testimony Book* is earlier in date than some of the earliest books of the New Testament; and that it . . . is also clear from the antiquity and wide diffusion of errors which can only have arisen in a written book. . . .

Setting Matthew on one side for the present, we may argue the antiquity of the *Testimony Book* even more forcibly by reference to the opening verses of Mark.[24]

According to the best and most ancient manuscripts, the text of Mark 1:2

is: "As it is written in the prophet Isaiah, 'See, I am sending my messenger ahead of you, who will prepare your way.'"

The quotation, however, is not from the book of Isaiah, but from Malachi 3:1. This quotation in Mark is immediately followed by another quotation in verse 3: "The voice of one crying out in the wilderness: 'Prepare the way of the Lord, make his paths straight,'" which is indeed a quotation from Isaiah 40:3. This is the type of error and confusion that Harris has found to be typical of numerous biblical and early Christian passages quoted from the *Book of Testimonies*. We should also be reminded that nearly all twentieth-century critical scholars are convinced that the gospel of Mark was written earlier than the gospel of Matthew, since Matthew and Luke both copied a great deal of material from Mark.

In a chapter near the end of his book, Harris presented an argument that a version of the *Book of Testimonies* used by a second-century Christian writer had been "compiled by Matthew the Apostle."[25]

In 1920, Harris published Part II of *Testimonies*, in which he explored additional evidence in support of his theory and further implications of the theory. In asking again just how early the *Book of Testimonies* originated, he commented:

> Now it is one thing to say that a collection of *Testimonies* was current in the Church in the time of Paul's first missionary journey, or at the time of his first imprisonment in Rome, and quite another thing to say that it was extant in the first days of the Church at Jerusalem.[26]

He did not appear to give a definitive solution to this matter, but rather went on to the ultimate question, which he formulated as the title of his chapter, "Did Jesus Use Testimonies?":

> When, therefore, we ask whether Jesus used *Testimonies*, we mean: Did Jesus use the Old Testament in an anti-Judaic manner? such as we find to prevail among his first disciples? and, Did Jesus employ the Old Testament in exposition of his own personal claims or character or being? These are the questions which require our attention.[27]

In discussing this question, he noted:

> It seems clear that the early Church believed that their method

of teaching by *Testimonies* could be traced back to the Lord: for we have definite statements by Luke to the effect that one of the duties discharged by Christ Risen to his disciples was that of opening their eyes to understand the Scriptures and of making them see what was written in the Prophets, the Law and the Psalms concerning himself; . . . the early Church believed that they had supreme authority for their method in dealing with the Old Testament.[28]

Harris did go as far as to "infer that one whole line of Christian testimonies (the line of the Stone of Stumbling and the Rock of Offence) was directed against the Jews, and the initial momentum came from Jesus Himself."[29] In response to the second half of his question (of using the Old Testament to support claims about himself), he diffidently suggested: "Where the difficulty occurs is in passing from what the disciples said about Him to what He said about Himself. In view of the consequences which result from the affirmative answer, it is well to be cautious and to move slowly."[30] He was not ready to make a conclusive answer "before referring the whole matter to a more definite and detailed enquiry by Biblical scholars."[31]

Perhaps the genius of Harris can be summed up in this combination of boldness in theorizing with caution in drawing final conclusions.

Some Friends were favorably impressed by Harris's views on the *Book of Testimonies*. In her *Memories of J. Rendel Harris*, Irene Pickard devoted nearly a page to a summary of his arguments in *Testimonies*, Part I and Part II.[32] In his book on the nature and inspiration of the Bible, Edward Grubb clearly accepted Harris's findings:

> Much evidence has recently been gathered, by Dr. Rendel Harris and others, that one of the first things they [the followers of Jesus] did was to make a collection of "Testimonies," or passages from the Old Testament which appeared to be prophecies of Christ. . . .
>
> They also seem to have compiled, very early in the history of the Apostolic Church, a collection of the remembered "sayings" of Jesus Himself. Neither of these compilations has come down to us in its original form; but, as we shall see later, they probably underlie some of the New Testament writings. They can only be reconstructed, with more or less probability, from these and other Christian documents in which they are quoted or used.[33]

Papias [an early second-century bishop] is quoted . . . as saying,

> "So then Matthew composed the oracles in the Hebrew language, and each one interpreted them as he could."

It was long supposed that Papias here referred to our First Gospel, and that therefore this was originally written in Hebrew (*i.e.*, Aramaic). But it is now practically certain that this Gospel was not written first in Hebrew.[34]

Prof. Burkitt has suggested that the "oracles" were not sayings of Jesus, but the "Testimonies" to Jesus in prophecies drawn from the Old Testament, to which I have already alluded, and that this compilation was what the Apostle Matthew made in the Hebrew language. This suggestion has been confirmed by fresh evidence collected by Dr. Rendel Harris.[35]

Grubb concluded that many Old Testament prophecies in the gospel according to Matthew were copied from these "oracles"—a *Book of Testimonies* compiled by the apostle Matthew.

On the other hand, most New Testament scholars for several decades paid little attention to the idea that the writers of the gospels drew from a *Book of Testimonies* as a written source. Harris had loved the quest for new, undiscovered manuscripts and documents. It is fitting that evidence supporting his theory should come through one of the major document discoveries of the twentieth century—the Dead Sea Scrolls. These scrolls were discovered in 1947 and following years, and then painstakingly deciphered. They proved to be from the library of a Jewish sect—the Essenes—about whom little had been known beyond brief mention of them by first-century historians Pliny the Elder, Philo, and notably Flavius Josephus. A number of the Dead Sea Scrolls contained commentaries on books from the Hebrew Bible, particularly the prophets. The Essenes used a style of interpretation that is technically known as *pesher*:

> The sect read the sacred writings, especially the prophetic books, in the belief that the words and events contained in them were written with specific reference to the events occurring in their own time. . . . It was not only their belief that the prophets were to be understood in terms of the sect's contemporary history that was important. Equally significant was the conviction that

the prophets' words referred to the last days before the final victory of God's kingdom. The Essenes believed they were living in those last days.[36]

I have already noted an example of the tendency of Gospel writers to treat apparently autobiographical or historical passages in the prophetic books as if they were predictions that were fulfilled in events in and around the life, death, and resurrection of Jesus. This odd practice can be readily explained and understood, if we infer that the gospel writers (or the compiler of a document used by the gospel writers) were using the same type of *pesher* interpretation as the Essenes were. Or that they were at least borrowing the Essene method in order to counter the Essene claims with their own claims about Jesus.

One of the documents from the Dead Sea collection, found in the early 1950s and known as the "Testimonia" text, is of particular interest:

> It is a short document. . . . The name "Testimonia" comes from an early type of Christian writing, which it resembles in literary style. The Christian Testimonia was a collection of verses from the Bible about the messiah, strung together to prove some kind of point. . . . The Testimonia from Qumran is not a Christian document, but does resemble the early Christian Testimonia because of its use of a number of verses dealing with a theme.
>
> The Qumran text includes five biblical quotations connected by interpretation. The first two quotations refer to the raising up of a prophet like Moses. The third quotation refers to a royal Messiah, the fourth to a priestly Messiah. The quotation from Joshua is connected to the coming of a time of great disaster, brought on by those dedicated to evil. The manuscript is usually dated to the middle of the first century B.C.E.[37]

Referring to this Qumran text and to a recently-discovered Christian manuscript from the third or fourth century—"a papyrus leaf with remains of excerpts of several OT texts in Greek (Jer. 38:24–26 [LXX]; Amos 9:11–12; Psa. 17:1–11)"—biblical scholar Larry Hurtado has observed:

> These items also have caused some scholars to revisit favorably the "testimony hypothesis" put forth by J. Rendel Harris in the early 20th century. This essentially involves the idea that earliest Christians collected proof-texts ("testimony texts") from the OT,

arranged them topically, and used them in conveying and defending their beliefs, especially about Jesus.[38]

I suggest that this evidence from Qumran would point to a significant modification of Harris's theory. In its origin, the *Book of Testimonies* likely came from the period when Christians still considered themselves to be a Jewish sect or party. Rather than being anti-Jewish, it was directed against competing Jewish parties—including the Essenes and possibly followers of John the Baptist—and in support of the claim that the followers of Jesus were "true Jews."

Elbert Russell

After six years of teaching at Earlham College, Elbert Russell was a student at the University of Chicago Divinity School from 1901 to 1903. In his autobiography he reported that in 1903,

> when I was admitted to candidacy for the doctor's degree, I discussed my thesis subject with Professor Burton. I had a vague idea of writing on the symbolism of the Book of Revelation. I had in mind a system of exposition which would interpret the book as a statement of the spiritual forces at work in Christian history. Dr. Burton thought it too extensive and too vague for a research project. A thesis had already been written on "Paranomasia in the Old Testament"; Dr. Burton thought it would be valuable to have a similar study for the New Testament. We finally agreed on the title, "Paranomasia and Kindred Phenomena in the New Testament." . . . It was to be thirty years before I got to work out my theories of the interpretation of Revelation.[39]

That spring Russell accepted a reappointment to the Earlham College faculty. "By the time of the June Convocation I had worked out the material for my thesis but had not time to organize it and write it out. . . . It was not until sixteen years later that I went back to Chicago for my doctor's degree."[40]

Between 1915 and 1917, Russell did further graduate study in Old Testament and Semitic languages at Johns Hopkins University, but he and his advisor were unable to agree on a dissertation topic. By the beginning of 1919,

It seemed easiest for me to try to finish my work for the doctor's degree at Chicago. My work at Johns Hopkins could be transferred to my credit. . . . I spent my spare time reviewing and organizing my thesis material. On May 1, 1919, we went to Chicago, where I received my degree in June.[41]

A private edition of his dissertation, *Paronomasia and Kindred Phenomena in the New Testament*—all of forty-six pages long—was distributed by the University of Chicago Libraries in 1920. A primary example of paronomasia is alliteration. For purposes of his dissertation, Russell used this definition: "Paronomasia includes all cases where resemblances in sound are used to give literary effect—to lend color or liveliness to a passage or to emphasize the thought."[42]

In 1909 Russell published *The Parables of Jesus*. The book was written as a ten-week course of lessons, with "the purpose . . . to introduce students to the teaching of Jesus as given in His recorded parables."[43] In 1928 he gave "a series of noonday talks on the beatitudes"[44] at a summer school "primarily for the benefit of the public school teachers of the mountain countries"[45] of North Carolina. These talks were expanded into a book, *The Beatitudes: A Series of Studies*, which he published in 1929. Neither of these books was written for the purpose of presenting original, ground-breaking research.

Russell had been impressed by "the most stimulating personality"[46] of J. Rendel Harris and had found himself challenged by the depth of Harris's scholarship to extend and deepen his own studies. Nevertheless, in his book, *The Message of the Fourth Gospel*, Russell came to conclusions that contrasted sharply with those of Harris, who had insisted that the gospel of John was based clearly on Jewish thought, rather than on Greek philosophy. Russell insisted that "in the Fourth Gospel . . . the Jewish element is minimized."[47] More explicitly:

> The Fourth Gospel . . . expresses Jesus' teaching largely in a style that is partly oriental and partly Greek. The allegory and symbol are half-oriental, while the dialectic and diatribe are Greek. It still uses the Jewish messianic and eschatological vocabulary, but fills the words as nearly as possible with Hellenistic and mystic ideas.[48]

In this book Russell also argued that the gospel of John provides no basis for a forensic—satisfaction or substitutionary—theory of the atonement:

> There is . . . in this Gospel no doctrine of a dualism between Jesus and God as some of our Reformation theologies asserted. Christ did not offer himself upon the cross to appease an angry God nor to induce a reluctant God to treat man with leniency and grace. . . . It is part of John's good news that the death of Jesus was not a victory of sin and the devil over him, but that his death was the triumphant climax of his mission of redeeming love.[49]

(It is doubtful that Russell was aware, when he wrote this final sentence, of the concept of a Christus Victor type of atonement theory; he wrote the preface to *The Message of the Fourth Gospel* in April 1931—earlier than the publication of Aulén's seminal work in English.)

> The cross of Jesus is thought of in this Gospel not so much as an altar of sacrifice as the focus of divine love or as the instrument of spiritual power: "And I, if I be lifted up from the earth, will draw all men unto myself." The writer apparently does not think of the death of Jesus in judicial or forensic terms.[50]

In 1934, Russell began writing

> on a project which had been in the back of my mind ever since my Chicago days. I wanted an exposition of the Book of Revelation, which would treat its figurative language as symbolism, setting forth the general aspects of the struggle of Christianity against the forces of evil.[51]

He completed this commentary, but it was never published. A typed manuscript, with final editing in ink, is available in the Duke University library.

Russell rejected the view, which has recurred through many centuries and is still popular in many Christian circles, that Revelation (also known as the Apocalypse) can be interpreted as a narrative that predicts many specific historical events in the distant future (usually in the time of the interpreter): He went as far as to propose that one use of symbolism in Revelation was "to cover up the author's ignorance of the future."[52] He clearly emphasized that "the writer's insistence on the contemporary significance of his book shows that it is not . . . a mysterious foretelling of events or personages in the far future."[53]

The Book of Revelation begins: "The revelation of Jesus Christ . . . to his servant John"—and the author names himself, "I, John" (Revelation 1:1, 9 RSV). From early on, the tradition of the church has maintained that this was the same John as the author of the gospel of John and the three epistles of John. Many modern critical biblical scholars have thrown doubt on this identity of authorship. Russell discussed this issue at some length and concluded: "The attitude of the gospel toward the Son of Zebedee and the mystery of the four Johns of Ephesus is most easily solved on the supposition that John the Apostle, John the Prophet and John the Elder are one and the same."[54] That is, in particular, that the book of Revelation and the gospel of John were both written by the same person. Two decades later, Reginald H. Fuller observed: "Most scholars today would assign the Apocalypse to a different author from the rest of the Johannine literature."[55] It would appear that in this instance, Russell was taking a position that went against the main stream of early twentieth-century New Testament scholarship.

Henry Joel Cadbury and Herbert George Wood

Henry Joel Cadbury was born in Philadelphia in December 1883. He was "the youngest child and fourth son of Joel Cadbury, Jr., and Anna Kaighn Lowry Cadbury. His parents were both birthright members of the Religious Society of Friends."[56] Henry Cadbury was by birth a member of the Orthodox meeting at Twelfth Street in Philadelphia. He graduated from Penn Charter School (a Quaker school in Philadelphia) in 1899 and from Haverford College in 1903. In 1902, his sister Elizabeth married Rufus Jones, who was then a member of the Haverford faculty.

In 1904, Henry Cadbury earned his MA at Harvard University and began teaching at the secondary school level. In 1908, he returned to Harvard for further study, earning his PhD in 1914. Beginning in 1910, he taught Greek, biblical studies, and New Testament at Haverford College, Andover Theological Seminary, and Bryn Mawr College. In 1916, he married a Quaker, Lydia Brown; they had four children. From 1933 until his retirement in 1954, Henry Cadbury was Hollis Professor of Divinity at Harvard Divinity School. He served as chairman of the board of the American Friends Service Committee from 1928 to 1934 and again from 1944 to 1960. In that capacity he traveled to Oslo, Norway, in 1947 to receive the Nobel Peace Prize, which had been awarded to AFSC. In 1954, Henry and Lydia Cadbury moved to Pendle Hill, southwest of Philadelphia, and two years later to Haverford, Pennsylvania, where Henry carried on an active retirement until his death in October 1974, following a fall down the stairs in his home.

Henry Cadbury's first published book was a portion of his doctoral dissertation, published in 1919 under the title, *The Style and Literary Method of Luke*. He made a major point in that book, examining the claim "that the language of the third Evangelist has a distinctively medical tinge, . . . 'that Luke strongly inclines to the use of medical language'"[57]—a claim that had "been very widely accepted by New Testament scholars."[58] After carefully examining the frequency of relevant Greek words in various biblical and classical writings, Cadbury concluded that "the style of Luke bears no more evidence of medical training and interest than does the language of other writers who were not physicians."[59] He made it clear that this conclusion did not disprove the traditional view that the gospel of Luke and the book of Acts were written by Luke, "the beloved physician." Throughout his career, he stuck to a steady agnosticism as to whether the two books were written by Luke or by another anonymous Christian, and he insisted:

> We do well also to realize how little our uncertainty about the author's identity interferes with our effort to make clear and complete the story which we have aimed to recover. The main lines in the picture are quite independent of any assurance about such less important matters as the author's name or occupation, or even about his quondam association with Paul.[60]

Henry Cadbury's one significant venture into Old Testament studies, *National Ideals in the Old Testament*, was "the natural outgrowth of an impulse given by the Great War for the comparison of national standards and aspirations."[61]

In 1927, Cadbury published *The Making of Luke-Acts*. In the foreword to the 1999 reprinting of the second edition of this work, Quaker Bible scholar Paul Anderson declared: "Especially if taken together with its sequel, *The Book of Acts in History*, *The Making of Luke-Acts* is undoubtedly Cadbury's most enduring single contribution to biblical studies." A particularly significant feature of this work, according to Anderson, is that "Cadbury analyzes the Gospel of Luke and Acts as a unified two-volume work—a sound judgment, which was novel at the time."[62]

One meaningful point in this book was Cadbury's emphasis on

Jesus' parables . . . as conforming exactly to the oral speech of his precise environment. Neither the Jewish literature that preceded, as in the Old Testament, nor that which followed much later, nor any contemporary or alien culture, offers such close literary parallels as do the sayings of the Jewish rabbis of Jesus' day, which are later recorded in the Talmud and kindred writings.[63]

He particularly emphasized that

the form of the Christian parable . . . plainly represents the contemporary Jewish technique and gives striking testimony that the Christian tradition, running its roots back to Palestinian soil, has been molded by that Jewish technique and has not been much revamped by Luke or the other Greek evangelists, so as to lose its Semitic form.[64]

He hammered home this point by comparing Luke's method with that of the Jewish historian Josephus: "The contrast is as great in style as it is in motive and subject matter. Josephus has translated the Jewish prophetic oracle into the Greek philosophic essay." When Josephus drew material from the Old Testament, "Many of the picturesque features of the original disappear, and instead of Jewish repetition we get the studied variation of phrase characteristic of the Hellenistic style."[65]

Cadbury was thus able to emphasize the remarkable restraint that Luke exercised in rewriting the material he found in his sources: "The procedure of Luke's contemporary reminds us forcibly of what Luke has refrained from doing with the traditions of Jesus' words, and emphasizes the extent to which the evangelist's underlying material has determined its ultimate form."[66]

In his chapter on social and religious attitudes in Luke and Acts, Cadbury wrote:

There is a triumphant joy about Luke's story. . . . The Greek words for "joy" or "rejoice" occur much more frequently in Luke's writings than in all the other evangelists put together.

So the word "grace" or "gratitude," which is allied in Greek to the word "joy," . . . occurs, noun and verb, frequently in Luke and Acts in the sense of human grace and gratitude as well as of the favor of God to men.[67]

In his chapter on theological attitudes, Cadbury insisted:

> In comparison with his resurrection, the death of Jesus has little evidential value in Luke-Acts. . . . It is curious how it [the cross of Jesus] is treated in the speeches of Acts. The death of Jesus was an act of ignorant wickedness and rejection on the part of the Jews. God, however, thwarted its effect by raising Jesus from the dead. The resurrection is therefore the significant thing about Jesus. His death is only the prelude. The resurrection is the great fulfillment of prophecy, the demonstration of Messiahship, the occasion for repentance in view of a coming judgment and resurrection for all mankind. . . .
>
> Luke strikingly omits passages in Mark which might seem to suggest a doctrine of atonement, as modern theology would name it.[68]

John Comly had argued that the story of the prodigal son (in Luke) was totally incompatible with a satisfaction theory of the atonement. Edward Grubb claimed that Isaiah 53 and the writings of Paul provided no support for substitutionary atonement theory. Elbert Russell explicitly insisted that the gospel of John provided no support for these forensic theories. Cadbury similarly implied here that, at the very least, Acts and the gospel of Luke offered no basis for satisfaction and substitutionary atonement theories.

In 1933, Cadbury and Kirsopp Lake published the last two volumes of a mammoth five-volume work, *The Beginnings of Christianity*. The originators and overall editors of the project were Lake and F. J. Foakes Jackson. Lake and Cadbury were the authors of the fourth volume, *English Translation and Commentary*, as well as editors of the fifth volume, *Additional Notes to the Commentary*. The main body of volume 5 consisted of nearly five hundred pages, made up of thirty-seven additional notes written by seven different scholars. Cadbury wrote eleven of those notes.

Cadbury wrote two books about Jesus: *The Peril of Modernizing Jesus*, published in 1937, and *Jesus: What Manner of Man* in 1947. In a chapter titled "Purpose, Aim and Motive in Jesus," he made this interesting suggestion:

> What I wish to propose is that Jesus probably had no definite, unified, conscious purpose. . . .
>
> The sense of purpose, objective, etc., as necessary for every good life is more modern than we commonly imagine. . . . My

impression is that Jesus was largely casual. He reacted to situations as they arose but probably he had hardly a program or plan.[69]

Cadbury noted a corresponding casualness, even vagabondage, in Jesus' style of life:

> There is no reason to suppose that in his freedom from worry, in his lack of a place to lay his head, in his life of roving, Jesus was much more of a vagabond or gipsy than many another in the land....
>
> In spite of the casualness of economic life in Jesus' environment, which may betoken a similar casualness in other respects towards the investment of time, modern writers have hardly considered the possibilities—even the artistic possibilities—of such an unreflective vagabondage as we have suggested.[70]

Cadbury was an accomplished practitioner of modernist rational methods in his work of biblical criticism. Nevertheless, he was more aware than many of his colleagues that the modernist outlook may not be the final truth or even necessarily the closest approximation thereto yet achieved. He may have been the advance guard of twenty-first century postmodernism, in at least one of its primary aspects—a firm cultural relativism that recognizes that no one time or culture can claim exclusive access to the fullest truth or even the firmest method of apprehending truth. This shows up clearly where he wrote of "the tacit assumption that our own outlook is correct and that Jesus inevitably shared it." He went on from there:

> We forget how many of our thought categories are distinctly modern. The rise of science, with its notions of cause and effect, evolution and natural law, has moulded our thinking. This is true quite as much in our study of past history as it is in natural science itself.... The ideas of impersonal law, of causation, of genetic development, or of progress come to us as part of our whole civilization, they are imbibed rather than studied, taken for granted rather than proved.[71]

One influential strand of Christian modernism was the social gospel movement, which held that the preaching of the Old Testament prophets and of Jesus was aimed primarily at the problems of society rather than of individuals—at providing remedies for the social structures that victimized those at the bottom of the social and economic hierarchy. Cadbury himself, as chairman of the board of the American Friends Service Committee, had been deeply involved in such social gospel reforms. He had overseen and supported the massive shift of AFSC's work toward empowering coal-mining communities in the Appalachians and had chaired race relations conferences that AFSC sponsored together with the Friends yearly meetings in Philadelphia.[72] And yet he insisted, in writing about Jesus:

> His thinking is not wholesale but individual. . . . The social group, social solidarity as we conceive it, is not an abstraction attributable to Jesus.
>
> Preachers of the modern social gospel deny this limitation with special vigor. . . .
>
> I think this form of social emphasis has turned our gospels the wrong way around. No doubt there were social implications and social results in the advice that Christ gave to individuals. But his aim was the unit and not the mass. General improvement could be at most a by-product of personal right behavior, not vice versa. . . . His concern was for personal repentance and reform.[73]

Most Quaker modernists understood Quakerism to have been from its beginnings a mystical movement, rooted in living experience of the presence of God. The leading proponent of this view, Rufus Jones, saw in Jesus a man of exceptionally intense religious experience:

> The Gospels have given us . . . the portrait of a Person who had a most extraordinary experience of God and of Oneness with Him.[74]
>
> "Primitive Christianity" is supremely this unique Person, Jesus Christ, with His experience of God, His insight into the meaning of Life, His consecration to the task of remaking man, and the extraordinary fellowship which His Spirit produced. . . .
>
> The direct impact and power of His life on His followers is the most extraordinary thing in the Gospels, and the continued power of His life over men is the most marvellous thing in human history. The source of this power is to be found in the fact . . . that by His life and death they have been drawn themselves into a personal experience of God in some degree like His own. He always taught His disciples to expect this, and it was their

attainment of this experience that made them the apostles of the new religion. Christianity is thus at its very heart a mystical religion—a religion which lives and flourishes because its members experience what its Founder experienced, the actual presence of God as the formative Spirit of a new creation.[75]

Jones thus looked on Jesus as a pioneer in the long tradition of mystical reformers:

> The entire teaching of the Kingdom of God has its mystical aspect. It is a society, or fellowship, both in earth and in heaven, both human and Divine. . . . The person who belongs to the Kingdom is a person in whom God lives and rules, and through whom the contagion of a love, caught from above, spreads through the world. . . .
>
> Christ brought a little group of men and women into a personal experience of God, similar to His own, and left them baptized in a consciousness of the Spirit's presence to form the Church. . . .
>
> The Church itself, then, as seen in its simplest conception, is a mystical fellowship, formed and gathered not by the will of man, nor schemes of flesh and blood, but by direct revelation from God to the soul.[76]

On the question of whether Jesus was a mystic or a person who valued the experience of God's presence, Cadbury disagreed pointedly with his friends:

> Probably Jesus neither taught nor felt the importance of a religious experience. He did not live in the ecstatic moment, nor glory in it, nor even in the more normal sense of abiding fellowship with God. . . .
>
> Jesus himself made religious experience no aim or goal in his own life or in his teaching. Never consciously at least would he have emphasized experience as something valuable and to be enriched. Nor should we attribute his own achievement to some peculiarly vigorous struggle for communication with God or peculiarly clear consciousness of God.[77]

Modernist Friends generally shared with Conservative and Hicksite

Friends a Quaker tradition that valued inward guidance instead of learning from external authorities about religious truth. In his second book about Jesus, Cadbury affirmed:

> There is much in the gospels as they stand to suggest that the kind of knowledge Jesus looked for was not so much imparted information as insight achieved. There is in fact reason to suppose that he did not refer so often to what his followers were to be told as to what they were to recognize and to discover.[78]

Was Cadbury beginning to soften his earlier iconoclasm and to discover a Jesus who was more compatible with his own Quaker heart?

In 1930, Cadbury received an invitation "to serve as one of nine New Testament scholars to produce a Revised Standard Version of the New Testament for the American Standard Bible Committee."[79] The membership of this committee changed over the years; Cadbury was one of three translators who served the entire time until the Revised Standard Version was published in 1946.[80]

Members of the revision committee also published a pamphlet, *An Introduction to the Revised Standard Version of the New Testament*, to accompany the appearance of the newly revised translation. Cadbury wrote the chapter on "The Vocabulary and Grammar of New Testament Greek."[81]

In 1949, the first edition of *Gospel of Parallels* was published. This work was a "synopsis"—that is, it consisted primarily of the text of the gospels of Matthew, Mark, and Luke, in the Revised Standard Version, printed side by side so that the similarities and differences in the three gospels can be readily seen. "The committee supervising the preparation of the Synopsis was composed of Henry J. Cadbury, . . . Frederick C. Grant, . . . and . . . Clarence T. Craig."[82]

In the noted twelve-volume commentary, *The Interpreter's Bible*, Cadbury wrote one of the general articles on the New Testament in Volume 7 (published in 1951). His article was titled "The New Testament and Early Christian Literature."[83]

In 1954, Cadbury wrote an article on "Acts and Eschatology"[84] in a *festschrift*, a collection of essays published in honor of the noted British New Testament scholar C. H. Dodd. Cadbury also contributed a thirteen-page essay on "The Acts of the Apostles"[85] as an entry in Volume 1 (published in

1962) of the four-volume encyclopedia on biblical subjects, *The Interpreter's Dictionary of the Bible*.

Cadbury was one Bible scholar who took seriously J. Rendel Harris's theory of the existence of an early *Book of Testimonies* as a written source used by the authors of New Testament books. In his article in *The Interpreter's Bible*, Cadbury wrote:

> It may well be that an early form of Christian composition was simply an ordered collection of Old Testament passages which could be used in the Christian propaganda. Such collections, later known as *testimonia*, may lie behind the formula of Matthew's citations and elsewhere.[86]

In *The Book of Acts in History*, published in 1955, Cadbury explicitly credited Harris as a source for this view:

> If the association of Old Testament passages was one of the earliest forms of Christian literary effort antedating the New Testament, there is no reason why the habit should not have been Jewish too, pre-Christian and non-Christian. Cf. Rendel Harris, *Testimonies*, I, 1916, *Testimonies*, II, 1920, and B. P. W. Stather Hunt, *Primitive Gospel Sources*, 1951.[87]

Cadbury also referred, in *The Book of Acts in History*, to "the scrolls from the Dead Sea area of which only a few have been published so far," and noted that "there is even coincidence with Acts in the Old Testament passages they quote."[88]

Cadbury was the author of several lectures and pamphlets about biblical subjects, which were addressed specifically to Quaker audiences. Two such lectures were the 1953 Ward Lecture, delivered at Guilford College in North Carolina—*A Quaker Approach to the Bible*[89]—and the 1961 Shrewsbury Lecture given at Shrewsbury Friends Meeting in New Jersey—*Jesus and Judaism and The Emphasis of Jesus*.[90] He also wrote two Pendle Hill pamphlets on biblical issues: *The Eclipse of the Historical Jesus*, published in 1964, and *Behind the Gospels*, published in 1968.

Biblical scholars in the nineteenth and early twentieth centuries had discovered that the writers of the four gospels often modified material that they copied from earlier writings or from oral tradition about Jesus. How can we get behind these modifications and find the "real" Jesus? This was the famous "quest of the historical Jesus." Early in the twentieth century,

Albert Schweitzer had showed how scholars who carried on the quest had each come up with a "modernizing" picture of Jesus—a Jesus who looked more like a contemporary Western thinker than the first-century Jew that he was; Cadbury sharpened this criticism in his book *The Peril of Modernizing Jesus*. Meanwhile, the Biblical Theology Movement had at first directed its attention away from this attempt and turned to the "Christ of faith," reconstructing the contents of the preaching (technically called by the Greek term *kerygma*) of the earliest Christians. By the 1950s they had taken a new turn, seeking out a deeper congruence between the recorded teachings of Jesus and the preaching (*kerygma*) of the early church. This attempt culminated in the publication of *A New Quest of the Historical Jesus*.[91] Cadbury's *The Eclipse of the Historical Jesus* was in large part a review of these developments and a criticism of the "new quest." He was convinced that the whole attempt to merge theology and history was wrong-headed from the outset:

> May I attempt . . . to give a somewhat simple definition of theology as we have known it in Christianity. It is a dramatic representation intended to describe religious experience.
>
> . . . The subject matter may be the supposed predicament of the human beings and the imagined intervention of the supernatural beings.[92]

He carried on this "drama" for a couple of pages:

> The protagonist God who is also stage manager. . . .
>
> The inclusion of an historical character . . . Jesus . . . gave the drama a feeling of reality. . . .
>
> Contact at one point with recorded history gives the whole drama a kind of verisimilitude. . . .
>
> Theology . . . wanted to have whatever advantage history could give its drama but was not fastidious about ascertaining the actual historical details.[93]

Perhaps the whole approach was an instance of Cadbury's famous whimsy, but even so there remains evidence of profound skepticism, a conviction that theology can have only a subjective basis. He had already insisted that the "concept [of] the actual participation of God in history" was a "feature which I am not prepared to defend."[94] His biographer has observed that "Henry Cadbury did not consider himself a mystic."[95] He had said in a talk on "My Personal Religion": "I find myself in moods that seem to me closely to resemble the moods of religious experience. But I do not . . . treat them as evidential."[96] I find it hard to avoid a surmise that Cadbury harbored a suspicion that there may be no firm "Reality of the Spiritual World"[97] to be found.

Henry George (H. G.) Wood was the son of John Roskruge (J. R.) Wood, a Baptist minister, and the former Frances Anne Wren, an Anglican. He was born in September 1879; his mother died when he was seven years old. J. R. Wood "was minister of the Upper Holloway Baptist Church [in England] for the greater part of his life."[98]

H. G. Wood was a student at Cambridge University from 1899 until 1904. He received an MA from London University in 1903; in 1904 he passed his Theological Tripos (an examination for a BA with honors at Cambridge). One of the faculty members at Cambridge, until 1903, was J. Rendel Harris. He and Wood "became firm friends, and Rendel Harris was to exert a powerful influence upon his later life and career."[99] In 1904 and 1905, Wood spent a year as a student lecturer at Woodbrooke, which had opened a year earlier with Harris as director of studies. At Woodbrooke he taught New Testament subjects and lectured on Tertullian, an early church father; he also fell in love with a young Quaker, Dorothea Wallis, who was studying at Woodbrooke. Wood began teaching history at Cambridge in 1906; in "June 1907, H. G. Wood and Dora Wallis were married in the Friends Meeting House at Scarborough."[100] In due time they had four children.

"Already in 1908 the Woodbrooke Council was writing to him to ask whether arrangements could be made for his return . . . in the near future."[101] To accept the invitation would mean leaving a secure position at a highly prestigious university and risking his career at a young institution whose future course was not clearly established. After pondering the offer for months and discussing it with his wife, Wood made his decision; in 1910 he left Cambridge and began teaching at Woodbrooke. Since his previous stay at Woodbrooke, several small, specialized colleges had opened in Woodbrooke's immediate neighborhood, the community of Selly Oak at the southern end of Birmingham; these colleges (including Woodbrooke) became known as the Selly Oak Colleges.

"From 1910 to 1940 Woodbrooke and the neighbouring colleges in Selly Oak were to be the centre of H. G.'s thought and work. The main courses which he himself conducted were in New Testament studies, but he lectured on a variety of subjects throughout the years."[102] "For reasons of health, Rendel Harris resigned his post of Director of Studies in 1915, and H. G. was appointed to succeed him. He held this position till 1940."[103] In 1923, he finally took the step of becoming a member of the Society of Friends. "His final commitment to the Society of Friends was felt as a great loss"[104] within the Baptist community.

Wood's contributions to New Testament scholarship were deeply recognized. He received honorary doctor of divinity degrees from the University of St. Andrews in 1937 and from the University of Birmingham in 1957.

> He was one of the founder members of the New Testament Society (the Studiorum Novi Testamenti Societas) and was elected President of the Society for the year 1957–58, . . . being succeeded in turn by another member of the Society of Friends, Dr. Henry J. Cadbury.[105]

The position of professor of theology was established in 1940 at the University of Birmingham, and Wood was appointed as the first holder of that position, which he "held . . . for five years, until he reached the age of retirement."[106]

Dora Wood died in June 1959. In December of that year, H. G. Wood "suffered a stroke, which left him . . . for three years . . . unable to communicate with others by speech or writing,"[107] until his death in March 1963.

His biographer observed: "Whatever he set out to investigate and examine brought him always back to a central point, to the unsearchable mystery of the love and the beauty and the eternal strength of God."[108] He clarified the specific thrust of this "central point" in some of his lecture notes:

> In the case of Christianity, I think the great historic facts are vastly more important than the great ideas. . . . The Christian message is not to proclaim the Fatherhood of God and the brotherhood of man, but to witness to the great act of love by which God at a particular time changed the course of human history.[109]

H. G. Wood did not share Edward Grubb's faith in progress; he insisted, rather, that "the idea of the Progress of Humanity . . . can be shown to be illusory and unsatisfying."[110]

In his 1934 book, *Christianity and the Nature of History*, H. G. Wood dealt with matters of biblical interpretation in his chapter on "The Prophetic

Interpretation of History." He took a look at Old Testament prophets as interpreters of history:

> The prophet is distinguished from his fellows by the strength of his moral conviction. His moral insight is quickened by his religious experience, and he perceives with a painful clearness the connection between sin and its consequences. . . . To convict the prophet of error in detail, even in important detail, does not itself suffice to deny the validity of the mode of interpreting history which prophecy represents. For the prophet, history is the scene of moral judgments.[111]

As a case in point, Wood examined prophetic judgments on the genocidal holy war that the general Jehu carried out (with the blessing of the prophet Elisha) against the descendants of King Ahab in the city of Jezreel:

> The bloody assassinations carried out by Jehu at Jezreel are approved by the writer of II Kings. . . . The writer's standard was clearly the purity of public worship. In so far as Jehu stood for Jahweh against Baal he was doing God's will and his crimes became virtues. . . . Hosea views the history with a different and surely with a deeper insight. . . . The judgment of Hosea is more fundamentally moral than that of the writer of the book of Kings. The clarifying of the prophetic interpretation of history is marked by a growing concern for the fundamental moralities, the condemnation of oppression and cruelty, of injustice and untruthfulness, and the confidence that history will in the long run enforce that condemnation.[112]

Wood devoted his 1938 book, *Did Christ Really Live?*, to a detailed refutation of arguments that some scholars had advanced in support of the claims that the crucifixion was not an actual event in history and that Jesus was not a historical individual, but rather a legendary figure. He concluded with chapter "What do we know of Jesus?" At the end of the chapter, he touched on the question of the atonement:

> Christ died for us. He died, not to purchase pardon from an angry God, but to save his people from their sins and to save us from our sins. . . . The death of Christ stands as a barrier between mankind and moral decadence. Christ died to convince us that God is not just an impersonal reality of which we may be aware in moments of mystic exaltation, but one who cares for the least

of his creatures and whose love desires not the death of a sinner but rather that he turn from his wickedness and live. Christ died to convince us that love to God and love to our neighbours are our highest loyalties. Christ died to challenge our moral cowardice and to undermine our self-complacency and pride. Christ died to convince us of the miracle of forgiveness and to save us from sinking as we are sinking now into barbarism and secularism. In short, Christ died to make us good.[113]

Wood expanded on this answer in his 1953 book, *Why Did Christ Die?* Without attempting to propose or support a fully-developed atonement theory, he applied himself to spelling out the implications of various New Testament themes related to the meaning of Christ's death. Some of the salient points that he made are these:

Christ died to change the world's standards of greatness. His death strikes at the root of our pride and love of power.[114]

Guilt and the need of expiation arise not because God is angry, but because He is Holy.[115]

Christ died to establish the new covenant. . . . In a covenant or agreement between God and men, the parties to the covenant are not equal. The initiative is with God, not with men. God establishes the covenant and invites men to join with Him.[116]

In a book published two years later, *Belief and Unbelief Since 1850*, Wood provided a recent historical context for his own thinking on the atonement. In the mid-nineteenth century, he observed, "As the record of the revelation of God's will and purpose for mankind, the Bible was treated as a manual of theology—a theology which could be presented in a defensible, rational and harmonious system." A key element in this system was the doctrine of the atonement:

The plan of salvation turned on Christ's vicarious sacrifice. The substitutionary view of the Atonement, involving the penal satisfaction of God's justice, was held to be the correct understanding of the Cross. . . . In the 1850s this outline of the plan of salvation was regarded in many quarters as the truth of the gospel.[117]

In contrast, Wood affirmed that

our present reading of the New Testament suggests that . . . in II Cor. v, St Paul says that God in Christ was reconciling the world to himself. Christ died to reconcile men to God, not to reconcile God to men. Christ died not to change God's attitude to men but to change men's relation to God, to deliver men from a predominantly legal relation to God as ruler and taskmaster, and to bring them into a true personal relation to God as Father. . . . The idea of appeasing God's anger had no place in the New Testament. . . . The time is ripe for a reformulation of the nature of the Atonement in the light of our present-day scholarship.[118]

He did propose,

the truth behind the heresy of a fictitious substituted penalty is that Christ in dying has done something for us which we could never do for ourselves, has done all that is needed to reconcile us to God. We may never be able to state this in terms which satisfy us intellectually.

In this context, he found it helpful to insist on the

distinction between a problem and a mystery. . . . A problem is a puzzle for which you may hope to find a solution, a question to which you may give a rational answer. A mystery is a fact of experience which you cannot hope to fathom or understand, with which and by which you have to live. It is a mistake to treat problems as mysteries and close down the search for rational solutions before you are obliged, and there are problems connected with the theme of Atonement which we may still try to unravel. But it is a mistake to treat mysteries as problems, and at long last the Atonement is not a problem but a mystery, a depth where all our thoughts are drowned.[119]

Wood's objections to the substitutionary/satisfaction views of the atonement had been long standing. In 1920, even before he had become a Friend, he was invited to deliver the Swarthmore Lecture at the time of the London Yearly Meeting sessions. In that lecture he made these perceptive comments:

During the past six years many, if not most, Christians have felt it to be their duty to maintain a feeling of righteous indignation and an attitude of unbending severity towards our late enemies. The same body of Christian opinion has welcomed the punitive character of the Peace. They even regard this insistence on meting out strict and terrible justice to a guilty but fallen nation as making a moral advance. It is suggested that had we failed to punish, the moral law itself would have been weakened. This point of view is akin to those doctrines of the Atonement which find in the death of Christ an objective satisfaction to the justice of holiness of God. In accordance with such doctrine, some formal recognition of justice through punishment is insisted upon. ... Those who find no place for anger in the Christian character are inclined to attribute their fellow-Christians' trust in moral indignation to the strength of primitive but unregenerate instincts and to the persistence of the imperfect morality of the Old Testament on into the realm of Christian ethic. ...

It seems to me that, ... from the Christian standpoint, indignation apart from compassion is always and necessarily sinful.[120]

In recognizing the connection between satisfaction doctrines of the atonement and the insistence by most Christians on the importance of punitive justice in human society, Wood anticipated by eight decades the brilliant arguments of Timothy Gorringe, who spelled out in convincing detail the impact of these atonement theories on the widespread belief—and practice—among Christians that retributive justice (rather than the ethics of the Sermon on the Mount) is the appropriate norm for law and government, a consequence that has been "grim indeed."[121]

I am struck by the insightfulness with which Wood followed up these remarks:

> A moral indignation seldom if ever works the righteousness of God. ... It is curious to reflect how many Christian people in 1918 really supposed that the temptation we should have to resist in making peace was the temptation to let the Germans off too lightly. ... Our real peril was never on the side of leniency. The teaching of the New Testament and the facts of history combined to warn us that our serious temptations were all on the other side. It is difficult to point to any Peace Treaty which has erred in the direction of moderation. There are few Peace Treaties which do not include deplorable injustices, which war-passion regarded as simply just. ... This was the true danger in making peace in 1919, and if in large measure we have succumbed to it, our failure is due in part to the ignorance of Christian people. Christians at least should have been fore-armed against such a

danger. In this conflict with principalities and powers we took elaborate precautions against giving way to pity, which could hardly have led us seriously astray, while we stood defenceless against the temptation to anger, which has made good men the catspaws and defenders of a reactionary state-craft that is bankrupt intellectually and morally. . . .

When then we recall the atmosphere in which peace was made, . . . the steady maintenance of the idea that the German nation is a kind of moral pariah, a people of different clay from ourselves—what is all this but sheer Pharisaism, a self-righteous goodness with no redemptive power in it, a moral conceitedness which does not move the sinner to anything but a justifiable contempt? The moral defence of the peace is that which makes me most suspicious of it. The punitive element in which so many of my fellow Christians see a moral achievement, seems to me a denial of Christianity.[122]

I find in these statements by Wood a confirmation and vindication of sentiments Henry Cadbury expressed in his October 1918 letter to the *Philadelphia Public Ledger* (which was to lead to Cadbury's loss of his faculty position at Haverford College):

Whatever the immediate result of the present German request for an armistice, the spirit of implacable hatred and revenge exhibited by many persons in this country indicates that it is our nation which is the greatest obstacle to a clean peace and the least worthy of it. . . .

Surely it behooves us at this hour, when not retaliation for the past but the assurance of a safer and saner international fellowship is the world's need, distinguishing justice and mercy from blind revenge, to keep ourselves in the mood of moderation and fair play. A peace on other terms or in any other spirit will be no peace at all, but the curse of the future.[123]

I see these words by Cadbury and Wood as clear instances of the "prophetic interpretation of history" Wood was to describe later in *Christianity and the Nature of History*. In hindsight, I believe that both Friends have exercised the gift of true prophecy. It is not difficult to trace a historical development from the harshness of the Treaty of Versailles to its reaction: the rise of the Nazi party to power in Germany and its ensuing totalitarian tyranny, genocide, and thrust for world-conquest. "They sow the wind, and they shall reap the whirlwind" (Hosea 8:7).

Jesus in the Twentieth Century is primarily a collection of addresses that Wood had previously delivered and essays that he had previously published, some as early as 1912—all of which were brought together in honor of his eightieth birthday in 1959. In these essays he advanced his own conclusions on a number of issues that have been matters of controversy among New Testament scholars.

One of these issues was the question of eschatology—the nature of the coming of the kingdom of God at the end of this age—in the teaching of Jesus. Wood argued that it was important

> to emphasize the dependence of Jesus on God's initiative. Jesus knew the End was coming because God had spoken again to his people through a prophet, John the Baptist, and because God had anointed him, Jesus, to proclaim the acceptable year of the Lord. To become a Son of God faith is the first essential, faith in the living God who is visiting and redeeming his people. . . . It was because Jesus knew that men might be Sons of God like him, that he knew the End was coming. . . . If Jesus used the terms of Apocalyptic writers, we must not assume that he meant by them exactly what they meant. His experience was not theirs, and in Jesus the consciousness of being God's Son is fundamental.[124]

A related question is that of the "messianic self-consciousness" of Jesus. Did Jesus believe—and claim—that he was the Messiah expected by the Jewish people? Wood concluded:

> It is most improbable that Jesus only began to think of himself as Messiah after Peter's confession. Either . . . Jesus did not regard himself as the Messiah but as the herald of the coming Kingdom, or else the Messianic consciousness of Jesus underlies his mission and his message from start to finish. I have no doubt myself that the second view is the right one.[125]

He clarified the point in his next lecture:

> Jesus identified himself with his message, and he was much more concerned that men should do what he said than that they should call him Lord. He was not eager to focus attention on himself or

on his status, if that would divert men from his essential message, the Gospel. . . .

The claim [that he was Messiah] is there, is really made, but . . . the humility of Christ helps to explain why the claim was not asserted more openly and constantly. . . .

It seems to me Paul's doctrine of God humbling himself to become equal to men is a conclusion drawn from the Gospel story, not a presupposition which colours and shapes the Synoptic tradition. . . . Because he left all to His Father's will and emptied himself, spent himself utterly in the service of sinful men, God has highly exalted him and given him the name that is above every name. This Christ of faith is the Jesus of history.[126]

Henry Cadbury insisted that Jesus showed no significant interest in economic institutions, social reform, or politics: "His judgment dealt with individuals rather than with the organized life in which they lived."[127] Wood thought it quite likely that Jesus did deal with political issues: "We may find that some sayings and incidents in the Gospels are best understood in relation to political conditions which existed for Jesus but which no longer existed for the Church after the fall of Jerusalem."[128]

He provided specific examples. But even more, Wood was able to detect sayings, which have not been generally recognized as relevant to the issue, that confirm Jesus' rejection of the political beliefs and strategy of the Zealot party—the use of military violence in their effort to win freedom from Roman domination:

> The time is indeed an opportunity for Israel, a veritable time for greatness. But if the opportunity is missed, disaster is inevitable. Israel is faced with the necessity of making momentous decisions. . . . There is the crisis arising from the growing tension between Jewry and Rome. How is this tension to be eased and the national disaster averted?
>
> In this setting, the saying about seeking agreement with one's adversary on the way to court becomes a warning to the nation to seek at all costs a way to peaceful coexistence with Rome.[129]
>
> It seems to me that *lêstês* in the Fourth Gospel must be understood in this way. In ch. 10:8, "all who came before me were thieves and robbers," the most natural interpretation is to take

the word as referring to violent revolutionary leaders, such as sprang up in the time of Archelaus. Athrongaios [a shepherd who became a guerilla leader at that time] is the typical hireling shepherd. False Messiahs are precisely the advocates and exponents of the Messianic War. The old idea, entertained by both orthodox and rationalist critics, that in John 10:8 all other religious teachers inside and outside Jewry are repudiated and condemned as false, is certainly mistaken.[130]

Wood finished his address as president of the Studiorum Novi Testamenti Societas with these thoughts:

> I am tempted sometimes to suggest a paradox, to the effect that the finality of Christian faith is to be discerned in the non-finality of any given formulation of it. The Fourth Gospel, which asserts the finality of the revelation of God's love in sending his Son to save mankind, presents us with a vision of greater works still to be done and of ever-deepening understanding of the truth as it is in Christ. . . . The recorded "teaching" of Jesus is incomplete, and perhaps this is why the teaching of the historical Jesus plays practically no role in Paul or John. But the non-terminated character of the "teaching" is certainly part of its very essence. . . . So I return to my paradox. The truth as it is in Jesus is final, because it is never finished.[131]

He did not explicitly draw the inference that I see here—that this is a *biblical* argument for the traditional Quaker avoidance of creeds.

I have noted points at which the thoughts of Wood and of Henry Cadbury reinforce each other, and points at which they sharply diverge. I discovered a further point of intersection in their thinking, in the lecture that Wood delivered at the University of Birmingham in 1940:

> If there be any genuine knowledge of God, it can only be through a divine self-disclosure. . . . I no longer believe, as I was once inclined to believe, that theology can be based on an induction from religious experience in general. . . . A theology starts from the acceptance of some particular occasion as revelatory.[132]

The belief about theology that he had abandoned is nearly identical with the view that Cadbury was to affirm in his 1963 Haverford Library Lectures: "Theology . . . is . . . intended to describe religious experience."[133] If some particular occasion in history is revelatory, I believe Wood would accept the implication that it was a moment when God actually participated in history—which would put him in direct opposition to Cadbury, who was simply unable to defend the idea of "the actual participation of God in history."[134]

Like Cadbury, Wood played a key role in the production of a major new translation of the Bible. For Wood, this was the New English Bible. The Joint Committee on the New Translation of the Bible was formed in 1947. Originally, it consisted of delegates appointed by the Church of England; the Church of Scotland; the Methodist, Baptist, and Congregational Churches; and the University Presses of Oxford and Cambridge.

By January 1948, when its third meeting was held, invitations to be represented had been sent to the Presbyterian Church of England, the Society of Friends, the Churches in Wales, the Churches in Ireland, the British and Foreign Bible Society, and the National Bible Society of Scotland: these invitations were accepted.[135]

In September 1947, H. G. was asked by the Society of Friends in Great Britain to give a further service to the wider Christian community. In that year he was appointed to serve as one of the two Quaker representatives on the committee of the churches formed to prepare a new translation of the Bible in modern English. . . . H. G. continued as a member of this body until his last illness.[136]

The committee he served on was the Joint Committee on the New Translation of the Bible. His last illness incapacitated him late in 1959.

The Joint Committee provided for the actual work of translation from the original tongues by appointing three panels, to deal, respectively, with the Old Testament, the Apocrypha, and the New Testament. Their members were scholars drawn from various British universities. . . . The Committee appointed a fourth panel, of trusted literary advisers, to whom all the work of the translating panels was to be submitted for scrutiny.[137]

Since January 1948 the Joint Committee has met regularly twice a year in . . . Westminster Abbey. . . . At these meetings the Committee has received reports on the progress of the work from the Conveners of the four panels, and its members have had in their hands typescripts of the books so far translated and revised. They have made such comments and given such advice or decisions as they judged to be necessary, and from time to time they have met members of the panels in conference.[138]

In these semi-annual meetings of the Joint Committee, Wood "was alert to the problems facing the translators. . . . A fellow member of the committee spoke of his helpful and critically constructive contributions, his ear for a graceful rendering, his quiet incisiveness and winning humour."[139] The translation of the New Testament was published in 1961; the New English Bible translations of the Old Testament and Apocrypha were published in 1970.

The second Friend appointed as a representative on the Joint Committee was George H. Boobyer. He also served a long stretch of time on this committee—until 1961, the year in which the New Testament portion of the New English Bible was published.

George Henry Boobyer

George Henry Boobyer was born in August 1902, in Stoke Saint Gregory, England. His father was a Baptist deacon and a businessman. After receiving degrees from the Universities of Bristol and London, Boobyer received a stipend for two years of theological study in Germany, from 1925 to 1927: one semester at Marburg and the rest at Heidelberg University, where he studied under the noted New Testament scholar Martin Dibelius. His dissertation for his PhD from Heidelberg was published in 1929.

In 1927, he married a pianist, Dorothy Keirle. They had two children, a son and a daughter. He also began serving as a Baptist pastor. In the 1930s, "In spite of his success, George felt increasingly uneasy with the Baptist ministry. He felt that it gave him an artificial status as a figure in authority. . . . More fundamentally, he became uneasy about some of the basic tenets of his church."[140] In 1935, he gave up his position as a Baptist pastor and joined the Society of Friends. He later stated:

> One of the reasons why I joined the Society of Friends . . . was that . . . they seemed to me to have grasped [that] . . . ancient formularies like the Apostles Creed and the Nicene Creed . . . are seriously lacking in reference to what for Jesus and the rest of the

New Testament is so central, namely, the necessity of . . . a personal repentance which makes self-commitment, not doctrinal commitment, the basic requirement.

That is, "Quakers . . . have seen, however imperfectly, where the priorities as Jesus stated them really lay."[141]

The Boobyers moved to Woodbrooke in 1935, where George first did research under the guidance of H. G. Wood and then became a tutor in New Testament and Greek. He was a member of Selly Oak Meeting from 1935 to 1946. During World War II, he had a couple of teaching jobs and was listed as a member of Staines Meeting (London & Middlesex) between 1947 and 1948.

George was a lecturer and later head of the department of divinity at the University of Newcastle upon Tyne from 1948 until he retired in 1967. During that period he was a member of Newcastle Meeting. In 1969, George and Dorothy retired to Sidcot; George moved his membership to Sidcot Meeting. "During 1967–68 and in 1970 he was visiting Professor of Theology at the University College of Rhodesia (Salisbury) lecturing in his special field in New Testament studies."[142]

Dorothy died in 1985. "For the last two years of his life [George] lived in a home for the elderly where he died in January 1999."[143]

The title of George Boobyer's 1929 PhD dissertation was *"Thanksgiving" and the "Glory of God" in Paul*. The thrust of his argument in this work was

> that Paul's statements about [thanksgiving increasing the glory of God] . . . are not mere rhetorical speech, but embody very realistic and concrete conceptions; that there was in fact conceived to be an actual material increase of the *doxa theou* [glory of God] occasioned by the *eucharistia* [thanksgiving] of the Christians.[144]

More specifically, "Paul . . . stood quite in line with the current conceptions of his day. . . . It is the *doxa theou* in this materialistic sense, the light-substance, or shining splendor of God which is affected, which in fact receives from *eucharistia* substantial increase."[145] By comparing Paul's terminology with that of other writings of and before his day, Boobyer concluded that

> Paul's conception of increasing the *doxa theou* with *eucharistia* is the result of a mingling of Iranian-Gnostic light speculation with more primitive ideas of the effect of sacrifice and praise upon a

deity. The conception of an effect is primitive; the conception of praise as light which increases the light or glory of God is Iranian-Gnostic.[146]

In *St. Mark and the Transfiguration Story* (1942), Boobyer frequently referred to the "parousia." This was a Greek word, meaning "arrival" or "presence," but often translated in the New Testament as "coming." In the New Testament, "parousia" usually referred to the expected return of Christ to earth at the end of this age. In this work, Boobyer spelled out an argument that "for Mark, . . . the transfiguration prophesies the parousia in the sense that it is a portrayal of what Christ will be at that day, and is in some degree a miniature picture of the whole second advent scene."[147]

In *Jesus as "Theos" in the New Testament* (1968), Boobyer argued that, although the Greek word *theos* ("God" or "divine") is used a number of times when referring to Jesus,

> What . . . is said of his life and functions as the celestial Christ neither means nor implies that in divine status he stands on a par with God himself and is fully God. On the contrary, in the New Testament picture of his heavenly person and ministry we behold a figure both separate from and subordinate to God.[148]

His argument implied that the creeds of the early Church had gone beyond the New Testament evidence when they characterized Jesus, the Son, as being "of the same substance" with the Father, or as "fully God and fully man."

We come now to three final writings by Boobyer, which were addressed directly to Quakers. The first of these, *The Bible and the Light Within*, was a study booklet published in 1973 by the Friends Home Service Committee, a committee of London Yearly Meeting. One point that he made in this booklet was "that modern textual and linguistic studies have of themselves made the conception of the Bible as a verbally inspired and infallible book untenable."[149]

Boobyer was invited to deliver a series of six Bible lectures at the July 1975 sessions of Friends United Meeting, held at Wilmington College in Ohio. The text of these messages was published as *Fruits of the Spirit: According to New Testament Teaching*. In these lectures he articulated an understanding of biblical inspiration or revelation that he saw as far more tenable than the concepts of verbal inspiration and infallibility. He referred to

> the validity of the gospel of God as presented in the New Testament—. . . this gospel is much more than a faith now embodied in a book which we call the Bible. It emerged in history before it appeared in writing; it was thought and experienced by people, before it became literature; it expressed itself in actual events prior to the account of it in Scripture. The total biblical faith of which the New Testament gospel of God is the culmination is, indeed, the product of a long period of history. Behind it lie nearly two thousand years of human experience, reckoning from, say, the time of Abraham to the days of the apostolic church. With varying degrees of vitality, it has continued to manifest itself in historical events and people down to our own time.[150]

The approach that we need to make, in order to understand the biblical message, is thus:

> If, as the New Testament maintains, the God we seek is the God who seeks us, the initial question is not: Where, or how, can I find God? But: How can God find me? This is what Fox had discovered, when in reference to his spiritual awakening he said: "The Lord did gently lead me along." And when this possibility is accepted, the process by which we apprehend the substance of the New Testament gospel of God is changed. The prior emphasis will no longer be upon our search, but upon our willingness to be sought; the first consideration becomes not the possibility of our finding God, but our readiness to be found.[151]

Boobyer insisted on

> the continuing reality of that to which those first Christians witnessed in . . . the New Testament. In it, they too were claiming that God is present; that where our minds and hearts are receptively open towards him, he is known as the God of the future and the God of the here and now. He is experienced as the source of greater spiritual strength, bringing new moral power and a new vision of life's true meaning in consequence of which we enter into a sure sense of the true and ongoing fulfillment of our lives.[152]

Boobyer's study of the New Testament brought him back to the truth that led him to the Society of Friends in the first place: "On Jesus' own authority, then, here is the essence of the matter: true religion as he interprets it is essentially a love affair. As I see it, this must surely mean that whom or what a person loves is more important than what that person believes."[153]

He unpacked and further developed this thought in his Rufus Jones Lecture, "Are the Scriptures 'Very Precious' Still?," which he delivered at Arch Street Meeting House in Philadelphia in April 1980, and which was subsequently published by the Religious Education Committee of Friends General Conference:

> Christianity is concerned with the kind of personalness in which we should believe and especially with personalness as exemplified in the life of Jesus of Nazareth. . . .
>
> The biblical call to us as persons invites to a loyalty, a way and an end. The loyalty is a personal loyalty to God and Jesus which transforms us; the way is a way of life in the world which is redemptive because it is rooted and grounded in love; and the end set before us is one which reaches its consummation in our salvation as individuals and communities to the greater glory of God.[154]

Alexander C. Purdy

Alexander C. Purdy was born in West Laurens, New York, in 1890. His father, Ellison Purdy, was a Quaker pastor. Alexander received a BA from William Penn College (Iowa) in 1910 and a PhD from Hartford Theological Seminary (Connecticut) in 1916. He was married in 1914. In 1916, he filled the position that had been vacated by Elbert Russell, teaching Bible and church history at Earlham College. From 1923 to 1960, he served on the faculty of Hartford Theological Seminary; he taught New Testament, from 1933 on as Hosmer Professor of New Testament, and from 1954 to 1960 as dean of the seminary. After he retired from Hartford, Alexander Purdy taught from 1960 to 1965 as professor of biblical studies at the newly-founded Earlham School of Religion. Wilmer Cooper, the first dean of ESR, attested that "Alexander Purdy was an important influence in the first five years of ESR and was my mentor in the early years of my deanship."[155] After his second retirement, from Earlham, he and his wife moved to Pennsylvania, where he died in Swarthmore in April 1976.

In 1918, while he was a faculty member at Earlham College, Alexander Purdy published a book for personal study and group discussion: *The Way of Christ*. In this book he affirmed "the Need for a Social Gospel."[156] He found the basis for the social gospel in the teachings of Jesus: "Jesus called the New Order the Kingdom of God. . . . *The New Order is an unseen and spiritual commonwealth seeking to create in the world appropriate political and social forms for its adequate expression.*"[157] He insisted that "Jesus . . . had nothing to say about individuals apart from this social ideal of a kingdom or rule of God. His picture of society was that of a family—a world-wide, peaceable, serviceable brotherhood. . . . It partakes of the very spirit of democracy."[158] This was the way of interpreting Jesus that Henry Cadbury rejected nearly two decades later, in *The Peril of Modernizing Jesus*, where he insisted that this "social gospel" view has "turned our gospels the wrong way around"![159] During his Earlham years, in 1922, Purdy published another book, *Pathways to God*.

While he was teaching New Testament at Hartford, Purdy published a lecture in 1934, "Spirit in the New Testament and Today." In 1936, Purdy and another New Testament scholar, G. H. C. Macgregor, published *Jew and Greek: Tutors unto Christ*. Purdy wrote the half of that book that dealt with the Jewish background to the New Testament. At the heart of his argument in this work, he emphasized that both Judaism and the New Testament writers centered their faith in the God who acts in history:

> The New Testament was created by the faith that something revolutionary had occurred, God had acted. This is the secret of the certainty and the joy of the New Testament. . . . It was the God who is known by His acts, i.e., the God of Judaism, revealed anew in the Christ and supremely in the great acts of the Death and Resurrection, who created and directed the new community according to the writers of the New Testament. . . . The controlling influence of the Jewish doctrine of God is never wholly lost.[160]

Like Henry Cadbury, Purdy wrote significant pieces for both *The Interpreter's Bible* and *The Interpreter's Dictionary of the Bible*. His chapter "The Epistle to the Hebrews: Introduction and Exegesis" appeared in volume 11 of *The Interpreter's Bible*, published in 1955. He contributed an entry on "Paul the Apostle" in volume 3 of *The Interpreter's Dictionary of the Bible*, published in 1962.

In his exegesis, Purdy's commentary on Hebrews 1:1 ("In many and various ways God spoke of old to our fathers by the prophets" [RSV]) came to this significant conclusion: "That our author regarded Jesus as the culmination of a historic process rather than as an isolated phenomenon is evident throughout his writing. . . . The one continuity he proclaims lies in the purpose of God and its outworkings in history."[161] This was an example of the point Purdy had made in *Jew and Greek: Tutors unto Christ.*

As a young adult Friend, I had become increasingly interested in reading and understanding the Bible. One book that I found especially difficult to appreciate was the letter to the Hebrews; with all of its language about priests and sacrifices, it seemed to be completely foreign to my understanding of Quakerism and its emphasis on the direct experience of God. Purdy's discussion of Hebrews changed all of that for me; he has made a contribution to the understanding of that letter that broke new ground. In his introduction, he wrote:

> Christ has not only fulfilled the requirements of priesthood; he has ended forever all outward priestly rites by achieving the goal they were designed to represent, that is, unhindered access to God. . . . Christ's offering of himself through the eternal Spirit . . . is the ultimate and perfect sacrifice which is never to be repeated, and which terminates all the shadowy rites and ceremonies associated with the Old Testament priesthood. . . .
>
> By presenting Christ in his humanity, and especially in his death, as the perfect priest who ended all outward rites by fulfilling their shadowy anticipations, he made a permanent contribution to Christian thought and experience for all who grasp his thought in its entirety.[162]

He expanded on this theme in his commentary on specific passages in the letter. Following the quotation of Jeremiah 31:31–34 (the passage on the new covenant), Hebrews 8:13 read, "In speaking of a new covenant he treats the first as obsolete. And what is becoming obsolete and growing old is ready to vanish away" (RSV). Purdy commented:

> He is not proposing a sacrificial system for the new covenant; he is arguing that the sacrificial principle has been perfected in Christ. The sacrificial system on earth is ended, not because it is repudiated, but because it is perfected. In his own way, the way of the liturgist, he presents religion in wholly spiritual terms.

Christ's priesthood was perfected because it met human needs in terms of spiritual reality.[163]

In regard to Hebrews 10:8–10,

When he said above, "Thou has neither desired nor taken pleasure in sacrifices and offerings and burnt offerings and sin offerings" (these are offered according to the law), then he added, "Lo, I have come to do thy will." He abolishes the first in order to establish the second. And by that will we have been sanctified through the offering of the body of Jesus Christ once for all (RSV).

Purdy commented:

God willed a nobler sacrifice than the futile offerings made by earthly priests—offerings made *according to the law*—so that law is set aside with the *sacrifices and offerings* it prescribes. The sacrifice he willed was the offering of the body of Christ. Accordingly, the second abolishes the first; the offering of Christ abolishes the offerings made in the earthly tabernacle.[164]

In his discussion of chapter 13 (the final chapter of Hebrews), Purdy wrote, "Hebrews never refers to the Lord's Supper. . . . The argument of Hebrews allows no logical place for the repetition of the Supper. Christ's sacrifice cannot be repeated; it was once for all."[165]

In short, he gave a clearly Quaker interpretation to this book. I presume that his own Quaker background and commitment enabled him to see the letter to the Hebrews in this light. Certainly he succeeded in recovering the use that early Friends like George Fox had made of that letter—for instance, "Christ's sacrifice ends all other sacrifices."[166] Jesus Christ was the "priest to end all priests," who made the "sacrifice to end all sacrifices."

In both *The Interpreter's Bible* and *The Interpreter's Dictionary*, Purdy discussed pertinent biblical evidence that could underlie various theories or views of the atonement. In his exegesis of Hebrews 2:17 ("Therefore he had to be made like his brethren in every respect, so that he might become a merciful and faithful high priest in the service of God, to make expiation for the sins of the people" [RSV]) he commented:

Theodore H. Robinson ventures to call this "atonement by sympathy," using the word sympathy, of course, in its deepest sense. If we understand the background of our author's thought, it is not inaccurate to use this striking phrase. But in itself the phrase hardly does justice to the sweep of the author's thought. Temptation, suffering, and death as experienced by Jesus are not just evidences of the divine sympathy which shares our lot and helps to slay sins; they are rather the divine necessity, what was "fitting" for him "for whom and by whom all things exist." This is an even more daring thought than the divine sympathy, which is indeed the impact made on man by the divine necessity. Our author's thought is at once more primitive and more potent than the phrase "atonement by sympathy" suggests. . . .

The author has moved from the heavenly Son to the earthly Jesus. His approach is not that Jesus in his words and deeds is man's empirical datum for faith in a Christlike God, but that God in his final word to men has spoken in a Son who shared God's nature and was the agent of creation and who, in Jesus the great high priest of the universe, entered into the experience of man when man was neediest—in temptation, suffering, and death.[167]

In his essay on Paul the apostle, Purdy examined Paul's thoughts about the Cross:

Why and how is the death of Christ on the cross effective for salvation? . . . Paul employs a number of metaphors to communicate what God has done for man's salvation in the death of Christ: It is a redemption, a ransoming, like a slave's release from bondage (Rom. 3:24; I Cor. 1:30). It is a sacrifice adequate for restoring favorable relations with deity (Rom. 3:25; 5:9). It is a victory over demonic powers who are competing for man's soul (Rom. 8:38–39; I Cor. 2:8; 15:25; Col. 2:15). It is the end of the old and the beginning of the new humanity (Rom. 5:12–21; I Cor. 15:20–22). . . .

Yet the Pauline imagery, varied though it is, is far from chaotic. God is always the author of salvation; there is no slightest hint that it is wrested from an unwilling God, even though the nature of sin is such as to involve estrangement, nor is there any suggestion that the death of Christ is the noble sacrifice of a good man over against an unfeeling or hostile world. . . . It is clear that the death of Christ reveals the nature and meaning of God's forgiveness. . . . His favorite words, "grace," "peace," "reconciliation," express the same deep sense of God's forgiving, restoring love. The death of Christ carries the note of the cost of sin and the costly character of God's act in Christ.[168]

Purdy here supplied evidence to suggest that the ancient ransom theory and the modern Christus Victor and perhaps covenant (the new humanity) theories can find support in Paul's writings; on the other hand, he saw little in Paul's thinking to support the forensic (satisfaction and substitutionary) theories or the moral influence theory of the atonement.

In 1963, while Purdy was teaching at Earlham School of Religion, the Five Years Meeting published "Recovering a Lost Radiance," a lecture he had given at the sessions of Five Years Meeting that year. In 1967, after he had fully retired, he wrote *The Reality of God: Thoughts on the "Death of God" Controversy*, which was published as a Pendle Hill pamphlet.

One comment made by Purdy struck me as having profound ramifications. In his exegesis of Hebrews 6:13–20, he stated,

> For when God made a promise to Abraham, since he had no one greater by whom to swear, he swore by himself. . . . When God desired to show more convincingly to the heirs of the promise the unchangeable character of his purposes, he interposed with an oath, so that through two unchangeable things, in which it is impossible that God should prove false, we who have fled for refuge might have strong encouragement to seize the hope set before us. We have this as a sure and steadfast anchor of the soul, a hope that enters into the inner shrine behind the curtain, where Jesus has gone as a forerunner on our behalf (RSV), he wrote, "If God is to be known, he must have revealed himself to the knower. The author assumes that God has so revealed himself. Yet the appeal to revelation, so constantly made in Hebrews, has an overtone that strikes the attentive ear. The ultimate appeal is to the nature of God."[169]

Purdy's suggestion that underlying revelation itself, "the ultimate appeal is to the nature of God," reminds me of Karl Barth's seminal early essay, "The Strange New World within the Bible" (originally delivered as a lecture in 1916). In that essay, Barth asked, "What is there within the Bible?"[170] After discussing several possibilities, he answered that what we find within the Bible is "the standpoint of God, . . . a new world, the world of God, . . . the history of God."[171] Barth noted that this answer gave rise to the next question: "Who then is God? . . . The contents of the Bible are 'God.' But what is the content of the contents?"[172] He reviewed a number of answers that have been proposed, then asked again: "Is not God—greater than that?"[173] He gave his own answer:

> Who is God? The heavenly Father! . . . He purposes naught but the establishment of a new *world*.
>
> Who is God? The Son who . . . is the redeemer of a humanity gone astray and ruled by evil spirits and powers. He is the redeemer of the groaning creation about us. . . .
>
> Who is God? The Spirit . . . (that love and good will) which . . . makes a new heaven and a new earth and, therefore, new men, new families, new relationships, new politics.[174]

Barth refined this answer in his more mature thinking, which is expressed in his *Church Dogmatics*. In a volume of that work that he produced in 1942, he wrote:

> The voice by which we were taught by God Himself concerning God, was the voice of Jesus Christ. . . . Theology must begin with Jesus Christ, and not with general principles. . . . Theology must also end with Him, and not with supposedly self-evident general conclusions from what is particularly enclosed and disclosed in Him.[175]

I will pick up for myself this line of thought, which Purdy and Barth have initiated, when I move toward the conclusion of the chapter titled "To 'Satisfy the Mind and Stir the Heart,'" in my third volume.

Moses Bailey

Moses Bailey, son of Melvin and Lettie Bailey, was born in 1892. Throughout his childhood, the Moses family lived in and near to Portland, Maine. In his memoirs, Moses wrote: "I was born a Friend, a Quaker. . . . Our Meeting had a pastor. . . . Two of our pastors, Elison Purdy and my cousin Charles Woodman, were a truly helpful influence upon my early years."[176] Ellison Purdy's son, Alex Purdy, "was a playmate of Moses in Portland."[177]

Moses enrolled as a student at Earlham College in 1911. He worked on accelerating his courses, so that "after three years Moses graduated from Earlham with honors in 1914 earning a Bachelor of Arts in Greek and Philosophy."[178] He stayed on at Earlham for a graduate year and earned a Master's degree in 1915. That fall he enrolled at Hartford Theological Seminary, where he enjoyed his studies in Hebrew, Arabic, and world religions, but was frustrated by the required courses in theology, in which "some of the professors were telling him what he should believe."[179] Moses decided to leave seminary, and in the fall of 1916, he began teaching "at the Oak Grove Seminary, a Friends School in East Vassalboro, Maine."[180]

In June 1917, Moses married Mabel Googins, of Portland, at her Free Will Baptist Church. Mabel persuaded him to return to Hartford Theological Seminary that fall. Their daughter, Marguerite, was born in June 1918. "In 1919 Moses graduated from the Seminary with a Bachelor of Divinity Degree. He accepted a two year commitment to teach at the Friends School in Ramallah, Palestine."[181] Because of post-war travel delays, Moses, Mabel, and Marguerite did not reach Ramallah until January 1920. On their arrival, Moses learned that he was to be principal of the boys school at Ramallah. In 1921, Moses learned that New England Yearly Meeting of Friends had recorded him as a minister.

Moses finished his tour at Ramallah and returned to Portland in 1921. "Henry J. Cadbury recommended that he study for a year at the Harvard Divinity School . . . Moses started graduate classes at Harvard in the Fall of 1921."[182] He earned a master of sacred theology from Harvard in 1922. From 1922 to 1932, he taught in the department of biblical literature at Wellesley College. He also earned a PhD in 1926 from Boston University's School of Theology. A son, Moses Omar, was born in February 1927.

> In 1932 Moses was offered the Nettleton Chair at the Hartford Theological Seminary. . . . Reverend Nettleton, an old time evangelist, had specified his own theological criteria for whoever took the Nettleton Chair. Moses did not believe in some of the criteria. He went to the lawyer on the Seminary Board of Trustees explaining his position. The lawyer told him not to worry about it. . . . Board members . . . wanted him on the faculty. . . .
>
> In 1932 Moses began 30 years of teaching at the Seminary.[183]

He taught Hebrew, Aramaic, and Old Testament studies at Hartford. His old childhood friend, Alexander Purdy, had been teaching New Testament at Hartford for nine years when Moses arrived. "In 1933 the Baileys and the five members of the Alex Purdy family started holding Friends Meetings for Worship in a room at the Hartford YWCA. In the late 1930s . . . they moved their Meetings to the faculty room at the Hartford Seminary." Attendance increased, and "in 1940 the Hartford Monthly Meeting of the Religious Society of Friends was formally organized."[184]

Two years after Purdy's retirement from Hartford Theological Seminary, Moses retired from the seminary in 1962. For several years he continued to teach part-time at various institutions. "Mabel Bailey . . . died in 1976 at the age of eighty three."[185] Later that year, Moses moved to Ellington, Connecticut (several miles from Hartford), where his daughter and son-in-law, Marguerite and Evan Lawn, lived. A year later he moved into an apartment in a converted tobacco shed behind Marguerite and Evan's home, where he lived for his final eighteen years. He traveled widely during those years. He was 101 years old when he died in March 1994.

Moses Bailey wrote a study book for classes and discussion groups, *The Prophetic Word: Ancient and Modern*. This book was published in 1968 by the Religious Education Committee of Friends General Conference. His distinctive style of thinking clearly showed up in the pages of that book.

He defined "myth" as "imaginative storytelling whose purpose is to present human values and meanings that are important."[186] He described two significant myths in the Old Testament. In one of these myths, "The quaking, thundering, flaming Sinai glorifies the covenant and produces feelings of horror at the breaking of it. The rules of loyalty could be read in a dull monotone, but the flaming mountain makes a mighty sermon of them."[187] In addition to this,

> There is a second myth from the Old Testament that is less familiar. . . .
>
> Yahweh, the god of the southern deserts, found a lovely shepherdess, Israel, caring for her flock. He loved her gentle goodness. So Yahweh married the shepherdess. As a gift to his new bride he promised her a land and a home. . . . The honeymoon was deeply happy. Then Yahweh brought his shepherdess bride, Israel, into her new home, the land of the Amorite, Canaanite, Gurgashite, Hivite, Hittite, Perizzite and Jebusite, where she found their husbands (baals), had adulterous affairs with them, and, in spite of Yahweh's urging, refused to return to him. Finally

Yahweh divorced his shepherdess (*Hosea* 2) but still offered to take her back if only she would come (*Jeremiah* 3).[188]

In the chapter titled "The Word of the Lord to the Prophet," Bailey observed a typical use of "Hebrew superlatives" in this type of language:

wind of God	for hurricane . . .
hill of God	great hill
house of God	great house, temple
food of God	delicious, or satisfying food . . .
fire of God	lightning"[189]

And so he suggested that the phrase "the word of God," in the prophetic books, was a "super-superlative":[190] either "the prophets, using superlatives in their excitement, say that they were quoting Yahweh," or "their editors, intent upon presenting the words of the prophets only in the strongest superlative, call each invective 'the word of Yahweh,'"[191] or perhaps both.

In a chapter titled "The Righteous Shall Live by His Faith," Bailey discussed the proper translation of Habakkuk 2:4. The King James Version translates the last portion of that verse as "the just shall live by his faith." The New Revised Standard Version translates it as "the righteous live by their faith" but offers an alternative translation: "the righteous live by their faithfulness." In other twentieth-century translations, we read: "The righteous man will live by being faithful" (NEB); "The upright will live through faithfulness" (NEB); and "The righteous man is rewarded with life for his fidelity" (*Jewish Study Bible*). Bailey argued that a more accurate translation would be "the loyal Jew lives by his character."[192]

Howard R. Macy

Two Quaker scholars have written significant books on humor in the Bible and in Christian life. The first of these books is *The Humor of Christ*, published in 1964 by Elton Trueblood. In his preface, Trueblood makes it clear "that the New Testament has not been my chief field of study, . . . this book is written more in the mood of a philosopher than in that of a New Testament critic."[193] In his study of Jesus' humor, he drew on the writings of several New Testament scholars—particularly the pioneering work of T. R. Glover.

From his philosophical viewpoint, he points out the views of such thinkers as Søren Kierkegaard and Henri Bergson on the importance of humor.

To this extent, Trueblood has been helpful. But I find something missing in this book: his writing is completely lacking in humor! In reading it, I plowed through one-hundred-plus pages of ponderous pontification.

What a contrast I found when I turned to the second of these books: *Laughing Pilgrims: Humor and the Spiritual Journey* (published in 2006), by Howard Macy. He notes that in his original intention for the book, "I had set out to suggest some principles for identifying and interpreting humor in the Bible. . . . What I was learning about humor and Scripture, however, soon took surprising directions. It intersected with important themes in spiritual formation."[194] His basic theological insight is: "We're made for humor—and God likes it."[195] And so he wrote a book that is as light in tone as it is profound in insight. This study of humor in Christian spirituality abounds in funny and witty comments: "It is not better to curse a candle than to light the darkness. . . . We don't have to attribute Deep Meaning to all the details of life."[196] "Laughing can also remind us that we don't have to be perfekt."[197]

In his chapters on humor in the Bible, Macy insists: "Seeing its humor can help us better understand the Bible's intended message. Biblical writers used humor . . . to reveal and emphasize truth, to make it stick."[198] In dealing with specific examples of humor in the Bible, the contrast between the approaches of Trueblood and of Macy shows up most sharply. Trueblood's explanations remind me of the laborious attempts many make in order to explain the point of a joke to someone who just doesn't get it. For example:

> Christ used deliberately preposterous statements to get his point across. When we take a deliberately preposterous statement and, from a false sense of piety, try to force some literal truth out of it, the result is often grotesque. The playful, when interpreted with humorless seriousness, becomes merely ridiculous. An excellent illustration of this is a frequent handling of the gigantic dictum about the rich man and the needle's eye, an elaborate figure which appears in identical form in all three of the Synoptics. "It is easier," said Jesus, "for a camel to go through the eye of a needle than for a rich man to enter the kingdom of God" (Mark 10:25). This categorical statement given with no qualifications whatever, follows, in all three accounts, the story of a wealthy man who came to Jesus to ask seriously how he might have eternal life. He

claimed to have kept the standard commandments, but he went away sorrowfully when told that, at least in his case, it would be necessary to divest himself of all of his possessions.

We are informed that Christ's hearers were greatly astonished, and well they might have been if they took the dictum literally, as they apparently did. Taken literally, of course, the necessary conclusion is that no one who is not in absolute poverty can enter the Kingdom, because most people have some riches, and it is impossible for a body as large as that of a camel, hump and all, to go through an aperture as small as the eye of a needle. For humorous purposes this is evidently the same camel swallowed by the Pharisee when he carefully rejected the gnat. That the listeners failed to see the epigram about the needle's eye as a violent metaphor is shown by their question, "Then who can be saved?"[199]

Macy regularly makes his explanations far more tersely, frequently cutting to the chase with a zinger of his own. He concludes his references to the humor in the stories of Samson: "In the end, of course, we learn that though Samson was not a stand-up comic, he could still bring down the house."[200] When he comes to the gospels, Macy tells us: "And there are fish stories. Who would enjoy a good fish story more than a fisherman? . . . The last is another story of nets nearly bursting after a night of dismal failure. It's such a good fish story that we even have the count of the catch—153 (John 21:1–14)."[201] Let the medium match the message.

Howard R. Macy is descended from the Macy family who were among the original Quaker settlers on Nantucket Island, Massachusetts. He was born in December 1944 in Berkeley, California. His parents were Mahlon and Hazel Macy. His father was a Friends pastor. Howard married Margi Astleford (daughter of former Friends missionaries) in June 1966, at Newberg (Oregon) Friends Church. Margi and Howard have a son and a daughter.

Howard Macy earned a BA from George Fox University in 1966, an MA from Earlham School of Religion in 1970, and a PhD from Harvard Graduate School of Arts and Sciences in 1975. He was "recorded as a minister in New England Yearly Meeting (1975) while serving as a pastor at Smith Neck Friends Meeting in South Dartmouth, MA."[202]

From 1976–78 Macy was a member of the pastoral team at Reedwood Friends Church (Portland, Oregon), where he was instrumental in founding its Center for Christian Studies. He taught religion and biblical studies (primarily Old Testament) at Earlham College (1975–76), at Friends University from 1978–90, and at George Fox University from 1990 until his retirement in 2011. Since 2012 he has been editor of *Quaker Religious Thought*.

In his master's thesis for Earlham School of Religion, "The Legal Metaphor in Oracles Against Foreign Nations in the Pre-Exilic Prophets," Macy bases his argument on the following generalization:

> One of the most widely accepted conclusions of modern Old Testament study is the fact that the concept of covenant is central to the Old Testament materials. The covenant idea is found in legal, historical, and prophetic texts as well as in the Psalms. . . . Many also see the covenant idea as one of the formative factors very early in Israel's history. Furthermore, the form of the covenant is understood to be analogous to the basic treaty form common to the ancient Near East.[203]

The details of his argument focus on the form of covenant treaties and lead to this conclusion:

> Prophetic indictment against Israel was stated in terms of violation by Israel, the vassal, of the covenant given by Yahweh, the Suzerain. . . . From examination of the prophetic oracles against the foreign nations, we can conclude that Israel's prophets drew from the same legal metaphor of treaty for oracles against both Israel and the foreign nations.[204]

In his *Quaker Religious Thought* article, "The Prophets in the Old Testament," Macy rejects a view of the prophets that had been popular among early twentieth-century liberal scholars:

> Scholars used to talk about the prophets as great innovators of "ethical monotheism." It is clear now that the prophets did not innovate very much, but instead spoke out of Israel's ancient tradition. They explicitly recalled the mighty acts of God on Israel's behalf and reminded Israel of her obligations under the ancient covenant. They charged Israel with breaking covenant—the covenant which was the very constitution of Israel as a people.[205]

The Biblical Theology Movement of the mid-twentieth century emphasized "mighty acts of God" and "covenant" as key themes in biblical (particularly Old Testament) thinking about God. In the 1970s, I became acquainted with Macy at Quaker Theological Discussion Group conferences, and it is clear that we were both influenced by the views of that movement. Macy took it as obvious that biblical theology was the most influential movement at that time in ecumenical Bible scholarship.

One type of biblical criticism biblical theology scholars have found especially congenial is word studies—the careful examination of the meaning and context of individual Hebrew and Greek words in the Old and New Testaments. The fruitful contribution of word studies to biblical theology is mentioned in *The Interpreter's Dictionary of the Bible*'s entry on "History of Biblical Theology":

> The ideal biblical theology in the Christian church must treat the witness and views of both OT and NT together. How much both testaments bear upon each other has become increasingly clear in the latest scholarship. We are now reaping the fruit of such unified research—e.g., in the articles in the *Theologisches Wörterbuch*, edited by G. Kittel and G. Friedrich.[206]

Theologisches Wörterbuch is a multi-volume encyclopedia of the results of word study scholarship. An excellent sampling, in English, of the fruits of biblical word study can be found in two brief volumes by William Barclay: *A New Testament Wordbook* (New York: Harper & Brothers, 1958) and *More New Testament Words* (New York: Harper & Brothers, 1958). The entry on "Biblical Theology" in *The Interpreter's Dictionary of the Bible: Supplementary Volume* observes that

> the positive position of the biblical theology movement included the following characteristic features. . . .
>
> iii. A contrast between Hebrew and Greek thought. . . .
>
> iv. An emphasis on the unity of the Bible. . . .
>
> v. An approach to biblical language in which word studies were much emphasized. . . .
>
> vii. An emphasis on revelation in history, which fits in with and embodies all of the above.[207]

Throughout his writing career, Howard Macy has displayed a manifest interest in word study as a critical method. In the 2006 *Quaker Bible Reader*, he contributed a chapter on "Learning to Read the Psalms." In that essay he wrote:

In reflecting on how I approach the Psalms, I find that I use three complementary but distinct approaches. The first is analytical or exegetical, the second is imaginative, and the third is prayerful. . . .

For me, careful exegesis is a valuable approach to engaging the Psalms. Simply put, exegesis uses a variety of analytical tools to discover how the original singers and hearers of these songs might have understood them.[208]

After discussing several other forms of analysis, he continued: "One of my favorite analytical tools is exploring the meanings of words, trying to reach behind the limitations of translation. (Almost anyone can do this by comparing translations and using study tools such as commentaries and theological wordbooks.)"[209]

Macy's 1972 booklet, *The Shalom of God*, is based on a word study of one Hebrew word, *shalom*, often translated as "peace":

Shalom is a fantastic word. It is at once filled with a diversity of meanings and yet is not fragmented, but whole. . . .

Shalom means completion, fulfillment, well-being, wholeness or making whole. I always think of a circle when I think of *shalom*. . . .

Above all, *shalom* is a concept of wholeness—in society—man with man, man with God, man with nature. It is very much tied up with concepts of justice, faithfulness, righteousness, truth, reliability. *Shalom* signifies that things are in right order.[210]

As a preface to this word study, he put it into a biblical context that contrasted with a popular Quaker view that the peace testimony grew out of faith in the fundamental goodness of human beings: "The hope we see in the Bible does not come from the idea that man is terrific and someday will put it all together. Instead, peace will come because God is so good and because he is trustworthy."[211]

Rhythms of the Inner Life, by Macy, was first published in 1988. This book is primarily about Christian spirituality, but the spirituality is centered on the book of Psalms in the Old Testament:

We shall pay particular attention to the ancient Hebrew singers who gave us the Psalms of the Old Testament. Composed over a period of several hundred years, these magnificent songs have endured now well over two millennia as a primary guide to the inner life, and for all their marks of antiquity, they are still fresh and striking today. . . .

Our interest in nurturing the inner life gives shape to this work. In using the Psalms, the book is thematic and selective.[212]

At one point in the book, Macy observes: "To know both God's power and God's Presence in the world does not in itself provide an adequate basis for trust. In fact, such convictions can easily bring fear, instead of hope, if we are not also convinced of God's love."[213] In order to bring out a full sense of the depth of God's love for us, he turns to a remarkable word study:

> The word the Hebrews used to talk of God's love is so sturdy and rich that we don't even have a single English word adequate to translate it. For this wonderful word, *hesed*, translators have used, among others, "love," "kindness," "steadfast love," "loving-kindness," and "grace." Yet none of these words fully conveys the Hebrews' sense of God's love. This love does not waver and is always loyal. It is about this love that the poet of the Shepherd Psalm sings when he writes, "Ah, how goodness and *hesed* pursue me, every day of my life" (23:6). *Hesed* is both strong and tender, a love that reaches as high as the heavens (36:5; 57:10; 103:11). . . .
>
> It is not surprising, then, that the psalmists often point to such reliable love as a reason to trust. . . . They even connect this conviction with the fortress language that is so common to the theme of trust in the Psalms: "My citadel is God himself, the God who loves [*hesed*] me" (59:17). . . .
>
> How much further ahead we would be if we could see that God pursues us with love![214]

If Macy can draw such riches and depth out of just two Hebrew words—*shalom* and *hesed*—what a wonderful instrument indeed must word study be, this exploration of the meaning of words in the Bible.

Macy explored the spirituality of Old Testament prophets in an essay, "Ordinary Prophets, Extraordinary Lives,"[215] published in the 1996 *festschrift* for Arthur Roberts. He wrote the introduction and commentary on the book of Psalms[216] in the *Renovaré Spiritual Formation Bible*, first published in 2005. The 2013 *Oxford Handbook of Quaker Studies* included a useful chapter by Macy, on "Quakers and Scripture."[217]

Daniel L. Smith-Christopher

Daniel L. Smith was born in April 1955 in Portland, Oregon. His parents, R'Dean and Virginia Smith, were active members of First Friends Church in Portland, which later became Reedwood Friends Church. R'Dean was a pharmacist, who owned a drug store that had belonged to his father-in-law. Daniel had two brothers: R'Dean Smith, Jr. and David Smith (who changed his name to David Christopher as a young adult).

Daniel earned a BA from George Fox University (Newberg, Oregon) in 1977, an MDiv from Associated Mennonite Biblical Seminaries (Elkhart, Indiana) in 1981, and a PhD from Oxford University (England) in 1986. He was recorded as a minister by Reedwood around 2005 "at the congregational level only,"[218] without going through the process at the yearly meeting level that is normally required in Northwest Yearly Meeting.

Daniel married Zsa Zsa Janine House in Los Angeles in June 1992. Zsa Zsa is from a Mexican-Hungarian family. At the time of his marriage, Daniel changed his name to Daniel L. Smith-Christopher. Daniel and Zsa Zsa have a son and a daughter.

In 1986, Daniel Smith-Christopher "volunteered to go to Israel for Quaker Peace and Service, and . . . worked for . . . nearly two years for London Yearly Meeting."[219] From 1987 to 1989 (filling the position of just-retired T. Canby Jones), he was assistant professor of theology and director of peace studies at Wilmington College of Ohio. Since 1989, Smith-Christopher has been on the faculty of Loyola Marymount University, a Jesuit university in Los Angeles—except for a one-year leave of absence in 2003-4, when he served as professor of biblical studies at Bluffton College in Ohio. At Loyola Marymount he is now professor of theological studies (Old Testament), director of peace studies, and director of graduate studies in theology.

From 1993 to 1995, he was an academic advisor for the Arts and Entertainment (A&E) Network television series *Mysteries of the Bible*, on which he made numerous appearances as a Bible scholar. In July 1995, he was guest Bible teacher at the sessions of New York Yearly Meeting of Friends, in Silver Bay, New York. In 2004, Roman Catholic Cardinal Roger Mahoney appointed Smith-Christopher as permanent consultant to the Theological Commission of the Archdiocese of Los Angeles. has retained his membership at Reedwood Friends Church.

In seeking to understand his thought as a biblical scholar, I have worked through his books and articles listed in the bibliography. I have read two books that he wrote as textbooks for Roman Catholic high schools: *The Old Testament: Our Call to Faith & Justice* (2005) and the Old Testament portion of *Sacred Scripture: A Catholic Study of God's Word* (2013a); both of these texts are published with a *Nihil Obstat* from a Roman Catholic censor and the *Imprimatur* of a bishop (official declarations that these books are "free of doctrinal or moral error" [Smith-Christopher 2005, 4]). I have also read working drafts of Smith-Christopher's not-yet-published commentary on the book of Micah.

The fact that a Quaker can write an officially approved textbook—about the Bible, of all subjects—for Roman Catholic schools seems miracle enough to me. I can remember when no Catholics were permitted at professional meetings like the American Academy of Religion, and when all Roman Catholic clergy and seminary professors were required to swear an oath against modernism (issued by Pope Pius X in 1910)—and then the days after the Second Vatican Council when Roman Catholic professors and scholars began attending meetings of the American Academy of Religion and the American Society of Christian Ethics.

Now we have students in Roman Catholic high schools learning from texts in which a Quaker teaches such thoughts as:

> The stories of Genesis 1–11 are not historical in the sense that they include verifiable names, facts, and dates. . . .
>
> The first three chapters of Genesis express the truths of creation. From a literary standpoint, these stories may have borrowed from several sources, including *myths* from the ancient Near East.[220]

And:

> The Genesis stories provide clear answers to . . . perpetual questions: . . . What is our origin? What is our end? Where does everything that exists come from and where is it going?

> In more recent times, scientific discoveries have cast more specific light on the details of creation, including the *evolution* of mankind. . . . Human intelligence is certainly already capable of finding an accurate answer to these questions. These studies only enhance our appreciation for God, the Creator.[221]

Giuseppe Verdi composed the opera *Nabucco* [Nebuchadnezzar] in 1841. The most famous number in that opera is the "Chorus of the Hebrew Slaves"—one of the most magnificent, deeply plaintive musical pieces in the entire classical music repertory. No opera lover bats an eyelid over whether the composer and librettist stick closely to actual historical facts in the details of their story and music.

Not the same for any self-respecting college or university professor! We go to any length to insure that we get our facts straight. During my teaching years in the 1960s and '70s, I frequently taught Introduction to the Old Testament. Not being a specialist in biblical studies myself, I depended on writings by the best Old Testament scholars in order to be sure my historical facts were correct. Depending on these scholars, I regularly told my students that many of the Jews in exile in Babylon had settled down and become relatively successful in business and secure in their new homes. The terrible thing for them was not any political or economic hardship, but a religious crisis: the despair and disillusion caused by the fall of Jerusalem and the destruction of the temple. Hardly the "slavery" that Verdi portrayed.

When Daniel Smith-Christopher published his doctoral dissertation in 1989, he observed: "It is often suggested in studies of the Babylonian Exile that the exiles were not slaves."[222] He went on to challenge this suggestion. He notes that, throughout history, not all forms of slavery were as cruel and severe as the slavery suffered by Africans and their descendants in America. "Clarifying the definition of slavery mitigates against over-confident assumptions that the Jews in Babylon were, or were not, slaves."[223] He concludes:

> The dismissive statement that the Jews were not slaves can be a hasty generalization, depending on the "type," or characteristics, of slavery that are suggested by the term "slave." . . . Slavery is a point on a "continuum of domination." The Babylonian exiles may not have been slaves, but evidence suggests they were most assuredly on this continuum.[224]

In his 1992 *Quaker Religious Thought* article, he repeats many of these points, as well as this further observation: "We have important hints that the exiles did face symbolic aspects of slavery, . . . and this insight must inform our view of the social conditions of the Exile." And he concludes: "Finally, even under the rule of the supposedly tolerant Persians, Ezra mentions in his prayer to God (Ezra 9) that 'we are slaves'!"[225]

In his 1996 article in the Arthur Roberts *festschrift*, Smith-Christopher expands on this thought that not only in their Babylonian exile, but even after their "release" by the Persians, who permitted them to return to Palestine, the condition of the Jews could be described as slavery: "In both Ezra 9:7–8 and Neh. 9, the editors have Ezra referring to the condition of the Jews as 'slavery.'"[226] He insists that these and other hints in the books of Ezra and Nehemiah take us to the conclusion that "the attitude of Ezra-Nehemiah to Persian rule was *not* a grateful subservience to enlightened foreign emperors. . . . There are simply too many 'tooth-marks' on the Persian hands that fed them!" Indeed, "the attitude of Ezra-Nehemiah toward their Persian overlords is . . . the realistic assessment of forced subservience."[227]

In his 2002 book, *A Biblical Theology of Exile*, Smith-Christopher becomes even more firm and forthright in his claim that the Jewish exiles were actually slaves:

> It is precisely these tendencies to presume a tame, even if not entirely comfortable, existence that needs to be challenged in the light of an analysis informed by the experience of exiles throughout history and the evidence of trauma in the Hebrew literature after the experience.
>
> A good example of this assumption is the view . . . that the exiles were not "slaves." . . . One must contend with the reality that the Bible certainly did consider the term to be appropriate to the condition of the Jews living under Persian rule (Neh. 9:36).[228]
>
> When this evidence of identity and work details is combined with biblical references to "slavery" and conditions of exile, the emerging picture is painted in dark colors.[229]

He adds to this picture by examining the use of such terms as "chains," "bonds," and "imprisonment" in biblical books written during and after the exile:

> Clearly, various forms of the Hebrew terms normally rendered "imprisonment" turn up as metaphors for exile, along with the various use of terms of binding and fetters. . . .

> In more detail, . . . note the frequent biblical motif that relates "sight to blind" and "release of prisoners" as metaphors of exile. This is found in many exilic and postexilic passages (e.g., Ps 146:7–8; Isa 42:7; 61:1; Zech 9:12). . . .
>
> The metaphor of imprisonment and reference to places of imprisonment do not grow more plentiful during the exilic period by pure chance, especially in view of its foreignness to the Israelite judicial system. Contemporary assessments of the exile must not simply dismiss this imagery as purely metaphorical with no historical basis.[230]

Smith-Christopher's understanding of the exile, and even of life under Persian rule, as being indeed slavery now becomes loud, clear, and confident—greatly matured from his tentativeness thirteen years earlier. He has indeed vindicated Verdi.

He telegraphs the maturity of his thinking in the opening chapter of *A Biblical Theology of Exile*:

> I choose to write a biblical theology that will not only use many of the critically accepted tools of historical and textual analysis of the Bible, but also to be forthright about the contemporary concerns, assumptions, and interests that inform my selection of texts and tools.[231]

In his commentary on the book of Micah, Smith-Christopher nicely demonstrates this forthrightness about his contemporary concerns in his translation of Micah 6:8. In this favorite "What does the Lord require of you?" passage, the New Revised Standard Version and New Jerusalem Bible both retain the King James language in the final line: "Walk humbly with your God." Smith-Christopher translates this line: "Walk mindfully with your God," and explains: "I favor 'mindfully' because it suggests stronger intentionality than 'humbly.'"[232]

In the commentary on Micah, Smith-Christopher also touches on a deeper issue, one that has been an ongoing concern of his: the relationship between theology and politics—and what a serious look at biblical texts and contexts might contribute to a redefining of this relationship. He suggests

> that, for Micah, policy should be rooted in the experience and discernment of God's leading, not merely in power. To critique policy, one begins by critiquing the theological foundations that

the policy is built upon. This is certainly an enduring message that too often goes unheeded, especially in Western tradition.[233]

Smith-Christopher takes seriously the claim made by John Howard Yoder and other Mennonite scholars, that Christian thought took a fateful turn when the Roman emperor Constantine co-opted the Christian church in the fourth century, so that Christian theology since that time has largely become an ideology on behalf of the political establishment. It was only with the early "peace churches"—Mennonites, Quakers, Church of the Brethren—that this marriage of Christendom and the state was first systematically challenged. For Smith-Christopher, this challenge finds a biblical rootage in Micah's critique, followed up and expanded when the experience of exile led Jewish writers to take seriously the possibility of a viable faith community not tied to the power of the monarchy. He thus proposes, in *A Biblical Theology of Exile*, a reading of biblical texts that "may inform a radical Christian theological resistance to our own history of imperial connivances and the theologies that have so long excused and supported them."[234] In particular, he writes: "I also suggest that a theology of abandoning Constantine, and Constantinian exegetical models of doing biblical theology, is to assert a postcolonialist, as well as exilic, biblical theology."[235]

As an alternative to "Constantinian" theology, he proposed

> readings of biblical texts ... that ... will presume the viability of a community in exile, and the ability to engage in resistance, even outside of nationalist aspirations or imperial connivance.[236]

> Christian exiles, Christian diasporas and minorities, and Christian subcultures have the biblical resources to live an alternative existence that affirms justice and peace, seeking to move forward God's holy experiment of creating an authentic humanity that is consciously gathered in non-conformity to the structures around them.[237]

In his commentary in *The New Interpreter's Bible*, Smith-Christopher reflects on the story of Nebuchadnezzar's dream and "conversion" in chapter 4 of the book of Daniel: "Is it even possible to have a state with such a transformed monarch who is now unwilling to oppress and ruthlessly exercise the power of the state?" This question led him to discuss the varying ways in which peace churches have attempted answers:

> In the radical reformation traditions of Christianity (Quakerism,

Mennonites, Church of the Brethren, among others), there is a long-standing debate about the possibility of Christian righteousness within the secular political systems of world states. The most radical rejection of this possibility is the nonconformity of such groups as the Amish, whose conception of the church is that it is a social reality in the world, but an entity entirely apart from the world. Such Christian communities would refuse almost any participation in a system that is apart from the church. The Quaker tradition, while aware of the import of these ethical questions, has always taken a more hopeful, and at times utilitarian, approach to this issue. Quakerism is utilitarian in that it accepts the present realities, even if less than ideal, but remains hopeful that God's transforming justice can at least influence partially any system of humanity. Therefore, lobbying, prophetically advocating, and perhaps even running for office within any governmental system may result in a bit more light in the world, even if it is never bright sunshine!

Smith-Christopher appears to appeal directly to Friends (in this unlikely context):

> A respectful eye on our more radical Christian brothers and sisters is necessary to maintain a clearheaded approach about the reality of the demands of God's justice, which must never be compromised for political expediency. The book of Daniel teaches that transformation is possible, but the very fact that we are dealing with fictional accounts of transformed emperors . . . makes one wonder whether the possibility for conscientious Christians to "rule" is an ethically viable choice. Perhaps the answer is that when we reach the point at which we find that such participation in the kingdoms of the world involves impossible compromise, Christians become, with Daniel, Hananiah, Mishael, and Azariah, a part of the prophetic resistance.[238]

Could this have been the point that John Woolman, Anthony Benezet, John Churchman, and Samuel Fothergill reached in 1775, at the risk of bringing "such a breach and division as never happened amongst us since we were a people"?[239]

In his commentary on the book of Daniel, Smith-Christopher makes a couple of fascinating observations. In an aside, he surprisingly calls the

"Magnificat" (Mary's song of praise in Luke 1:47-55) a "dramatic anti-Roman polemic."[240] His second thunderbolt is: "Visionary religion has always been dangerous and uncontrolled for any institutional status quo"—upending Karl Marx's charge that religion is "the opiate of the people." This observation is made as part of Smith-Christopher's reflections on apocalyptic literature (such as Daniel 7-12 and the book of Revelation). He goes on to unpack his prize gem:

> Visionary religion draws deep from the hopes and passions of people, especially in dire and despairing conditions. Visionary religion speaks to the failure of established attitudes and traditions, and it opens the way to new possibilities. It accomplishes this by prying open the sealed doors of tradition and imagining possibilities beyond the realities dictated by world powers. Apocalyptic visions can lead to hope—and hopes have the potential of giving birth to *plans*. For Christians, to live with a constant sense of the advent of Christ is . . . a life-style *within* the world that is built on the vision of God's true kingship and dominion. It is to live as if the sentence on the beasts has already been carried out, despite the fact that their lives appear to be "prolonged for a season and a time."[241]

This is the mystery that underlies Christus Victor views and theories of the atonement; it is the secret that empowered the early Quaker vision of the Lamb's War.

Not far from the end of his Old Testament textbook for Catholic schools, Smith-Christopher suggests that it would be "interesting to consider which was the better response of the Jews to foreign rulers." He notes that in the Bible (including the Apocrypha), "We have no literature that represents the position of total compromise—that is, Jewish writings about Jews who totally abandoned their faith in order to embrace Hellenistic religion and culture."[242] He observes: "The military option was certainly one that was available, and exercised, by some Jewish groups,"[243] such as the followers of Judas Maccabeus in the second century BCE and the Zealots in the first century CE. He continues:

> Another way of responding to foreign rule was to focus on maintaining a strong religious commitment in spite of the political challenges. . . .
>
> In this tradition, peacefulness was admired, and *spiritual*

resistance rather than violent resistance was praised—even if it resulted in martyrdom. . . .

Passages representing the tradition of spiritual resistance are offered in much of Wisdom literature. . . .

In the first century A.D., Jesus himself seemed to adopt the path of spiritual resistance. . . . Jesus affirms the wisdom tradition of peace . . . , and St. Paul echoes him.[244]

Smith-Christopher follows up this review of options in the Bible with a modern example: "Dorothy Day was a Catholic layperson of the twentieth century. She was founder of the Catholic Worker Movement that served the poor. She was also opposed to war and promoted nonviolence throughout her life."[245]

Smith-Christopher explained his intention to me:

My life has been with the Catholics—but I remain a Quaker.

Those who know what to look for see my Quakerism expressed here and there. In the Textbook for Catholic High Schools that I wrote on the Old Testament, there is a . . . spread, with photo, of Dorothy Day and the Catholic Worker Movement. That was *my* way of "balancing" the Bishop's insistence that the "Just War" doctrine be addressed.[246]

In *The Religion of the Landless*, Smith-Christopher took his first steps toward "the construction of a contemporary 'theology of exile,' "[247] rooted in Old Testament writings from the period of the exile and afterward. This theology had to be expressed through active nonviolence:

To live as exiles, therefore, is to renounce violence. Indeed, nonviolence is an ethical value that has its roots in the Hebrew Scriptures, as illustrated in the exilic ethic preached by Jeremiah over against Hananiah, or Ezra's rejection of armed guards in favor of the protection of God (Ezra 8:21–23). . . .

At its root, violence is a form of idolatry because it is an attempt to make Babylon into the New Jerusalem by means of our own strength. To worship a place, to give it our allegiance and reverence, when that place is not the Reign of God, is idolatry.[248]

As Smith-Christopher worked out this theme, he recognized that any genuine theology of exile must begin by recognizing the depths of suffering that are at the heart of the experience of exile and that lead to profound emotional crisis. The writings of the prophet Ezekiel provide a significant case study. He notes that many Old Testament scholars have shown a strong interest in "Ezekiel's psychological state."[249] Some, for example, feel that a Freudian analysis is called for. One scholar "believes that Ezekiel's turning a sword on himself to shave the hair of his beard is a veiled reference to pubic hair, and off we go into an analysis of the psychosexual implications of this." Smith-Christopher sees this explanation as a needlessly convoluted way of analyzing what drove Ezekiel to shave with a sword, and so he ironically exclaims: "What drove him indeed! What appears to have driven Ezekiel the man to act out the horrors of conquest. . . . When analyzing a refugee's paranoia, surely a sword is sometimes actually a sword."[250] The real point, he insists, is this:

> Such tendencies to read the psychological state of Ezekiel totally apart from the social and political experiences he suffered are symptoms of the same avoidance in other biblical scholarly analyses of the exile as a real event where human beings deeply suffered. Any psychological assumptions about Ezekiel derived apart from serious attention to the exile are thus tantamount to blaming the victim.[251]

Smith-Christopher suggests that a far more relevant psychological approach to Ezekiel would take into account the growing attention being lavished on studies of post-traumatic stress disorder. "Of particular interest to" him is "the amount of PTSD research conducted with refugees."[252] He recommends:

> A synoptic reading of the exile through Ezekiel and the book of Lamentations forces us to take a fresh look at the actions and behavior of Ezekiel. Lamentations, of course, consists of poetic memories of the fall of Jerusalem. To read Ezekiel with an eye to Lamentations suggests that many of Ezekiel's "bizarre" actions can be seen as modeling the trauma of the fall of Jerusalem.[253]

Smith-Christopher went back to this beginning in his reflections on the stories in the book of Daniel—chapter 3 (the fiery furnace) and chapter 6 (the lion's den). He focuses on "the anger of the suffering. . . . These stories in Daniel often reflect the physical and spiritual crises brought about by the conquerors and rulers in the ancient Near East from 587 through the

Hellenistic despots of the second century BCE." He goes on to clarify this point—and then to go further:

> It is precisely the angry details that open a historical window onto the emotions of occupied Palestine and diaspora Judaism. It is not the people of God in their finest moment, but it is the reality of social conditions. Their ability eventually to embrace nonviolence and even to welcome the foreigner is all the more amazing—and all the more a witness to the involvement of revelation![254]

Smith-Christopher summed up his argument about anger and nonviolence in the ringing conclusion to his reflections on Daniel 6:

> Our call is to understand anger and to accept it as a reality in people's lives, precisely because our nonviolent action must be based on the realities of human life and not on fantasy worlds.
> . . .
>
> It is particularly disturbing when Christians, in false attempts to identify with the sufferers, somehow suspend their convictions of peace and nonviolence and find ways to justify the violence of those who have suffered, saying, "There is no peace without justice." But understanding anger is not an invitation to suspend commitment to the way of peace. Rather, it is an invitation to prophetic endurance of anger while not compromising the gospel of nonviolence. Ultimately, there is no justice without peace.[255]

In his commentary on the book of Micah, Smith-Christopher shows how Micah laid stress on the evil consequences of war:

> Reading Micah involves listening to the cries against the "peripheral damage," "unintended casualties," the "civilian losses," and all the other euphemisms the modern media use to mention, always in passing, the suffering of noncombatants in modern warfare. . . . The book of Micah . . . stands with the peripheral, the unintended, and the doubly affected noncombatants.

He emphasizes that Micah's words are as relevant today as in his own time:

> Micah . . . is not caught up in nationalist bravado used to rouse history's masses for battle. He knows what is coming and tries

to warn others. There is no higher calling for modern Christian prophetic preaching than standing against all idolatrous patriotism and violent nationalism.[256]

Smith-Christopher proposes that the famous "swords into plowshares" passage in Micah 4:1–5 was not so much a prediction of an ideal future time as it was a message for his own day:

> Beating swords into plowshares, when read as part of a bitter sociopolitical agenda against the Jerusalem elite, no longer remains in the realm of "utopian sentiments" and is restored to its proper place within a "People's History" of Judah, representing some of the sentiments of the subordinated classes as revealed in their spokespersons, such as Micah and later Jeremiah. . . .
>
> By transforming our reading of Mic. 4:1–5 from a "pacifist sentiment" (which it is not) to an agrarian antiwar protest (which it is), we restore the angry voice to Micah the Moresheti.[257]

In this context, I find Smith-Christopher's commentary on Micah 4:4 to be of particular interest. In my doctoral dissertation, I had taken this verse: "they shall sit every man under his vine and under his fig tree," in conjunction with Zechariah 3:10: "In that day, says the LORD of hosts, every one of you will invite his neighbor under his vine and under his fig tree," to be key ingredients of the biblical pictures of the final "goal of human history."[258] But Smith-Christopher noticed a connection Smith-Christopher I had missed in the speech of one of the Assyrian officials (the Rabshakeh) to the people of Judah, when the Assyrian army was besieging Jerusalem:

> Perhaps most significantly, . . . the promise of a "vine and fig tree" was proposed to the surrendering Israelites as a benefit of Assyrian occupation in the Rabshakeh's speech: "Then every one of you will eat from your own vine and your own fig tree, and drink water from your own cistern" (2 Kings 18:31; Isa. 36:16). . . . Here is an unavoidable hint that Micah may be directly citing the Rabshakeh's promise—and thus may indicate that *Micah proposes to accept the offer!*[259]

A little over a century later, Jeremiah would wear an iron ox-yoke as a sign to the rulers and people of Jerusalem of God's command that they should surrender to the Babylonians.

After the Babylonian exile came life under Persian rule. Even though the

Persians permitted a few Jews to return to Palestine, Ezra admitted in prayer that "we are slaves" (Ezra 9:9; see also Nehemiah 9:36). Smith-Christopher claimed that Ezra and Nehemiah, realistically assessing this situation, advocated neither violent revolt nor passive submission, but rather "a faithful non-violent resistance to any idea that Persian power or authority is greater than God's spiritual armament of the faithful."[260]

The book of Daniel was probably completed two or three centuries after Ezra's time. Smith-Christopher maintains that this book influenced Ezra's message of encouraging nonviolent resistance and civil disobedience as a response to tyranny and oppression. He notes that Gandhi found great support for his own non-violent resistance campaigns in the book of Daniel:

> Mahatma Gandhi made interesting comments, between 1909 and 1937, on the book of Daniel in his work in both South Africa and India. Gandhi stated that he had "found much consolation in reading the book of the prophet Daniel in the Bible" and declared Daniel to be "one of the greatest passive resisters that ever lived." Gandhi appears to have been particularly intrigued with chap. 6, the story of Daniel in the lions' den. . . . Gandhi suggested that Daniel was a model of resistance to South African "pass laws" for Indian South Africans. . . .
>
> Gandhi's comments suggest a number of possibilities for understanding Daniel 6 and, by implication, the other stories as well. . . . From a South African prison, Daniel 6 made perfect sense to one engaged in nonviolent resistance to unjust laws. Here, perhaps, we have an important clue to reordering our own reading of the text in the modern era. Stories of resistance were written by a diaspora community who faced such trials often enough to identify with the fate of the heroes in these stories.[261]

Smith-Christopher read the story of the fiery furnace (Daniel 3) as another example of nonviolent civil disobedience: Daniel's three friends "boldly express civil disobedience to the law of the king."[262] And again: "A martyr legend is intended to promote action—to embolden faith—and in the case of Daniel 3, to call people to active, nonviolent resistance to the symbols of worldly power."[263]

Daniel 6:10 portrays Daniel praying to the true God, with his windows open toward Jerusalem. Smith-Christopher suggests: "The story, in short, represents an act of civil disobedience on Daniel's part. . . . Daniel was openly declaring his disobedience by keeping open, or even throwing open, his windows.[264]

Commenting on "a little help" in Daniel 11:34, and comparing this with "the violent men among your own people" (Daniel 11:14 NIV), Smith-Christopher summarizes: "These texts are further evidence of the nonviolent orientation of Daniel's visionary attitude to foreign power. The book of Daniel *does* call for resistance, but nonviolent resistance."[265] The book of Daniel was almost certainly written at the time when the Maccabees revolted against the rule of the emperor Antiochus Epiphanes; in this context, Smith-Christopher added: "To read Dan. 11:34 as a further condemnation of the Maccabean option is hardly stretching historical credibility."[266]

Smith-Christopher pushes this analysis to far deeper and more comprehensive levels in the reflections that conclude his commentary on the book of Daniel:

> To take Daniel seriously as a basis for contemporary theology, we must be prepared for a call to arms, for we are called to nothing less than spiritual warfare with material realities; what the early Quakers called "The Lamb's War" (borrowing the image from the other biblical apocalyptic work, Revelation). Daniel's final vision is a description of the powers of this world and the struggles of the "covenanted people" within the orbit of these powers.
>
> "Speaking truth to power" is a recent Quaker ideal that is the equivalent of Daniel's imagery of Michael's taking up the sword of truth against the foreign powers. Speaking truth is not mere advocacy as opposed to action. Speaking truth *is* action because truth empowers, inspires, and guides. If God is our emperor and Christ is our victorious general, then no earthly power will command our total loyalty again. Truth, if taught, will not be defeated. The most revolutionary act under Antiochus IV, according to Daniel, was for one to *be* a Jew and to teach others to be a Jew. The most revolutionary act in the modern world is first of all to be a woman or a man of faith—to reject violence, to reject the abuse of the weak, and to embrace the gospel of life and teach it to others. . . . How can a democracy emerge from a militaristic, hierarchical, disciplined culture of unquestioned obedience to superiors? Truth rules by the power of the many. It is inherently

democratic, because its power derives from the convictions of the masses, and not from the forced obedience of the masses. It is, in short, war by angelic power—a lamb's war. It is the way of Daniel the wise.[267]

With the phrase "Daniel the wise," we see a direction in Smith-Christopher's thought that he developed more fully in the next few years. In *A Biblical Theology of Exile*, we read, "Daniel defeats his enemies by means of wisdom—he is the quintessential wisdom warrior."[268] Smith-Christopher discovered a type of nonviolence in wisdom books of the Bible—notably Proverbs and Ecclesiastes—and saw parallels with this in the stories about Daniel. But this was an unusual variety of nonviolence: "Wisdom ethics are subcultural ethics in Proverbs, Ecclesiastes, and Daniel. Whatever nonviolent witness there may be, I would argue, is also subcultural." It differed from Gandhi's nonviolent resistance campaigns: "Where is the nonviolent witness of the Hebrew Bible? If we look for a Hebrew Gandhi, we will not find him/her." In particular, the goal of Gandhi's nonviolent campaigns in India was to achieve independence for India as a nation. In contrast,

> Principled nonviolence as a tactic of national politics is not a diasporic virtue and thus arguably not the Hebraic form of nonviolence. . . .
>
> The nonviolence of the Hebrew diasporic ethics is a nonviolence of radical doubt and irreverence to the self-proclaimed state power and piety, a nonviolence based on the fact that God's plans are centered on the people of God primarily, and the nation-state is not the center of the universe. In other words, for the wisdom warrior, the nonviolence of the Hebrew Diaspora is a nonviolence based on the wise awareness that the empire, despite all its attempts to convince itself otherwise, is not of ultimate significance.[269]

Smith-Christopher suggests that this wisdom-nonviolence of Proverbs, Ecclesiastes, and Daniel

> is the clever and wise insight of the diaspora community that their life as the people of God is far more important than the success or failure of the empire. . . .
>
> The irreverence toward the state and the advice to keep one's wits in relation to the state are quite simply the practical wisdom

of the Diaspora. Such wisdom does not believe in the myths of the state. It is, however, the embodiment of Jesus' classic advice to his minority, subcultural followers: "See, I am sending you out like sheep into the midst of wolves; so be wise as serpents and innocent as doves" (Matt 10:16).[270]

In his essay "Political Atheism and Radical Faith," Smith-Christopher points out another (perhaps interrelated) strand in the Hebrew traditions of nonviolence that emerged in the centuries after the exile. In the writings of "Second Isaiah," he observes

> a renewal not limited only to the restoration of the Israelite peoples themselves, but which also sought to redefine their relationship to their former enemies (Isa. 2; 19:24–25; 49:6). Included in this developing Hebraic theology of nonviolence and universal mission are the following: the stories of Jonah (a *midrash* based on Isa. 49:6); the little book of Ruth's redefinition of "foreigners" (Ruth, a foreigner, gained acceptance and succeeded). . . .
>
> The powerful story of Jonah moves in an entirely new direction. It radically redefines the nature of being the people of God, a people of mission with a message of reconciliation (see Isa. 2 wherein this reconciliation will lead to the destruction of all weapons).[271]

This is in sharp contrast to the nonviolence of Ezra, which was positioned within a "pure," separated community in which a covenant was made to divorce foreign wives (Ezra 10:1–12).[272]

In the face of all this evidence, Smith-Christopher draws

> the conclusion . . . that there is not one singular and consistent answer in the Hebrew Scriptures to the problem of war and relations to the enemy. In fact, there are conflicting interpretations of the tradition of violence, even within the canon of the Hebrew texts. Jesus . . . can be identified as standing faithfully in one, but not all, of these differing post-exilic, Hebraic traditions.
>
> Jesus did not create the Hebrew tradition of nonviolence. He stands in this peace tradition with other early rabbinic teachers. . . . However, Jesus clearly radicalizes Hebrew nonviolence and clarifies its central importance for the character of his movement.[273]

Smith-Christopher sharpened some of these points in *Jonah, Jesus, and Other Good Coyotes*:

> A debate takes place between biblical books (and sometimes within a single biblical book) over this question of what it means to be the people of God now, when one is living in the shadow of Exile or in the diaspora, living away from the old homeland. A related, and equally interesting, question also presents itself. If we must rethink who we are, must we not also rethink who *the nations* are? . . . With regard to both of these questions, then—"who are we?" as God's people, and "who are they?" as *the nations*—there are signs of intense debate after the time of the Exile.[274]

He cites examples of contrasting answers to these questions:

- The passages from Isaiah (2:2–4; 19:24–25; 49:6) which he had already referred to in "Political Atheism and Radical Faith."

- Proverbs 30:24–28: "Four things on earth are small, yet they are exceedingly wise: the ants; . . . the badgers; . . . the locusts; . . . the lizard. . . ." In each case, the animals represent the condition of the Hebrew people after 587 BCE.[275]

- The face-off between the prophets Jeremiah and Hananiah over the question of whether to revolt against Babylonian rule.[276]

Smith-Christopher summarizes:

> The devastation of the exile created partisan struggles, infighting, and disagreements about what it meant to be the people of God after the Exile. For some, as we will see, the language of revenge, violence, and regaining power became uppermost in their minds. These voices are definitely part of the biblical record. But there are other voices in the debate, too.[277]

If we are to learn from the Bible, how are we to handle these continuing debates—and the extreme diversity within biblical writings? This is the overarching question of biblical interpretation, of how we are to understand, deal with, and apply the Bible in its entirety to our lives today. This will be the thrust of the final chapter in my third volume. I will be bringing Smith-Christopher back to join the discussion in that chapter.

Epilogue

The earliest Friends looked on university education "at Oxford or Cambridge" as being unnecessary to qualify themselves for Christian ministry or to make wise use of the Bible. And yet one of their number, Samuel Fisher, was an Oxford graduate and—both before and after his conversion to Quakerism—a brilliant Bible scholar, who used his learning effectively to advance and defend the Quaker movement.

By the late nineteenth and twentieth centuries, large groups of Friends either insisted that critical scholarship was an enemy to true Christian faith or had come to believe that scripture was so secondary to guidance by the Spirit that they had little interest in formal Bible study. Even so, with Samuel Fisher as an example, it should not be totally surprising that critical and constructive Bible scholars have again emerged among Friends in these modern times. If anything is surprising, it is that such a small body should have produced a considerable number of Bible scholars and that several of these have been counted among the leading and most influential scholars of their times.

Even more remarkably, a number of these scholars have drawn on their own Quaker faith and heritage as a source of insights that have become significant, original contributions to our understanding of the Bible. I see this as validation that there has always been tremendous vitality at the heart of Quakerism—a vitality that supports the claim that the Quaker vision is indeed a restoration of the earliest Christian vision.

These Quaker Bible scholars and the results of their studies have turned out to be extremely diverse. In order to give justice to the thinking of each of these persons, my writing has extended to too great a length to be included within a single chapter. I made a decision to divide it into two chapters. To balance the length of these chapters as closely as I could, the original chapter on "Quaker Bible Scholars" concludes with my study of the work of Daniel Smith-Christopher.

And so this second book ends, as it were, in mid-stream. The next chapter, titled "More Quaker Bible Scholars," will be the opening chapter in my third volume. Relevant works by the scholars covered in that chapter were all published within the last three decades of the twentieth century and the first two decades of the twenty-first century.

Notes

Introduction

1. Robert Barclay, *An Apology for the True Christian Divinity: being an explanation and vindication of the principles and doctrines of the people called Quakers*, stereotype ed. (1678; Philadelphia: Friends Book Store, 1908), 88.
2. Henry W. Wilbur, *The Life and Labors of Elias Hicks* (Philadelphia: Friends' General Conference Advancement Committee, 1910), 231.
3. Joseph John Gurney, *Essays on the Evidences, Doctrines, and Practical Operation, of Christianity* (1825; repr., n.p.: Kessinger, 2008), 83–84.
4. Bliss Forbush, *Elias Hicks: Quaker Liberal* (New York: Columbia University Press, 1956), 218.
5. Joseph John Gurney, *A Peculiar People: The Rediscovery of Primitive Christianity*, with an introduction by Donald Green, 7th ed. (1824; repr., Richmond, IN: Friends United Press, 1979), 474.
6. John Wilbur, *Journal of the Life of John Wilbur. . . .* (Providence, RI: George H. Whitney, 1859), 158.

7. Jonathan Dymond, *Essays on the Principles of Morality and on the Private and Political Rights and Obligations of Mankind*, abr. ed. (1829; repr., Philadelphia: Philadelphia Yearly Meeting of Friends, 1896), 89.
8. Ibid., 100.
9. Lucretia Mott, *Lucretia Mott: Her Complete Speeches and Sermons*, Studies in Women and Religion 4 (New York and Toronto: Edwin Mellen, 1980), 125.
10. Ibid., 129.
11. Hugh Barbour and J. William Frost, *The Quakers*, Denominations in America 3 (Westport, CT: Greenwood, 1988), 304.
12. David B. Updegraff, *Old Corn; or, Sermons and Addresses on the Spiritual Life* (Boston: McDonald & Gill, 1892), 205.
13. Dougan Clark, *The Holy Ghost Dispensation*, 4th ed. (New York: Fleming H. Revell, 1891), 10.
14. Ibid., 149.
15. Ibid., 150.
16. Luke Woodard, *What Is Truth?* (Auburn, NY: Knapp, Peck & Thomson, 1901), 127.
17. Ibid., 130.
18. Luke Woodard, *Sketches of a Life of 75: In Three Parts; Biographical, Historical and Descriptive* (Richmond, IN: Nicholson, 1907), 235.
19. Luke Woodard, *The Morning Star: A Treatise on the Nature, Offices, and Work of the Lord Jesus Christ* (1875; repr., n.p.: Kessinger, 2007), 96n.
20. Dougan Clark and Joseph H. Smith, *David B. Updegraff and His Work* (Cincinnati: M. W. Knapp, 1895), 243.
21. Rufus M. Jones, *John William Rowntree*, (1942; repr., LaVergne, TN: Kessinger, 2010), 9th (unnumbered) page.
22. H. G. Wood, *Belief and Unbelief Since 1850* (Cambridge: Cambridge University Press, 1955), 43.
23. George Fox, *The Works of George Fox*, New Foundation Publication (1831; repr., State College, PA: George Fox Fund, 1990), 4:290.
24. Daniel L. Smith-Christopher, "Resistance in a 'Culture of Permission': Sociological Readings of the Correspondence with Persian Authorities in Ezra 1–7" in *Truth's Bright Embrace: Essays and Poems in Honor of Arthur O. Roberts*, eds. Paul N. Anderson and Howard R. Macy (Newberg, OR: George Fox University Press, 1996), 35.

Notes

Chapter One

1. T. Vail Palmer, Jr., "Some Issues from Nineteenth-Century Quakerism," *Quaker Religious Thought* 29, no. 2 (January 1999): 9–10.
2. Joseph John Gurney, *Essays on the Evidences, Doctrines, and Practical Operation of Christianity* (1825; repr., n.p.: Kessinger, 2008), ix.
3. Palmer, "Some Issues," 10.
4. Gurney, *Essays on the Evidences*, 83–84.
5. Robert Barclay, *An Apology for the True Christian Divinity*. . . . , stereotype ed. (1678; Philadelphia: Friends' Book Store, 1908), 23.
6. Ibid., 33.
7. Palmer, "Some Issues," 11.
8. George Fox, *The Works of George Fox*, 8 vols. New Foundation Publication (1831; repr., State College, PA: George Fox Fund, 1990), 3:255.
9. Ibid., 5:229.
10. Ibid., 3:209.
11. George Fox, *"The Power of the Lord Is Over All": The Pastoral Letters of George Fox*, ed. with introduction by T. Canby Jones (Richmond, IN: Friends United Press, 1990), 96.
12. Palmer, "Some Issues," 12.
13. Job Scott, *The Knowledge of the Lord, the Only True God*. . . . (Philadelphia: Emmor Kimber, 1824), 35. Digital Quaker Collection, Earlham School of Religion, http://esr.earlham.edu/dqc.
14. Palmer, "Some Issues," 12.
15. Fox, *Works of George Fox*, 3:284.
16. Arthur J. Mekeel, *Quakerism and a Creed* (Philadelphia: Friends' Book Store, 1936), 32–33.
17. Fox, *Works of George Fox*, 3:502.
18. Ibid., 3:503.
19. Ibid., 3:180.
20. Ibid., 3:139–40.
21. Ibid., 5:89.
22. Ibid., 5:317.
23. Fox, *Power of the Lord*, 100.
24. Fox, *Works of George Fox*, 2:285.
25. Ibid., 3:209.
26. Fox, *Power of the Lord*, 90.
27. Ibid., 199–201.

28. Ibid., 83.
29. G. Ernest Wright, *God Who Acts: Biblical Theology as Recital*, Studies in Biblical Theology 8 (London: SCM Press, 1952), 109.
30. Ibid., 110–11.
31. Palmer, "Some Issues," 12.
32. Ibid.
33. Mekeel, *Quakerism*, 59.
34. Ibid., 62.
35. Henry W. Wilbur, *The Life and Labors of Elias Hicks* (Philadelphia: Friends' General Conference Advancement Committee, 1910), 231.
36. Bliss Forbush, *Elias Hicks: Quaker Liberal* (New York: Columbia University Press, 1956), 218.
37. Mekeel, *Quakerism*, 127–28.
38. Os Cresson, "Roots and Flowers of Quaker Nontheism," *Nontheist Friends* (January 23, 2007): http://www.nontheistfriends.org.
39. Palmer, "Some Issues," 12.
40. Ibid.
41. Ibid., 12–13.
42. Gustaf Aulén, *Christus Victor: An Historical Study of the Three Main Types of the Idea of Atonement*, trans. A. G. Herbert (1931; repr., Eugene, OR: Wipf and Stock, 2003), 4.
43. Gurney, *Essays on the Evidences*, 427.
44. Ibid., 433.
45. Ibid., 437.
46. Palmer, "Some Issues," 15.
47. T. Vail Palmer, Jr., "Theorising a Quaker View of the Atonement," *Quaker Studies* 16, no. 1 (September 2011): 113.
48. Palmer, "Some Issues," 18.
49. Palmer, "Theorising," 120.
50. Ibid., 121.
51. Anthony Benezet, letters reprinted in George S. Brookes, *Friend Anthony Benezet* (Philadelphia: University of Pennsylvania Press, 1937), 225.
52. George Crosfield, *Memoirs of the Life and Gospel Labours of Samuel Fothergill . . . Some of His Descendants*, 2nd ed. (1843; London: William and Frederick G. Cash, 1857), 450.
53. Scott, *Knowledge of the Lord*, 31.
54. Ibid., 42.
55. Ibid., 41.

Notes

56. John Comly, *Journal of the Life and Religious Labours of John Comly late of Byberry, Pennsylvania* (Philadelphia: T. Ellwood Chapman, 1853), 577–78.
57. Ibid., 580–81.
58. R. Larry Shelton, *Christ and Covenant: Interpreting the Atonement for 21st Century Mission* (Tyrone, GA: Paternoster, 2006), 64.
59. Ibid., 206–7.
60. Fox, *Power of the Lord*, 4.
61. Ibid., 183.
62. Ibid., 282.
63. Ibid., 468.
64. Ibid., 351.
65. Walter R. Williams, *The Rich Heritage of Quakerism*, rev. ed. (1962; Newberg, OR: Barclay Press, 1987), 166.
66. Wilbur, *Life and Labors*, 232.
67. Elias Hicks, *Letters of Elias Hicks . . . Produce of Their Labor* (Philadelphia: T. Ellwood Chapman, 1861), 127–28.
68. Ibid., 99.
69. Elias Hicks, *The Journal of Elias Hicks*, ed. Paul Buckley (San Francisco: Inner Light Books, 2009), 175.
70. Hicks, *Letters*, 67.
71. Ibid.,124.
72. Ibid., 170.
73. Ibid.
74. Ibid., 216.
75. Hicks, *Journal*, 11.

Chapter Two

1. T. Vail Palmer, Jr., "Some Issues from Nineteenth-Century Quakerism," *Quaker Religious Thought* 29, no. 2 (January 1999): 18.
2. Henry Tuke, *The Principles of Religion, As Professed by the Society of Christians, Usually Called Quakers. . . .*, 7th ed. (1805; n.p.: Kessinger, 2005), 179–80.
3. Ibid., 39.
4. Joseph John Gurney, *A Peculiar People: The Rediscovery of Primitive Christianity*, 7th ed. (1824; repr., Richmond, IN: Friends United Press, 1979), 327.

5. Ibid., 347.
6. Ibid., 271–72.
7. George Fox, *The Journal of George Fox*, rev. ed. by John L. Nickalls (Cambridge: Cambridge University Press, 1952), 667.
8. Ibid., 27.
9. See Lisa Bieberman Kuenning, "Christ's Wife: A Vision for All Women," *Quaker Religious Thought* 18, no. 2 (Summer 1979): 14–15.
10. Fox, *Journal*, 665.
11. George Fox, *"The Power of the Lord Is Over All": The Pastoral Letters of George Fox*, ed. with introduction by T. Canby Jones (Richmond, IN: Friends United Press, 1990), 357.
12. Gurney, *Peculiar People*, 460–61.
13. Robin Scroggs, "Woman in the New Testament," in *The Interpreter's Dictionary of the Bible*, Supplementary Volume, ed. Keith Crim et al. (Nashville: Abingdon, 1976), 966.
14. Gurney, *Peculiar People*, 474.
15. Pink Dandelion, *An Introduction to Quakerism* (Cambridge: Cambridge University Press, 2007), 158.
16. See Rebecca Larson, *Daughters of Light: Quaker Women Preaching and Prophesying in the Colonies and Abroad, 1700–1775* (Chapel Hill, NC: University of North Carolina Press, 2000), 34.
17. See Larson, *Daughters of Light*, 344–45n44; T. Vail Palmer, Jr., "Quaker Peace Witness: The Biblical and Historical Roots," *Quaker Religious Thought* 23, no. 2 (Summer 1988): 47; and especially Bonnelyn Young Kunze, *Margaret Fell and the Rise of Quakerism* (Stanford: Stanford University Press, 1994), 143–68.
18. Edward Hicks, *Memoirs of the Life and Religious Labors of Edward Hicks, Late of Newtown, Bucks County, Pennsylvania* (Philadelphia: Merrihew & Thompson, 1851), 15.
19. Bliss Forbush, *Elias Hicks: Quaker Liberal* (New York: Columbia University Press, 1956), 289.
20. Hicks, *Memoirs of the Life*, 21.
21. Eleanore Price Mather, *Edward Hicks Primitive Quaker: His Religion in Relation to His Art*, Pendle Hill Pamphlet 170 (Wallingford, PA: Pendle Hill, 1970): 11.
22. Ibid., 13.
23. Ibid., 9.
24. Hicks, *Memoirs of the Life*, 267.
25. Ibid., 270–71.

26. H. Larry Ingle, *Quakers in Conflict: The Hicksite Reformation*, 2nd ed. (1986; Wallingford, PA: Pendle Hill, 1998), 110–11.
27. Hicks, *Memoirs of the Life*, 46.
28. See John Churchman, *An Account of the Gospel Labours . . . John Churchman*. . . . (Philadelphia: Joseph Crukshank, 1779), 9, 44, 187–88.
29. Job Scott, *Journal of the Life, Travels, and Gospel Labours . . . Job Scott* (1798; repr., n.p.: Kessinger, 2007), 75.
30. Hicks, *Memoirs of the Life*, 69.
31. Ibid., 30.
32. Ibid., 31–32.
33. Ibid., 47–48.
34. Ibid., 180.
35. John Wilbur, *Journal of the Life of John Wilbur*. . . . (Providence, RI: George H. Whitney, 1859), 46.
36. Ibid., 69.
37. John Wilbur, *A Narrative and Exposition . . . New England Yearly Meeting*. . . . (New York: Piercy & Reed, 1845), 240. Digital Quaker Collection, Earlham School of Religion, http://esr.earlham.edu/dqc.
38. Wilbur, *Journal of the Life*, 156.
39. Ibid., 118.
40. Ibid., 139–40.
41. Ibid.
42. John Wilbur, *Letters to a Friend, On Some of the Primitive Doctrines of Christianity* (1832; repr., n.p.: Kessinger, 2007), 34.
43. Ibid., 37.
44. Ibid., 16.
45. Ibid., 14–15.
46. Ibid., 5.
47. Ibid., 5n.
48. Alexander C. Purdy, "The Epistle to the Hebrews: Introduction and Exegesis," in *The Interpreter's Bible*, ed. George Arthur Buttrick et al. (New York and Nashville: Abingdon, 1955), 11:652–53.
49. Wilbur, *Letters to a Friend*, 10.
50. Ibid., 11.
51. Ibid., 12.
52. Wilbur, *Journal of the Life*, 158.
53. Ibid., 182.

54. Ibid., 280.
55. Ibid., 269.
56. Palmer, "Quaker Peace Witness," 48–53.
57. Peter Brock, "The Peace Testimony in 'A Garden Enclosed,'" *Quaker History* 54, no. 2 (Fall 1965): 69.
58. Jonathan Dymond, *Essays on the Principles of Morality and on the Private and Political Rights and Obligations of Mankind*, abridged and reprinted (1829; repr., Philadelphia: Book Committee of the Philadelphia Yearly Meeting of Friends, 1896), 10.
59. Ibid., 15.
60. Ibid., 21.
61. Ibid., 29.
62. Ibid., 34.
63. Ibid.
64. Jonathan Dymond, *An Inquiry into the Accordancy of War with the Principles of Christianity . . . on Some of Its Effects* (1823; repr., New York: William Wood, 1870), 63.
65. Dymond, Essays on the Principles (1896), 21.
66. Ibid., 22.
67. Ibid., 89.
68. Ibid., 96.
69. Ibid., 100.
70. Ibid., 68–69.
71. Ibid., 20.
72. Ibid., 80.
73. Ibid., 61.
74. Ibid., 80.
75. Ibid., 81.
76. Ibid., 428.
77. Ibid., 210.
78. Ibid., 208.
79. Ibid., 41.
80. Ibid., 40.
81. Ibid., 203–4.
82. Dymond, *Inquiry into the Accordancy*, 87–88; also in Jonathan Dymond, *Observations on the Applicability of the Pacific Principles of the New Testament. . . .*, Tract 7 of the Society for the Promotion of Permanent and Universal Peace (London: Hamilton, Adams, 1835), 17.
83. Ibid., 14n.

84. Jonathan Dymond, *Essays on the Principles of Morality and on the Private and Political Rights and Obligations of Mankind* (1829; repr., New York: Robert B. Collins, 1850), 249–50.
85. Dymond, *Essays on the Principles* (1896), 309.
86. Ibid.
87. Ibid., 294.
88. Ibid., 296.
89. Ibid., 321.
90. Dymond, *Essays on the Principles* (1850), 31.
91. Dymond, *Inquiry into the Accordancy*, 69.
92. Ibid., 85.
93. Dymond, *Essays on the Principles* (1896), 90.
94. Ibid., 116.
95. Ibid., 115.
96. Ibid., 24.
97. Dymond, *Essays on the Principles* (1850), 15–16.
98. Dymond, *Essays on the Principles* (1896), 8.
99. Dymond, *Inquiry into the Accordancy*, 87.
100. Dymond, *Essays on the Principles* (1896), 473.
101. Ibid., 25.
102. Ibid., 26.
103. Dymond, *Inquiry into the Accordancy*, 41.
104. Dymond, *Essays on the Principles* (1896), 49.
105. Dymond, *Inquiry into the Accordancy*, 40.
106. Dymond, *Essays on the Principles* (1896), 41.
107. Dymond, *Essays on the Principles* (1850), 325.
108. Ibid., 441.
109. Dymond, *Inquiry into the Accordancy*, 37.
110. Ibid., 89.
111. Dymond, *Essays on the Principles* (1896), 99–100.
112. Ibid., 333–34.
113. Dymond, *Inquiry into the Accordancy*, 93.
114. Dymond, *Essays on the Principles* (1896), 443.
115. Ibid., 470.
116. Dymond, *Essays on the Principles* (1850), 508.
117. Robert Barclay, *An Apology for the True Christian Divinity. . . .* , stereotype ed. (1678; Philadelphia: Friends' Book Store, 1908), 76 [Prop. 3, Sect. 2].
118. Dymond, *Essays on the Principles* (1850), xiv.

119. Margaret Hope Bacon, *Valiant Friend: The Life of Lucretia Mott* (1980; Philadelphia: Friends General Conference, 1999), 22.
120. Ibid., 185.
121. Ibid., 54.
122. Lucretia Mott, *Slavery and "The Woman Question". . . .*, in *Journal of the Friends' Historical Society*, Supplement 23, ed. Frederick B. Tolles (London: Friends' Historical Society, 1952).
123. Bacon, *Valiant Friend*, 100.
124. Mott, *Slavery*, 22.
125. Bacon, *Valiant Friend*, 108.
126. Ibid., 143.
127. Ibid., 145.
128. Lucretia Mott, *Lucretia Mott: Her Complete Speeches and Sermons*, ed. with introduction by Dana Greene (New York and Toronto: Edward Mellen, 1980), 38.
129. Ibid., 125.
130. Ibid., 131.
131. Ibid., 71.
132. Ibid., 72.
133. Ibid., 110.
134. Ibid., 214.
135. Ibid., 95.
136. Ibid., 128.
137. Ibid., 173.
138. Ibid., 229.
139. Lucretia C. Mott, *Selected Letters of Lucretia Coffin Mott*, ed. Beverly Wilson Palmer (Urbana: University of Illinois Press, 2002), 175–76.
140. Ibid., 461.
141. Mott, *Complete Speeches*, 109.
142. Ibid., 111.
143. Ibid., 105.
144. Mott, *Selected Letters*, 234.
145. Mott, *Complete Speeches*, 26–27.
146. Ibid., 27.
147. Ibid., 28.
148. Thomas D. Hamm, "'A Protest Against Protestantism': Hicksite Friends and the Bible in the Nineteenth Century," *Quaker Studies* 6, no. 2 (March 2002): 190.
149. Mott, *Complete Speeches*, 229–30.

150. Ibid., 235.
151. Ibid., 129.
152. Ibid., 164.
153. Ibid., 53.
154. Ibid., 83.
155. Ibid., 107.
156. Thomas Hamm, email message to Michael Birkel and author, January 20, 2010.
157. Abraham Lawton, *Some Testimonies of Truth, Set Forth for the Healing of the Nations* (1866; repr., n.p.: Kessinger, 2007), 50.
158. Ibid., 48.
159. Ibid., 62.
160. Ibid., 32.
161. Ibid., 54.
162. Ibid., 26.
163. Ibid., 28.
164. Ibid., 38.
165. Ibid., 73.
166. Ibid., 101.
167. Ibid., 102.
168. Ibid., 103.
169. Ibid., 43–59.
170. Ibid., 44.
171. Ibid., 46.
172. Ibid.
173. Ibid., 48.
174. Ibid., 51.
175. Ibid., 52.
176. Ibid., 97.

Chapter Three

1. Thomas D. Hamm, *The Transformation of American Quakerism: Orthodox Friends, 1800–1907*, Religion in North America (Bloomington, IN: Indiana University Press, 1992), 77–78.
2. Ibid., 125.
3. Dougan Clark and Joseph H. Smith, *David B. Updegraff and His Work* (Cincinnati: M. W. Knapp, 1895), 38–39.

4. J. Brent Bill, *David B. Updegraff, Quaker Holiness Preacher* (Richmond IN: Friends United Press, 1983), 13.
5. Ibid., 17.
6. Ibid., 19.
7. Clark and Smith, *David B. Updegraff*, 220.
8. Ibid., 228.
9. Ibid., 229.
10. Ibid., 230.
11. David B. Updegraff, *Old Corn; or, Sermons and Addresses on the Spiritual Life*, introduction by Joseph H. Smith (Boston: McDonald & Gill, 1892), 230.
12. Ibid., 233.
13. Ibid., 235.
14. Ibid., 236.
15. Ibid., 125.
16. Ibid., 123.
17. Ibid., 200–201.
18. Ibid., 198.
19. Ibid., 204.
20. Ibid., 205–6.
21. Ibid., 204.
22. Ibid., 205.
23. Ibid.
24. Clark and Smith, *David B. Updegraff*, 243.
25. Bill, *David B. Updegraff*, 38.
26. Ibid., 33–34.
27. Clark and Smith, *David B. Updegraff*, 223.
28. Ibid., 224.
29. Ibid.
30. Ibid., 225–26.
31. Ibid., 19–20.
32. Ibid., 25–26.
33. Ibid., 96.
34. Ibid., 102.
35. Ibid., 115.
36. Clark and Smith, *David B. Updegraff*, 9.
37. Hugh Barbour and J. William Frost, *The Quakers*, Denominations in America (Westport, CT: Greenwood, 1988), 3:304.

38. Elbert Russell, *Elbert Russell, Quaker: An Autobiography* (Jackson, TN: Friendly Press, 1956), 80.
39. Dougan Clark, *The Offices of the Holy Spirit*, ed. Anna Louise Spann (1878; Portland, OR: Evangel, 1945), 10.
40. Ibid., 208.
41. Dougan Clark, *Instructions to Christian Converts* (1889; repr., Salem, OH: Schmul, 1978), 15.
42. Dougan Clark, *The Theology of Holiness* (1893; San Diego: ICON Group International, 2008), 52.
43. Ibid., 1.
44. Clark, *Offices*, 207–8.
45. Ibid., 214.
46. Hamm, *Transformation*, 127.
47. Dougan Clark, *The Holy Ghost Dispensation*, 4th ed. (New York: Fleming H. Revell, 1891), 148.
48. Ibid., 150.
49. Ibid., 149.
50. Ibid., 10–11.
51. Ibid., 15–16.
52. Ibid., 65.
53. Ibid.
54. Ibid., 67.
55. Ibid., 67–68.
56. Ibid., 66.
57. Ibid., 68.
58. Ibid., 86.
59. Rufus M. Jones, *Finding the Trail of Life* (1926; repr., New York: Macmillan, 1931), 138–39.
60. Ibid., 139.
61. Elizabeth Gray Vining, *Friend of Life: The Biography of Rufus M. Jones* (Philadelphia: J. B. Lippincott, 1958), 34.
62. Rufus M. Jones, *The Trail of Life in College* (New York: Macmillan, 1929), 39.
63. Ibid., 89.
64. Margaret Hope Bacon, *Valiant Friend: The Life of Lucretia Mott* (1980; Philadelphia: Friends General Conference, 1999), 120.
65. Ibid., 133.
66. Ralph Waldo Emerson, *Essays: First and Second Series* (New York: A. L. Burt, [1900?]), 46.

67. Ibid., 201.
68. Ibid., 392.
69. Ralph Waldo Emerson, *Representative Men* (1883; repr., Honolulu: University Press of the Pacific, 2010), 94–95.
70. Ibid., 113.
71. Ibid., 119.
72. Jones, *Trail of Life in College*, 90–91.
73. T. Vail Palmer, Jr., "Response" [to Calvin J. Keene, "Historic Quakerism and Mysticism"], *Quaker Religious Thought* 7, no. 2 (Autumn 1965): 30.
74. Rufus M. Jones, *The Great Succession of Torch Bearers* (Philadelphia: Young Friends Movement of Philadelphia, 1946), 5.
75. Jones, *Trail of Life in College*, 189.
76. Ibid., 133.
77. Vining, *Friend of Life*, 39.
78. Rufus M. Jones, *Eli and Sybil Jones: Their Life and Work* (Philadelphia: Henry T. Coates, 1889), 301.
79. Vining, *Friend of Life*, 64.
80. Ibid., 68.
81. Caroline Emelia Stephen, *Quaker Strongholds*, Centenary ed. (1890; Chula Vista, CA: Wind and Rock, 1995), 3.
82. Ibid., 13.
83. Ibid., 13–14.
84. Ibid., 16.
85. Ibid., 90.
86. Ibid., 11.
87. Caroline Emelia Stephen, *Light Arising: Thoughts on the Central Radiance* (1908; repr., Lexington, KY: University of Michigan Library, 2010), 47–49.
88. Ibid., 60–61.
89. Ibid., 62.
90. Irene Pickard, coll., *Memories of J. Rendel Harris, Collected by Irene Pickard* (Sutton, Surry: Express Lithographic, 1978), 3.
91. James Rendel Harris, *Union with God: A Series of Addresses*, 2nd ed. (1895; repr., Breinigsville, PA: Bibliolife, 2010), 129–30.
92. Ibid., 131.
93. Ibid., 67–68.
94. Ibid., 33.
95. Ibid., 42.

Notes

96. Ibid., 46–47.
97. Martin Davie, *British Quaker Theology Since 1895* (Lewiston, NY: Edwin Mellen, 1997), 1.
98. Rufus M. Jones, *The Later Periods of Quakerism* (1921; repr., n.p.: Kessinger, 2008), 2:976–77.
99. The Society of Friends, *Report of the Proceedings of the Conference of Members of the Society of Friends . . . 1895* (London: Headley Brothers, 1896).
100. Ibid., 42–48.
101. Ibid., 75–83.
102. Ibid., 176–83.
103. Ibid., 218–26.
104. Ibid., 240–46.
105. Ibid., 307–15.
106. Ibid., 220.
107. Ibid., 222–23.
108. Ibid., 246.
109. Stephen Allott, *John Wilhelm Rowntree, 1868–1905, and the Beginnings of Modern Quakerism* (York, England: Sessions Book Trust, 1994), 3.
110. Ibid., 25.
111. Rufus M. Jones, *John Wilhelm Rowntree* (1942; repr., LaVergne, TN: Kessinger, 2010), 4th [unnumbered] page.
112. Allott, *John Wilhelm Rowntree*, 26.
113. Ibid., 22.
114. Jones, *John Wilhelm Rowntree*, 6th [unnumbered] page.
115. Allott, *John Wilhelm Rowntree*, 22.
116. Vining, *Friend of Life*, 71.
117. Ibid.
118. Jones, *John Wilhelm Rowntree*, 8th [unnumbered] page.
119. Vining, *Friend of Life*, 71.
120. Jones, *Trail of Life in College*, 190.
121. Jones, *John Wilhelm Rowntree*, 9th [unnumbered] page.
122. Allott, *John Wilhelm Rowntree*, 61.
123. Davie, *British Quaker Theology*, 83.
124. Vining, *Friend of Life*, 87.
125. Allott, *John Wilhelm Rowntree*, 79.
126. Ibid., 92.
127. Ibid., 80.

128. Rufus M. Jones, *The Trail of Life in the Middle Years* (New York: Macmillan, 1934), 82.
129. Allott, *John Wilhelm Rowntree*, 107.
130. John Wilhelm Rowntree, *Palestine Notes: And Other Papers*, ed. Joshua Rowntree (London: Headley Brothers, 1906), 255.
131. John Wilhelm Rowntree, *Essays and Addresses*, ed. Joshua Rowntree (1906; repr., n.p.: General Books, 2010), 91.
132. Ibid., 92.
133. Ibid., 143.
134. Ibid., 144–46.
135. Allott, *John Wilhelm Rowntree*, 86.
136. Rowntree, *Essays and Addresses*, 22–56.
137. Vining, *Friend of Life*, 116.
138. Jones, *Middle Years*, 85.
139. Vining, *Friend of Life*, 116.
140. Jones, *Middle Years*, 89.
141. Ibid., 90.
142. Ibid., 100.
143. Rufus M. Jones, *The Double Search: Studies in Atonement and Prayer* (1906; repr., n.p.: General Books, 2009), 3.
144. Ibid., 7.
145. Ibid.
146. Ibid., 9.
147. Ibid., 10.
148. Ibid., 11–12.
149. Ibid., 12–14.
150. Ibid., 14–15.
151. Rowntree, *Essays and Addresses*, 145.
152. Jones, *Double Search*, 16–17.
153. Gregory Anderson Love, *Love, Violence, and the Cross: How the Nonviolent God Saves Us through the Cross of Christ*, Cascade Books (Eugene, OR: Wipf and Stock, 2010), 89.
154. Ibid., 104.
155. Ibid.
156. Ibid., 104–6.
157. Luke Woodard, *Sketches of a Life of 75: in Three Parts; Biographical, Historical and Descriptive* (Richmond, IN: Nicholson, 1907), 7–8.
158. Ibid., 9–10.
159. Ibid., 124.

160. Luke Woodard, *What Is Truth?* (Auburn, NY: Knapp, Peck & Thomson, 1901), 11.
161. Luke Woodard, *The Morning Star: A Treatise on the Nature, Offices, and Work of the Lord Jesus Christ* (1875; repr., n.p.: Kessinger, 2007), 35.
162. Woodard, *What Is Truth?*, 96.
163. Luke Woodard, *A Panorama of Wonders: A Brief Discussion of Some of the Principal Doctrines of the Christian Religion* (Richmond, IN: Nicholson, 1921), 64.
164. Ibid., 85.
165. Woodard, *Morning Star*, 170.
166. Ibid., 126–63.
167. Ibid., 129.
168. Ibid., 135–36.
169. Ibid., 139.
170. Ibid., 158.
171. Woodard, *What Is Truth?*, 94–130.
172. Ibid., 99–100.
173. Ibid., 103–13.
174. Ibid., 113–14.
175. Ibid., 117.
176. Ibid., 118.
177. Woodard, *Morning Star*, 103.
178. Ibid., 225.
179. Woodard, *Panorama of Wonders*, 73.
180. J. Denny Weaver, *The Nonviolent Atonement* (Grand Rapids, MI: William B. Eerdmans, 2001), 201; T. Vail Palmer, Jr., "Theorising a Quaker View of the Atonement," *Quaker Studies* 16, no. 1 (September 2011): 115.
181. Woodard, *What Is Truth?*, 112.
182. Ibid., 116.
183. Ibid., 116n.
184. Ibid., 127.
185. Ibid., 130.
186. Margaret J. Benefiel, "The Doctrine of the Atonement: The Quaker Contribution—A Revisionist View," *Quaker Religious Thought* 23, no. 4 (Winter 1988–89): 22.
187. Palmer, "Theorising," 113.
188. Woodard, *Sketches of a Life*, 235.
189. Woodard, *Morning Star*, 96n.

190. William Penn, *The Select Works of William Penn*, 3 vols. 4th ed. (1825; repr., New York: Kraus Preprint, 1971), 1:129.
191. Ibid., 1:133.
192. Woodard, *Morning Star*, 96–97.
193. George Fox, *The Works of George Fox*, 8 vols. New Foundation Publication (1831; repr., State College, PA: George Fox Fund, 1990), 3:180.
194. Ibid., 5:126.
195. T. Vail Palmer, Jr., "Some Issues from Nineteenth-Century Quakerism," *Quaker Religious Thought* 29, no. 2 (January 1999): 16.
196. Woodard, *Morning Star*, 104.
197. James Dudley, *The Life of Edward Grubb, 1854–1939: A Spiritual Pilgrimage* (London: James Clark, 1946), 43.
198. Ibid., 58.
199. Ibid., 59.
200. Ibid., 71.
201. Ibid., 106.
202. Ibid., 108–9.
203. Ibid., 127.
204. Ibid., 138.
205. Edward Grubb, *The Personality of God: And Other Essays in Constructive Christian Thought* (London: Headley Brothers, 1911), 36.
206. Ibid., 70–71.
207. Edward Grubb, *The Bible: Its Nature and Inspiration*, 2nd ed. (1920; London: Swarthmore Press, 1933), 51.
208. Ibid., 55.
209. Edward Grubb, *Authority in Religion* (London: Swarthmore Press, 1924), 60–61.
210. Grubb, *Bible*, 223.
211. Grubb, *Authority in Religion*, 107.
212. Grubb, *Bible*, 238.
213. Grubb, *Authority in Religion*, 110.
214. Grubb, *Bible*, 239.
215. Ibid., 230.
216. Ibid., 238.
217. Ibid., 243.
218. Grubb, *Authority in Religion*, 107.
219. Grubb, *Bible*, 244–46.
220. Ibid., 246–47.

221. Dudley, *Edward Grubb*, 110.
222. Edward Grubb, *What Is Quakerism?: An Exposition of the Leading Principles and Practices of the Society of Friends, as Based on the Experience of "The Inward Light"* (1917; repr., Lexington, KY: University of Michigan Library, 2011), 218.
223. Edward Grubb, *Christianity as Truth*, The Nature of Christianity (London: Swarthmore Press, 1928), 2:107–31.
224. Ibid., 130.
225. Ibid., 129–30.
226. Grubb, *What Is Quakerism*, 43.
227. Edward Grubb, *The Meaning of the Cross: A Study of the Atonement* (London: George Allen & Unwin, 1922), 15.
228. Ibid., 16.
229. Ibid., 47–48.
230. Ibid., 69.
231. Ibid., 98.
232. Ibid., 140–41.
233. Ibid., 141–42.
234. Ibid., 152–53.
235. Ibid., 153–54.
236. Ibid., 156.
237. Woodard, *What Is Truth?*, 63–66.
238. Grubb, *Authority in Religion*, 62–65.
239. Ibid., 67.
240. Ibid., 69–72.
241. Ibid., 74–75.
242. Ibid., 78–80.
243. Woodard, *Panorama of Wonders*, 29–30.
244. D. M. Baillie, *God Was in Christ: An Essay on Incarnation and Atonement* (New York: Charles Scribner's Sons, 1948), 95.
245. Ibid., 94–95.
246. Ibid., 95–96.
247. Ibid., 12–13.
248. Russell, *Autobiography*, 82.
249. Ibid., 74.
250. Ibid., 11–13.
251. Ibid., 91.
252. Ibid., 96.
253. Ibid., 97.

254. Ibid., 101–2.
255. Ibid., 99.
256. Ibid., 103.
257. Ibid., 105.
258. Ibid., 117.
259. Elbert Russell, *Jesus of Nazareth in the Light of Today* (1909; repr., n.p.: Nabu Press, 2011), 9–10.
260. Russell, *Autobiography*, 143.
261. Ibid., 144.
262. Russell, *Jesus of Nazareth*, 27–29.
263. Weaver, *Nonviolent Atonement*, 43.
264. R. Larry Shelton, *Christ and Covenant: Interpreting the Atonement for 21st Century Mission* (Tyrone, GA: Paternoster, 2006), 83, 99.
265. Elbert Russell, *The Christian Life*, William Penn Lecture (Philadelphia: Walter H. Jenkins, 1916), 43.
266. Ibid., 45–46.
267. Russell, *Autobiography*, 240.

Chapter Four

1. Martin Davie, *British Quaker Theology Since 1895* (Lewiston, NY: Edwin Mellen, 1997), 83.
2. Ibid., 81.
3. J. Rendel Harris, *Fragments of the Commentary of Ephrem Syrus upon the Diatessaron* (1895; repr., Lexington, KY: University of Michigan Library, 2012), 1.
4. Ibid., 7.
5. Ibid., 8.
6. J. Rendel Harris, *The Diatessaron of Tatian: A Preliminary Study* (1890; repr., n.p.: Nabu Public Domain Reprints, n.d.), 56.
7. Rendel Harris, *The Origin of the Prologue to St. John's Gospel* (1917; repr., Lexington, KY: Cornell University Library, 2012), 8–9.
8. Ibid., 18.
9. Ibid., 28.
10. J. Rendel Harris, *The Newly-Recovered Gospel of St. Peter: With a Full Account of the Same* (1893; repr., Eugene, OR: Wipf and Stock, 2006), 16.
11. Ibid., 60.

12. Ibid., 61–62.
13. Rendel Harris with Vacher Burch, *Testimonies*, Part 1 (1916; repr., n.p.: Nabu Public Domain Reprints, 2010), 40.
14. Ibid., 41.
15. Ibid., 48–49.
16. Ibid., 52.
17. Sherman E. Johnson, "The Gospel According to St. Matthew: Introduction and Exegesis," in *The Interpreter's Bible*, ed. George Arthur Buttrick et al. (New York and Nashville: Abingdon-Cokesbury, 1951), 7:593.
18. Harris and Burch, *Testimonies* 1, 54.
19. Ibid., 55.
20. Ibid., 56.
21. Ibid., 60.
22. Ibid., 67.
23. Ibid., 74.
24. Ibid., 21.
25. Ibid., 122.
26. Rendel Harris with Vacher Burch, *Testimonies*, Part 2 (1920; repr., n.p.: Nabu Public Domain Reprints, 2010), 80.
27. Ibid., 95.
28. Ibid., 96–97.
29. Ibid., 96.
30. Ibid., 97.
31. Ibid., 82.
32. Irene Pickard, coll., *Memories of J. Rendel Harris, Collected by Irene Pickard* (Sutton, Surry: Express Lithographic, 1978), 32.
33. Edward Grubb, *The Bible: Its Nature and Inspiration*, 2nd ed. (1920; London: Swarthmore Press, 1933), 27.
34. Ibid., 195.
35. Harris, *Testimonies* 1, 108ff; Grubb, *Bible*, 196.
36. Howard Clark Kee, Franklin W. Young, and Karlfried Froehlich, *Understanding the New Testament*, 3rd ed. (Englewood Cliffs, NJ: Prentice–Hall, 1973), 61.
37. Marilyn J. Lundberg, "Testimonia," West Semitic Research Project, accessed July 17, 2012, http://usc.edu/dept/LAS/wsrp/educational_site/dead_sea_scrolls/4QTestimonia.shtml.

38. Larry Hurtado, "Early Christian 'Testimonia' Texts," *Larry Hurtado's Blog*, April 14, 2011, http://larryhurtado.wordpress.com/2011/04/14/early-christian-testimonia-texts/.
39. Elbert Russell, *Elbert Russell, Quaker: An Autobiography* (Jackson, TN: Friendly Press, 1956), 107.
40. Ibid., 108.
41. Ibid., 177.
42. Elbert Russell, *Paronomasia and Kindred Phenomena in the New Testament*, PhD dissertation, University of Chicago (1920; repr., Lexington, KY: Forgotten Books, 2012), 6.
43. Elbert Russell, *The Parables of Jesus: A Course of Ten Lessons Arranged for Daily Study* (New York: National Board of the Young Women's Christian Association of the United States of America, 1909) 5.
44. Elbert Russell, *The Beatitudes: A Series of Studies* (Garden City, NY: Doubleday, Doran, 1929), vii.
45. Russell, *Autobiography*, 261.
46. Ibid., 100.
47. Elbert Russell, *The Message of the Fourth Gospel* (Nashville: Cokesbury, 1932), 15.
48. Ibid., 20.
49. Ibid., 157–58.
50. Ibid., 159.
51. Russell, *Autobiography*, 338.
52. Elbert Russell, "The Book of Revelation: With an Introduction, Paraphrase and Notes" (unpublished manuscript, Duke University Library), Intro. 63.
53. Ibid., Comm. 4.
54. Ibid., Intro. 91.
55. G. Ernest Wright and Reginald H. Fuller, *The Book of the Acts of God: Contemporary Scholarship Interprets the Bible*, Anchor Books ed. (1957; Garden City, NY: Doubleday, 1960), 375.
56. Margaret Hope Bacon, *Let This Life Speak: The Legacy of Henry Joel Cadbury* (Philadelphia: University of Pennsylvania Press, 1987), 1.
57. Henry J. Cadbury, *The Style and Literary Method of Luke: The Diction of Luke and Acts*, Harvard Theological Studies 6 (1919; repr., n.p.: Kessinger, 2007), 39.
58. Ibid., 40.
59. Ibid., 50.

60. Henry J. Cadbury, *The Making of Luke-Acts*, 2nd ed. with new introduction by Paul N. Anderson (1927; Peabody, MA: Hendrickson, 1999), 360.
61. Henry J. Cadbury, *National Ideals in the Old Testament* (New York: Charles Scribner's Sons, 1920), vii.
62. Paul N. Anderson, "Foreword," in *The Making of Luke-Acts*, by Henry J. Cadbury, 2nd ed. (1927; Peabody, MA: Hendrickson, 1999), vii–viii.
63. Cadbury, *Making of Luke-Acts*, 149.
64. Ibid., 152.
65. Ibid., 153.
66. Ibid., 154.
67. Ibid., 267–68.
68. Ibid., 280.
69. Henry J. Cadbury, *The Peril of Modernizing Jesus* (1937; repr., Eugene, OR: Wipf and Stock, 2006), 141.
70. Ibid., 124–25.
71. Ibid., 72–73.
72. Bacon, *Let This Life Speak*, 84, 86, 102.
73. Cadbury, *Peril of Modernizing Jesus*, 98–99.
74. Rufus M. Jones, *Studies in Mystical Religion* (London: Macmillan, 1909), 3.
75. Ibid., 4–5.
76. Ibid., 6–7.
77. Cadbury, *Peril of Modernizing Jesus*, 186–87.
78. Henry J. Cadbury, *Jesus: What Manner of Man*, with new foreword by Paul N. Anderson (1947; repr., Eugene, OR: Wipf and Stock, 2008), 94.
79. Bacon, *Let This Life Speak*, 88.
80. Luther A. Weigle with members of the Revision Committee, *An Introduction to the Revised Standard Version of the New Testament* (n.p.: The International Council of Religious Education, 1946), 6–7.
81. Ibid., 44–52.
82. Burton H. Throckmorton, Jr., ed., *Gospel Parallels: A Synopsis of the First Three Gospels*, 2nd ed. (1949; repr., New York: Thomas Nelson & Sons, 1965), iii.
83. Henry J. Cadbury, "The New Testament and Early Christian Literature," in *The Interpreter's Bible*, ed. George Arthur Buttrick et al. (New York and Nashville: Abingdon–Cokesbury, 1951), 7:32–42.

84. Henry J. Cadbury, "Acts and Eschatology," in *The Background of the New Testament and Its Eschatology: Studies in Honor of C. H. Dodd*, ed. W. D. Davies and D. Daube (1954; repr., Cambridge: Cambridge University Press, 1964), 300–21.
85. Ibid.
86. Cadbury, "New Testament," 35–36.
87. Henry J. Cadbury, *The Book of Acts in History* (1955; repr., Eugene, OR: Wipf and Stock, 2004), 108–9n37.
88. Ibid., 96.
89. Henry J. Cadbury, "A Quaker Approach to the Bible" (Ward Lecture, Guilford College, Greensboro, NC, 1953).
90. Henry J. Cadbury, *Jesus and Judaism and the Emphasis of Jesus*, Shrewsbury Lecture (Indianapolis: John Woolman Press, 1962).
91. James M. Robinson, *A New Quest of the Historical Jesus*, Studies in Biblical Theology 25 (London: SCM Press, 1959).
92. Henry J. Cadbury, *The Eclipse of the Historical Jesus*, Pendle Hill Pamphlet 133 (Wallingford, PA: Pendle Hill, 1964): 23.
93. Ibid., 24–25.
94. Ibid., 22.
95. Bacon, *Let This Life Speak*, 199.
96. Quoted in Bacon, *Let This Life Speak*, 117–18.
97. Thomas R. Kelly, *Reality of the Spiritual World*, Pendle Hill Pamphlet 21 (Wallingford, PA: Pendle Hill, 1942): 24.
98. Richenda C. Scott, *Herbert G Wood: A Memoir of His Life and Thought* (London: Friends Home Service Committee, 1967), 7.
99. Ibid., 19.
100. Ibid., 40.
101. Ibid., 45.
102. Ibid., 47.
103. Ibid., 54.
104. Ibid., 81.
105. Ibid.
106. Ibid., 89.
107. Ibid., 99.
108. Ibid., 52.
109. Ibid., 133–34.
110. H. G. Wood, *Christianity and the Nature of History*, Hulsean Lectures 1933–34 (Cambridge: Cambridge University Press, 1934), 197.
111. Ibid., 110–11.

112. Ibid., 134–35.
113. H. G. Wood, *Did Christ Really Live?* (London: Student Christian Movement, 1938), 184.
114. Herbert G. Wood, *Why Did Christ Die?*, Study Broadcasts (London: Epworth, 1953), 16.
115. Ibid., 33.
116. Ibid., 42.
117. H. G. Wood, *Belief and Unbelief Since 1850* (Cambridge: Cambridge University Press, 1955), 9.
118. Ibid., 42–43.
119. Ibid., 43.
120. Herbert G. Wood, *Quakerism and the Future of the Church*, Swarthmore Lecture (1920; repr., LaVergne, TN: Bibliolife, 2011), 31–32, 36–37.
121. Timothy Gorringe, *God's Just Vengeance: Crime, Violence and the Rhetoric of Salvation*, Cambridge Studies in Ideology and Religion 9 (1996; digital pr., Cambridge: Cambridge University Press, 2002), 103; see T. Vail Palmer, Jr., "Theorising a Quaker View of the Atonement," *Quaker Studies* 16, no. 1 (September 2011): 115.
122. Wood, *Quakerism and the Future*, 39–42.
123. Quoted in Bacon, *Let This Life Speak*, 44.
124. H. G. Wood, *Jesus in the Twentieth Century* (London: Lutterworth, 1960), 126.
125. Ibid., 128.
126. Ibid., 146–48.
127. Cadbury, *Peril of Modernizing Jesus*, 96.
128. Wood, *Twentieth Century*, 153.
129. Ibid., 155.
130. Ibid., 157–58.
131. Ibid., 185–86.
132. Ibid., 197.
133. Cadbury, *Eclipse*, 23.
134. Ibid., 22.
135. Donald Ebor, "Preface to the New English Bible," in *The New English Bible: With the Apocrypha*, 2nd ed. New Testament; 1st ed. Old Testament and Apocrypha (1961; Oxford: Oxford University Press and Cambridge University Press, 1970), v.
136. Scott, *Herbert G. Wood*, 202–3.
137. Ebor, "Preface," v.
138. Ibid., vi.

139. Scott, *Herbert G. Wood*, 203.
140. Aubrey F. Hill, "George Henry Boobyer: Born 29 vi 1902 Died 17 i 1999," testimony in *Britain Yearly Meeting Proceedings, 2000*, 50.
141. George Boobyer, *Fruits of the Spirit: According to New Testament Teaching* (Richmond, IN: Friends United Press, 1975), 63.
142. George H. Boobyer, *The Bible and the Light Within*, Study in Fellowship 34 (London: Friends Home Service Committee, 1973), 2nd [unnumbered] page.
143. Jennifer Hughes, "George Boobyer, 1902–1999," (obituary) *The Friend* 26 (November 1999): 11.
144. George Henry Boobyer, *"Thanksgiving" and the "Glory of God" in Paul* (Borna-Leipzig, Germany: Universitatsverlag von Robert Noske, 1929), 4.
145. Ibid., 14.
146. Ibid., 89.
147. G. H. Boobyer, *St. Mark and the Transfiguration Story* (Edinburgh: T. & T. Clark, 1942), 87.
148. G. H. Boobyer, "Jesus as 'Theos' in the New Testament," *Bulletin of the John Rylands Library* 50, no. 2 (Spring 1968): 258–59.
149. Boobyer, *Light Within*, 44.
150. Boobyer, *Fruits of the Spirit*, 54.
151. Ibid., 57–58.
152. Ibid., 24.
153. Ibid., 64.
154. George H. Boobyer, *Are the Scriptures "Very Precious" Still?*, Rufus Jones Lecture, April 18, 1980 (Philadelphia: Religious Education Committee of Friends General Conference, 1981), 17.
155. Wilmer A. Cooper, *Growing Up Plain, Among Conservative Wilburite Quakers: The Journey of a Public Friend* (Richmond, IN: Friends United Press, 1999), 96.
156. Alexander C. Purdy, *The Way of Christ: Studies in Discipleship* (1918; repr., San Bernardino, CA: New York Public Library, 2013), 120.
157. Ibid., 58, 60.
158. Ibid., 122.
159. Cadbury, *Peril of Modernizing Jesus*, 99.
160. G. H. C. Macgregor and A. C. Purdy, *Jew and Greek; Tutors unto Christ: The Jewish and Hellenistic Background of the New Testament* (London: Ivor Nicholson and Watson, 1936), 163–64.

161. Alexander C. Purdy, "The Epistle to the Hebrews: Introduction and Exegesis," in *The Interpreter's Bible*, ed. George Arthur Buttrick et al. (New York and Nashville: Abingdon, 1955), 11:598.
162. Ibid., 586.
163. Ibid., 682–83.
164. Ibid., 705.
165. Ibid., 757–58.
166. George Fox, *The Works of George Fox*, 8 vols. New Foundation Publication (1831; repr., State College, PA: George Fox Fund, 1990), 4:290.
167. Purdy, "Hebrews," 618.
168. Alexander C. Purdy, "Paul the Apostle," in *The Interpreter's Dictionary of the Bible*, ed. George Arthur Buttrick et al. (New York and Nashville: Abingdon, 1962), 3:695.
169. Purdy, "Hebrews," 659.
170. Karl Barth, *The Word of God and the Word of Man*, trans. Douglas Horton, 1st Harper Torchbook ed. (1928; New York: Harper & Brothers, 1957), 34.
171. Ibid., 44–45.
172. Ibid., 45–46.
173. Ibid., 47.
174. Ibid., 48–50.
175. Karl Barth, *The Doctrine of God*, ed. G. W. Bromiley and T. F. Torrance, trans. G. W. Bromiley et al., Church Dogmatics (1942; Edinburgh: T. & T. Clark, 1957), 2:4.
176. Lawrence Cockcroft Cargill, *Moses Bailey: Memoir of a Friend* (Bethlehem, CT: LCC Publishing, 2000), 4.
177. Ibid., 14.
178. Ibid., 29.
179. Ibid., 30.
180. Ibid., 31.
181. Ibid., 36.
182. Ibid., 42.
183. Ibid., 47.
184. Ibid., 47–49.
185. Ibid., 57.
186. Moses Bailey, *The Prophetic Word: Ancient and Modern* (Philadelphia: Religious Education Committee, Friends General Conference, 1968), 4.

187. Ibid., 5.
188. Ibid., 5–6.
189. Ibid., 52.
190. Ibid., 49.
191. Ibid., 51.
192. Ibid., 80–82.
193. Elton Trueblood, *The Humor of Christ* (New York: Harper & Row, 1964), 12.
194. Howard R. Macy, *Laughing Pilgrims: Humor and the Spiritual Journey* (Milton Keynes, UK and Waynesboro, GA: Paternoster, 2006), xiii.
195. Ibid., 14.
196. Ibid., 15.
197. Ibid., 24.
198. Ibid., 90.
199. Mark 10:26; Trueblood, *Humor of Christ*, 46–47.
200. Macy, *Laughing Pilgrims*, 95.
201. Ibid., 108.
202. Howard R. Macy, email message to author, December 16, 2013.
203. Howard R. Macy, "The Legal Metaphor in Oracles Against Foreign Nations in the Pre-Exilic Prophets" (master's thesis, Earlham School of Religion, 1970), George Fox University Library.
204. Ibid., 57.
205. Howard R. Macy, "The Prophets in the Old Testament," *Quaker Religious Thought* 16, no. 1–2 (winter 1974–75): 12.
206. Otto Betz, "History of Biblical Theology," in *The Interpreter's Dictionary of the Bible*, ed. George Arthur Buttrick et al. (New York and Nashville: Abingdon, 1962), 1:437.
207. James Barr, "Biblical Theology," in *The Interpreter's Dictionary of the Bible*, Supplementary Volume, ed. Keith Crim et al. (Nashville: Abingdon, 1976), 105.
208. Paul Buckley and Stephen W. Angell, ed., *The Quaker Bible Reader* (Richmond, IN: Earlham School of Religion Publications, 2006), 106.
209. Ibid., 108.
210. Howard R. Macy, *The Shalom of God* (Dublin, IN: Friends United Press, 1972), 3–4.
211. Ibid., 3.
212. Howard R. Macy, *Rhythms of the Inner Life: Yearning for Closeness with God* (Colorado Springs: Chariot Victor, 1999), 14–15.

213. Ibid., 113.
214. Ibid., 114.
215. Howard R. Macy, "Ordinary Prophets, Extraordinary Lives," in *Truth's Bright Embrace, Essays and Poems in Honor of Arthur O. Roberts*, ed. Paul N. Anderson and Howard R. Macy (Newberg, OR: Barclay Press, 1996), 3–13.
216. Howard R. Macy, "Psalms: Introduction and Commentary," in *The Renovaré Spiritual Formation Bible*, ed. Richard J. Foster et al. (San Francisco: HarperSanFrancisco, 2005).
217. Howard R. Macy, "Quakers and Scripture," in *The Oxford Handbook of Quaker Studies*, ed. Stephen W. Angell and Pink Dandelion (Oxford, UK: Oxford University Press, 2013), 187–201.
218. Daniel Smith-Christopher, email message to author, November 17, 2013.
219. Ibid.
220. Daniel Smith-Christopher, *The Old Testament: Our Call to Faith and Justice* (Notre Dame, IN: Ave Maria, 2005), 60.
221. Ibid., 62.
222. Daniel L. Smith, *The Religion of the Landless: The Social Context of the Babylonian Exile* (Bloomington, IN: Meyer-Stone Books, 1989), 38.
223. Ibid., 39.
224. Ibid., 41.
225. Daniel L. Smith, "On a Theology for Modern Babylonians: The Exile as a Basis for Doing 'Biblical Theology,'" *Quaker Religious Thought* 26, no. 1 (November 1992): 14.
226. Daniel L. Smith-Christopher, "Resistance in a 'Culture of Permission': Sociological Readings of the Correspondence with Persian Authorities in Ezra 1–7," in *Truth's Bright Embrace, Essays and Poems in Honor of Arthur O. Roberts*, ed. Paul N. Anderson and Howard R. Macy (Newberg, OR: George Fox University Press, 1996), 33.
227. Ibid., 34–35.
228. Daniel L. Smith-Christopher, *A Biblical Theology of Exile*, Overtures to Biblical Theology (Minneapolis: Fortress, 2002), 66.
229. Ibid., 68.
230. Ibid., 72–73.
231. Ibid., 4.
232. Daniel L. Smith-Christopher, *Micah: A Commentary*, The Old Testament Library (Louisville, KY: Westminster John Knox, 2015), 193.

233. Ibid., 92.
234. Smith-Christopher, *Biblical Theology*, 25.
235. Ibid., 195.
236. Ibid., 25.
237. Ibid., 195.
238. Daniel L. Smith-Christopher, "The Book of Daniel: Introduction, Commentary, and Reflections" and "The Additions to Daniel: Introduction, Commentary, and Reflections," in *The New Interpreter's Bible*, ed. Leander E. Keck (Nashville: Abingdon, 1966), 7:77–78.
239. George Crosfield, *Memoirs of the Life and Gospel Labours of Samuel Fothergill . . . Some of His Descendants*, 2nd ed. (1843; London: William and Frederick G. Cash, 1857), 198.
240. Smith-Christopher, "Book of Daniel," 52.
241. Ibid., 108.
242. Smith-Christopher, *Old Testament*, 241.
243. Ibid., 242.
244. Ibid., 242–43.
245. Ibid., 244.
246. Smith-Christopher, email message to author, November 17, 2013.
247. Smith, *Religion of the Landless*, 204.
248. Ibid., 210–11.
249. Smith-Christopher, *Biblical Theology*, 83.
250. Ibid., 88.
251. Ibid., 89.
252. Ibid., 92.
253. Ibid., 95.
254. Smith-Christopher, "Book of Daniel," 95.
255. Ibid., 96.
256. Smith-Christopher, *Micah*, 79.
257. Ibid., 144–45.
258. T. Vail Palmer, Jr., "Eschatology and Foreign Policy in the Thought of Reinhold Niebuhr, William Ernest Hocking, and John Courtney Murray" (doctoral thesis, University of Chicago, 1965), 343–44.
259. Smith-Christopher, *Micah*, 137.
260. Ibid., 35.
261. Smith-Christopher, "Book of Daniel," 94–95.
262. Ibid., 64.
263. Ibid., 66.
264. Ibid., 92.

Notes

265. Ibid., 144.
266. Ibid., 146.
267. Ibid., 151–52.
268. Smith-Christopher, *Biblical Theology*, 186.
269. Ibid., 187.
270. Ibid., 188.
271. Daniel L. Smith-Christopher, "Introduction: 'Everything Is Different Now': Reflections on the Tenth Anniversary Edition of *Subverting Hatred*," and "Political Atheism and Radical Faith: The Challenge of Christian Nonviolence in the Third Millennium," in *Subverting Hatred: The Challenge of Nonviolence in Religious Traditions*, ed. Daniel L. Smith-Christopher (Maryknoll, NY: Orbis Books, 2007), 182–83.
272. See Smith-Christopher, *Biblical Theology*, 150.
273. Smith-Christopher, *Subverting Hatred*, 183.
274. Daniel L. Smith-Christopher, *Jonah, Jesus, and Other Good Coyotes: Speaking Peace to Power in the Bible* (Nashville: Abingdon, 2007), 34–35.
275. Ibid., 34.
276. Ibid., 35.
277. Ibid., 36

Bibliography

Allot, Stephen. *John Wilhelm Rowntree, 1868–1905, and the Beginnings of Modern Quakerism.* York, England: Sessions Book Trust, 1994.

Aulén, Gustaf. *Christus Victor: An Historical Study of the Three Main Types of the Idea of Atonement.* Translated by A. G. Herbert. 1931. Eugene, OR: Wipf and Stock, 2003.

Bacon, Margaret Hope. *Let This Life Speak: The Legacy of Henry Joel Cadbury.* Philadelphia: University of Pennsylvania Press, 1987.

———. *Valiant Friend: The Life of Lucretia Mott.* 1980. Philadelphia: Friends General Conference, 1999.

Bailey, Moses. *The Prophetic Word: Ancient and Modern.* Philadelphia: Religious Education Committee, Friends General Conference, 1968.

Baille, D. M. *God Was in Christ: An Essay on Incarnation and Atonement.* New York: Charles Scribner's Sons, 1948.

Barbour, Hugh and J. William Frost. *The Quakers.* Denominations in America 3. Westport, CT: Greenwood, 1988.

Barclay, Robert. *An Apology for the True Christian Divinity: being an explanation and vindication of the principles and doctrines of the people called Quakers.* Stereotype ed. 1678. Philadelphia: Friends Book Store, 1908.

Barr, James. "Biblical Theology." In *The Interpreter's Dictionary of the Bible.* Supplementary Volume. Edited by Keith Crim et al., 104-11. Nashville: Abingdon, 1976.

Barth, Karl. *The Doctrine of God.* Edited by G. W. Bromiley and T. F. Torrance. Translated by G. W. Bromiley et al. Vol. 2, part 2 of *Church Dogmatics.* 1942. Edinburgh: T. & T. Clark, 1957.

———. *The Word of God and the Word of Man.* Translated by Douglas Horton. 1928. New York: Harper & Brothers, 1957.

Benefiel, Margaret J. "The Doctrine of the Atonement: The Quaker Contribution—a Revisionist View." *Quaker Religious Thought* 23, no. 4 (Winter 1988–89): 21-25.

Benezet, Anthony. Benezet Letters. Reprinted in *Friend Anthony Benezet,* by George S. Brookes, 207-411. Philadelphia: University of Philadelphia Press, 1937.

Betz, Otto. "History of Biblical Theology." In Vol. 1 of *The Interpreter's Dictionary of the Bible.* Edited by George Arthur Buttrick et al., 432-37. New York and Nashville: Abingdon, 1962.

Bill, J. Brent. *David B. Updegraff, Quaker Holiness Preacher.* Richmond, IN: Friends United Press, 1983.

Boobyer, George. *Fruits of the Spirit: According to New Testament Teaching.* Richmond, IN: Friends United Press, 1975.

———. *"Thanksgiving" and the "Glory of God" in Paul.* Inaugural-Dissertation zur Erlangung der Doktorwürde der Theologischen Fakultät der Badischen Ruprecht-Karls-Universität zu Heidelberg. Borna-Leipzig, Germany: Universitätsverlag von Robert Noske, 1929.

Boobyer, George H. *Are the Scriptures "Very Precious" Still?* Rufus Jones Lecture given in the Arch Street Meeting House, Philadelphia, PA, April 18, 1980. Philadelphia: Religious Education Committee of Friends General Conference, 1981.

———. *The Bible and the Light Within.* Study in Fellowship 34. London: Friends Home Service Committee, 1973.

Boobyer, G. H. *Jesus as "Theos" in the New Testament.* Bulletin of the John Rylands Library 50, no. 2 (Spring 1968). Manchester, England: The John Rylands Library, 1968.

Bibliography

———. *St. Mark and the Transfiguration Story*. Edinburgh: T. & T. Clark, 1942.

Brock, Peter. "The Peace Testimony in 'A Garden Enclosed.'" *Quaker History* 54, no. 2 (Fall 1965): 67-80.

Buckley, Paul, and Stephen W. Angell, eds. *The Quaker Bible Reader*. Richmond, IN: Earlham School of Religion Publications, 2006.

Cadbury, Henry J. "Acts and Eschatology." In *The Background of the New Testament and Its Eschatology*. Edited by W. D. Davies and D. Daube, 300-321. Studies in Honour of C. H. Dodd. 1954. Reprint, Cambridge: Cambridge University Press, 1964.

———. *Behind the Gospels*. Pendle Hill Pamphlet 160. Wallingford, PA: Pendle Hill, 1968.

———. *The Book of Acts in History*. 1955. Reprint, Eugene, OR: Wipf and Stock, 2004.

———. *The Eclipse of the Historical Jesus*. Pendle Hill Pamphlet 133. Wallingford, PA: Pendle Hill, 1964.

———. *Jesus and Judaism and the Emphasis of Jesus*. Shrewsbury Lecture. Indianapolis: John Woolman Press, 1962.

———. *Jesus: What Manner of Man*. 1947. Reprinted with a new foreword by Paul N. Anderson. Eugene, OR: Wipf and Stock, 2008.

———. *The Making of Luke-Acts*. 2nd ed. with a new introduction by Paul N. Anderson. 1927. Peabody, MA: Hendrickson, 1999.

———. *National Ideals in the Old Testament*. New York: Charles Scribner's Sons, 1920.

———. "The New Testament and Early Christian Literature." In Vol. 7 of *The Interpreter's Bible*, edited by George Arthur Buttrick et al. 32-42. New York and Nashville: Abingdon-Cokesbury, 1951.

———. *The Peril of Modernizing Jesus*. 1937. Reprint, Eugene, OR: Wipf and Stock, 2006.

———. "A Quaker Approach to the Bible." Ward Lecture, Guilford College, Greensboro, NC, 1953.

———. *The Style and Literary Method of Luke: The Diction of Luke and Acts*. Harvard Theological Studies 6. 1919. Reprint, n.p.: Kessinger, 2007.

Cargill, Lawrence Cockcroft. *Moses Bailey: Memoir of a Friend*. Bethlehem, CT: LCC Publishing, 2000.

Churchman, John. *An Account of the Gospel Labours and Christian Experiences of a Faithful Minister of Christ, John Churchman. . . .* Philadelphia: Joseph Crukshank, 1779.

Clark, Dougan. *The Holy Ghost Dispensation*. 4th ed. New York: Fleming H. Revell, 1891.

———. *Instructions to Christian Converts*. 1889. Reprint, Salem, OH: Schmul, 1978.

———. *The Offices of the Holy Spirit*. Edited by Anna Louise Spann. 1878. Reprint, Portland, OR: Evangel, 1945.

———. *The Theology of Holiness*. 1893. San Diego: ICON Group, 2008.

Clark, Dougan, and Joseph H. Smith. *David B. Updegraff and His Work*. Cincinnati: M. W. Knapp, 1895.

Comly, John. *Journal of the Life and Religious Labours of John Comly, late of Byberry, Pennsylvania*. Philadelphia: T. Ellwood Chapman, 1853.

Cooper, Wilmer A. *Growing Up Plain, Among Conservative Wilburite Quakers: The Journey of a Public Friend*. Richmond, IN: Friends United Press, 1999.

Crosfield, George. *Memoirs of the Life and Gospel Labours of Samuel Fothergill with Selections from his Correspondence*. . . . 2nd ed. 1843. London: William and Frederick G. Cash, 1857.

Dandelion, Pink. *An Introduction to Quakerism*. Cambridge, UK: Cambridge University Press, 2007.

Davie, Martin. *British Quaker Theology Since 1895*. Lewiston, NY: Edwin Mellen, 1997.

Dudley, James. *The Life of Edward Grubb, 1854–1939: A Spiritual Pilgrimage*. London: James Clarke, 1946.

Dymond, Jonathan. *Essays on the Principles of Morality and on the Private and Political Rights and Obligations of Mankind*. 1829. Reprint, New York: Robert B. Collins, 1850.

———. *Essays on the Principles of Morality and on the Private and Political Rights and Obligations of Mankind*. 1829. Abridged and reprinted, Philadelphia: Book Committee of the Philadelphia Yearly Meeting of Friends, 1896.

———. *An Inquiry into the Accordancy of War with the Principles of Christianity*. . . . 1823. Reprint, New York: William Wood, 1870.

———. *Observations on the Applicability of the Pacific Principles of the New Testament*. . . . Tract 7 of the Society for the Promotion of Permanent and Universal Peace. London: Hamilton, Adams, 1835.

Ebor, Donald. "Preface to the New English Bible." In *The New English Bible: With the Apocrypha*. 2nd ed. New Testament; 1st ed. Old Testament and Apocrypha, v-vii. 1961. Oxford: Oxford University Press and Cambridge University Press, 1970.

Bibliography

Emerson, Ralph Waldo. *Essays: First and Second Series, Complete in One Volume.* New York: A. L. Burt, [1900?].

———. *Representative Men.* 1883. Reprint, Honolulu: University Press of the Pacific, 2010.

Forbush, Bliss. *Elias Hicks: Quaker Liberal.* New York: Columbia University Press, 1956.

Fox, George. *The Journal of George Fox.* Rev. ed. by John L. Nickalls. Cambridge: Cambridge University Press, 1952.

———. *"The Power of the Lord Is Over All": The Pastoral Letters of George Fox.* Introduced and edited by T. Canby Jones. Richmond, IN: Friends United Press, 1990.

———. *The Works of George Fox.* 8 vols. New Foundation Publication. 1831. Reprint, State College, PA: George Fox Fund, 1990.

Gorringe, Timothy. *God's Just Vengeance: Crime, Violence and the Rhetoric of Salvation.* Cambridge Studies in Ideology and Religion 9. 1996. Digital printing, Cambridge: Cambridge University Press, 2002.

Grubb, Edward. *Authority in Religion.* London: Swarthmore Press, 1924.

———. *The Bible: Its Nature and Inspiration.* 4th imp., 2nd ed. 1920, 1924. London: Swarthmore Press, 1933.

———. *Christianity as Truth.* Vol. 2 of The Nature of Christianity. London: Swarthmore Press, 1928.

———. *The Meaning of the Cross: A Study of the Atonement.* London: George Allen & Unwin, 1922.

———. *The Personality of God: And Other Essays in Constructive Christian Thought.* London: Headley Brothers, 1911.

———. *What Is Quakerism? An Exposition.* . . . 1917. Reprint, Lexington, KY: University of Michigan Library, 2011.

Gurney, Joseph John. *Essays on the Evidences, Doctrines, and Practical Operation, of Christianity.* 1825. Reprint, n.p.: Kessinger, 2008.

———. *A Peculiar People: The Rediscovery of Primitive Christianity.* 1824. Reprint of 7th edition with introduction by Donald Green. Richmond, IN: Friends United Press, 1979.

Hamm, Thomas D. "'A Protest against Protestantism': Hicksite Friends and the Bible in the Nineteenth Century." *Quaker Studies* 6, no. 2 (March 2002): 175-94.

———. *The Transformation of American Quakerism: Orthodox Friends, 1800–1907.* Religion in North America. 1st Midland Book ed. 1988. Bloomington, IN: Indiana University Press, 1992.

Harris, James Rendel. *Union with God: A Series of Addresses*. 1895. Reprint of 2nd ed., Breinigsville, PA: Bibliolife, 2010.

Harris, J. Rendel. *Codex Bezae: A Study of the So-Called Western Text of the New Testament*. Texts and Studies: Contributions to Biblical and Patristic Literature. 1891. Reprint, Nendeln, Liechtenstein: Kraus Reprint, 1967.

———. *The Diatessaron of Tatian: A Preliminary Study*. 1890. Reprint, n.p.: Nabu Public Domain Reprints, n.d.

———. *The Doctrine of Immortality in the Odes of Solomon*. 1909. Reprint, n.p.: Kessinger, n.d.

———. *Fragments of the Commentary of Ephrem Syrus upon the Diatessaron*. 1895. Reprint, Lexington, KY: University of Michigan Library, 2012.

———. *Hermas in Arcadia: And Other Essays*. 1896. Reprint, n.p.: Kessinger, n.d.

———. *Newly-Recovered Gospel of St. Peter: With a Full Account of the Same*. 1893. Reprint, Eugene, OR: Wipf and Stock, 2006.

Harris, Rendel. *The Origin of the Prologue to St. John's Gospel*. 1917. Reprint, Lexington, KY: Cornell University Library, 2012.

Harris, Rendel with the assistance of Vacher Burch. *Testimonies*. Part 1. 1916. Reprint, n.p.: Nabu Public Domain Reprints, 2010.

———. *Testimonies*. Part 2. 1920. Reprint, n.p.: Nabu Public Domain Reprints, 2010.

Hicks, Edward. *Memoirs of the Life and Religious Labors of Edward Hicks*. . . . Philadelphia: Merrihew & Thompson, 1851.

Hicks, Elias. *The Journal of Elias Hicks*. Edited by Paul Buckley. San Francisco: Inner Light Books, 2009.

———. *Letters of Elias Hicks. Including also Observations on the Slavery of the Africans*. . . . Philadelphia: T. Ellwood Chapman, 1861.

Hill, Aubrey F. "George Henry Boobyer: Born 29 vii 1902 Died 17 i 1999." Testimony in *Britian Yearly Meeting Proceedings 2000*.

Hughes, Jennifer. "George Boobyer, 1902–1999." Obituary in *The Friend*, November 26, 1999, 11.

Ingle, H. Larry. *Quakers in Conflict: The Hicksite Reformation*. 2nd ed. 1986. Wallingford, PA: Pendle Hill, 1998.

Johnson, Sherman E. "The Gospel According to St. Mathew: Introduction and Exegesis." In Vol. 7 of *The Interpreter's Bible*, edited by George Arthur Buttrick et al., 229-625. New York and Nashville: Abingdon-Cokesbury, 1951.

Bibliography

Jones, Rufus M. *The Double Search: Studies in Atonement and Prayer*. 1906. Reprint, n.p.: General Books, 2009.

———. *Eli and Sybil Jones: Their Life and Work*. Philadelphia: Henry T. Coates, 1889.

———. *Finding the Trail of Life*. 1926. Reprint, New York: Macmillan, 1931.

———. *The Great Succession of Torch Bearers*. Philadelphia: Young Friends Movement of Philadelphia, 1946.

———. *John Wilhelm Rowntree*. 1942. Reprint, LaVergne, TN: Kessinger, 2010.

———. *The Later Periods of Quakerism*. Vol. 2. 1921. Reprint, n.p.: Kessinger, 2008.

———. *Studies in Mystical Religion*. London: Macmillan, 1909.

———. *The Trail of Life in College*. New York: Macmillan, 1929.

———. *The Trail of Life in the Middle Years*. New York: Macmillan, 1934.

Kee, Howard Clark, Franklin W. Young, and Karlfried Froehlich. *Understanding the New Testament*. 3rd ed. 1957. Englewood Cliffs, NJ: Prentice-Hall, 1973.

Kelly, Thomas R. *Reality of the Spiritual World*. Pendle Hill Pamphlet 21. Wallingford, PA: Pendle Hill, 1942.

Kuenning, Lisa Bieberman. "Christ's Wife: A Vision for All Women." *Quaker Religious Thought* 18, no. 2 (Summer 1979): 4-32.

Kunze, Bonnelyn Young. *Margaret Fell and the Rise of Quakerism*. Stanford, CA: Stanford University Press, 1994.

Lake, Kirsopp and Henry J. Cadbury. *Additional Notes to the Commentary*. Vol. 5 of *The Beginnings of Christianity: The Acts of the Apostles*. Edited by F. J. Foakes Jackson and Kirsopp Lake. 1933. Reprint, Eugene, OR: Wipf and Stock, 2002.

———. *English Translation and Commentary*. Vol. 4 of *The Beginnings of Christianity: The Acts of the Apostles*. Edited by F. J. Foakes Jackson and Kirsopp Lake. 1933. Reprint, Eugene, OR: Wipf and Stock, 2002.

Larson, Rebecca. *Daughters of Light: Quaker Women Preaching and Prophesying in the Colonies and Abroad, 1700-1775*. Chapel Hill, NC: University of North Carolina Press, 2000.

Lawton, Abraham. *Some Testimonies of Truth, Set Forth for the Healing of the Nations*. 1866. Reprint, n.p.: Kessinger, 2007.

Love, Gregory Anderson. *Love, Violence, and the Cross: How the Nonviolent God Saves Us through the Cross of Christ*. Cascade Books. Eugene, OR: Wipf and Stock, 2010.

Macgregor, G. H. C. and A. C. Purdy. *Jew and Greek; Tutors unto Christ: The Jewish and Hellenistic Background of the New Testament*. London: Ivor Nicholson and Watson, 1936.

Macy, Howard R. *Laughing Pilgrims: Humor and the Spiritual Journey*. Milton Keynes, UK and Waynesboro, GA: Paternoster, 2006.

———. "The Legal Metaphor in Oracles Against Foreign Nations in the Pre-Exilic Prophets." Master's thesis, Earlham School of Religion, 1970. In George Fox University library.

———. "Ordinary Prophets, Extraordinary Lives." In *Truth's Bright Embrace: Essays and Poems in Honor of T. Canby Jones*, edited by Paul N. Anderson and Howard R. Macy, 3-13. Newberg, OR: George Fox University Press, 1996.

———. "The Prophets in the Old Testament." In *Quaker Religious Thought* 16, no. 1 and 2 (Winter 1974-75): 4-19.

———. "Psalms: Introduction and Commentary." In *The Renovaré Spiritual Formation Bible*, edited by Richard J. Foster et al., 773-900. San Francisco: HarperSanFrancisco, 2005.

———. "Quakers and Scripture." In *The Oxford Handbook of Quaker Studies*, edited by Stephen W. Angell and Pink Dandelion, 187-201. Oxford: Oxford University Press, 2013.

———. *Rhythms of the Inner Life: Yearning for Closeness with God*. 1988. Colorado Springs: Chariot Victor, 1999.

———. *The Shalom of God*. Dublin, IN: Friends United Press, 1972.

Mather, Eleanore Price. *Edward Hicks Primitive Quaker: His Religion in Relation to His Art*. Pendle Hill Pamphlet 170. Wallingford, PA: Pendle Hill, 1970.

Mekeel, Arthur J. *Quakerism and a Creed*. Philadelphia: Friends' Book Store, 1936.

Mott, Lucretia. *Lucretia Mott: Her Complete Speeches and Sermons*. Edited with an introduction by Dana Greene. Studies in Women and Religion 4. New York and Toronto: Edwin Mellen, 1980.

———. *Slavery and "The Woman Question": Lucretia Mott's Diary of Her Visit to Great Britain to Attend the World's Anti-Slavery Convention of 1840*. Edited by Frederick B. Tolles. Supplement 23 to *Journal of the Friends' Historical Society*. London: Friends' Historical Society, 1952.

Mott, Lucretia C. *Selected Letters of Lucretia Coffin Mott*. Edited by Beverly Wilson Palmer. Urbana, IL: University of Illinois Press, 2002.

Bibliography

Palmer, T. Vail, Jr. "Eschatology and Foreign Policy in the Thought of Reinhold Niebuhr, William Ernest Hocking, and John Courtney Murray." PhD diss., University of Chicago, 1965.

———. "Quaker Peace Witness: The Biblical and Historical Roots." *Quaker Religious Thought* 23, vols. 2 & 3 (Summer 1988): 36-55.

———. "Response" [to Calvin J. Keene, "Historic Quakerism and Mysticism"]. *Quaker Religious Thought* 7, no. 2 (Autumn 1965): 30-33.

———. "Some Issues from Nineteenth-Century Quakerism." *Quaker Religious Thought* 29, no. 2 (January 1999): 5-40.

———. "Theorising a Quaker View of the Atonement." *Quaker Studies* 16, no. 1 (September 2011): 105-123.

Penn, William. *The Select Works of William Penn*. Fourth ed. 3 vols. 1825. Reprint, New York: Kraus Reprint, 1971.

Pickard, Irene, coll. *Memories of J. Rendel Harris*. Sutton, Surrey: Express Lithographic Supplies, 1978.

Purdy, Alexander C. "The Epistle to the Hebrews: Introduction and Exegesis." In Vol. 11 of *The Interpreter's Bible*. Edited by George Arthur Buttrick et al., 577-763. New York and Nashville: Abingdon, 1955.

———. *Pathways to God*. New York: The Womans Press, 1922.

———. "Paul the Apostle." In Vol. 3 of *The Interpreter's Dictionary of the Bible*. Edited by George Arthur Buttrick et al., 681-704. New York and Nashville: Abingdon, 1962.

———. "Spirit in the New Testament and Today." John Brown Lecture, n.p., 1934.

———. *The Way of Christ: Studies in Discipleship*. 1918. Reprint, San Bernardino, CA: New York Public Library, 2013.

Robinson, James M. *A New Quest of the Historical Jesus*. Studies in Biblical Theology 25. London: SCM Press, 1959.

Rowntree, John Wilhelm. *Essays and Addresses*. Edited by Joshua Rowntree. 1906. Reprint, n.p.: General Books, 2010.

———. *Palestine Notes: And Other Papers*. Edited by Joshua Rowntree. London: Headley Brothers, 1906.

Russell, Elbert. *The Beatitudes: A Series of Studies*. Garden City, NY: Doubleday, Doran, 1929.

———. *The Book of Revelation: With an Introduction, Paraphrase and Notes*. Unpublished manuscript, Duke University Library.

———. *The Christian Life*. William Penn Lecture. Philadelphia: Walter H. Jenkins, 1916.

———. *Elbert Russell, Quaker: An Autobiography.* Jackson, TN: Friendly Press, 1956.

———. *Jesus of Nazareth in the Light of Today.* 1909. Reprint, n.p.: Nabu Press, 2011.

———. *The Message of the Fourth Gospel.* Nashville: Cokesbury, 1932.

———. *The Parables of Jesus: A Course of Ten Lessons Arranged for Daily Study.* New York: National Board of the Young Women's Christian Associations of the United States of America, 1909.

———. *Paronomasia and Kindred Phenomena in the New Testament.* PhD diss., University of Chicago. 1920. Reprint, Lexington, KY: Forgotten Books, 2012.

Scott, Job. *Journal of the Life, Travels, and Gospel Labours, of that Faithful Servant and Minister of Christ, Job Scott.* 1798. Reprint, n.p.: Kessinger, 2007.

———. *The Knowledge of the Lord, the Only True God. To Which Is Added, Remarks upon the Doctrine of Perseverance.* Philadelphia: Emmor Kimber, 1824. Digital Quaker Collection, Earlham School of Religion, http://esr.earlham.edu/dqc.

Scott, Richenda C. *Herbert G Wood: A Memoir of His Life and Thought.* London: Friends Home Service Committee, 1967.

Scroggs, Robin. "Woman in the New Testament." In *The Interpreter's Dictionary of the Bible.* Supplementary Volume. Edited by Keith Crim et al., 966-68. Nashville: Abingdon, 1976.

Shelton, R. Larry. *Christ and Covenant: Interpreting the Atonement for 21st Century Mission.* Tyrone, GA: Paternoster, 2006.

Smith, Daniel L. "On a Theology for Modern Babylonians: The Exile as a Basis for Doing 'Biblical Theology.'" *Quaker Religious Thought* 26, no. 1 (November 1992): 7-18.

———. *The Religion of the Landless: The Social Context of the Babylonian Exile.* Bloomington, IN: Meyer-Stone Books, 1989.

Smith-Christopher, Daniel. *The Old Testament: Our Call to Faith and Justice.* Notre Dame, IN: Ave Maria, 2005.

Smith-Christopher, Daniel L. *A Biblical Theology of Exile.* Overtures to Biblical Theology. Minneapolis: Fortress, 2002.

———. "The Book of Daniel: Introduction, Commentary, and Reflections" and "The Additions to Daniel: Introduction, Commentary, and Reflections." In Vol. 7 of *The New Interpreter's Bible*, edited by Leander E. Keck et al., 17-194. Nashville: Abingdon, 1996.

———. "Introduction: 'Everything Is Different Now': Reflections on the Tenth Anniversary Edition of *Subverting Hatred*" and "Political Atheism and Radical Faith: The Challenge of Christian Nonviolence in the Third Millennium." In *Subverting Hatred: The Challenge of Nonviolence in Religious Traditions*, edited by Daniel L. Smith-Christopher, xiii-xxvii and 171-96. 1998. Reprint, Maryknoll, NY: Orbis Books, 2007.

———. *Jonah, Jesus, and Other Good Coyotes: Speaking Peace to Power in the Bible*. Nashville: Abingdon, 2007.

———. *Micah: A Commentary*. The Old Testament Library. Louisville, KY: Westminster John Knox, 2015.

———. "Nationalism" and "Peace in the Old Testament." In Vol. 4 of *The New Interpreter's Dictionary of the Bible*, edited by Katharine Doob Sakenfeld et al., 228-31 and 423-25. Nashville: Abingdon, 2009.

———. "Resistance in a 'Culture of Permission': Sociological Readings of the Correspondence with Persian Authorities in Ezra 1-7." In *Truth's Bright Embrace: Essays and Poems in Honor of Arthur O. Roberts*, edited by Paul N. Anderson and Howard R. Macy, 15-35. Newberg, OR: George Fox University Press, 1996.

Smith-Christopher, Daniel L. and Stephen J. Spignesi. *Lost Books of the Bible for Dummies*. Hoboken, NJ: Wiley, 2008.

Society of Friends. *Report of the Proceedings of the Conference of Members of the Society of Friends . . . 1895*. London: Headley Brothers, 1896.

Stephen, Caroline Emelia. *Light Arising: Thoughts on the Central Radiance*. 1908. Reprint, Lexington, KY: University of Michigan Library, 2010.

———. *Quaker Strongholds*. 1890. Centenary edn., Chula Vista, CA: Wind and Rock, 1995.

Throckmorton, Burton H. Jr., ed. *Gospel Parallels: A Synopsis of the First Three Gospels*. 2nd ed. 1949. Revised reprint, New York: Thomas Nelson & Sons, 1965.

Trueblood, Elton. *The Humor of Christ*. New York: Harper & Row, 1964.

Tuke, Henry. *The Principles of Religion, as Professed by the Society of Christians, Usually Called Quakers*. . . . 1805. Reprint, n.p.: Kessinger, 2005.

Updegraff, David B. *Old Corn; or, Sermons and Addresses on the Spiritual Life*. Introduction by Joseph H. Smith. Boston: McDonald & Gill, 1892.

Vining, Elizabeth Gray. *Friend of Life: The Biography of Rufus M. Jones*. Philadelphia: J. B. Lippincott, 1958.

Weaver, J. Denny. *The Nonviolent Atonement*. Grand Rapids, MI: William B. Eerdmans, 2001.

Weigle, Luther A., with members of the Revision Committee. *An Introduction to the Revised Standard Version of the New Testament*. N.p.: The International Council of Religious Education, 1946.

Wilbur, Henry W. *The Life and Labors of Elias Hicks*. Philadelphia: Friends General Conference Advancement Committee, 1910.

Wilbur, John. *Journal of the Life of John Wilbur*. . . . Providence, RI: George H. Whitney, 1859.

———. *Letters to a Friend, On Some of the Primitive Doctrines of Christianity*. 1832. Reprint, n.p.: Kessinger, 2007.

———. *A Narrative and Exposition of the Late Proceedings of New England Yearly Meeting* . . . New York: Piercy & Reed, 1845. Digital Quaker Collection, Earlham School of Religion, http://esr.earlham.edu/dqc.

Williams, Walter R. *The Rich Heritage of Quakerism*. 1962. Edited reprint with Epilogue by Paul Anderson. Newberg, OR: Barclay Press, 1987.

Wood, Herbert G. *Quakerism and the Future of the Church*. Swarthmore Lecture. 1920. Reprint, LaVergne, TN: Bibliolife, 2011.

———. *Why Did Christ Die?* Study Broadcasts. London: Epworth, 1953.

Wood, H. G. *Belief and Unbelief Since 1850*. Cambridge: Cambridge University Press, 1955.

———. *Christianity and the Nature of History*. Hulsean Lectures 1933–34. Cambridge: Cambridge University Press, 1934.

———. *Did Christ Really Live?* London: Student Christian Movement, 1938.

———. *Jesus in the Twentieth Century*. London: Lutterworth, 1960.

Woodard, Luke. *The Morning Star: A Treatise on the Nature, Offices, and Work of the Lord Jesus Christ*. 1875. Reprint, n.p.: Kessinger, 2007.

———. *A Panorama of Wonders: A Brief Discussion of Some of the Principal Doctrines of the Christian Religion*. Richmond, IN: Nicholson, 1921.

———. *Sketches of a Life of 75: In Three Parts; Biographical, Historical and Descriptive*. Richmond, IN: Nicholson, 1907.

———. *What Is Truth?* Auburn, NY: Knapp, Peck & Thomson, 1901.

Wright, G. Ernest. *God Who Acts: Biblical Theology as Recital*. Studies in Biblical Theology 8. London: SCM Press, 1952.

Wright, G. Ernest and Reginald H. Fuller. *The Book of the Acts of God: Contemporary Scholarship Interprets the Bible*. 1957. Anchor Books edition, Garden City, NY: Doubleday, 1960.

Index

Old Testament

Genesis		
1-11	233	
3:15	11	
3:16	48	
3:24	48	
3:28	16	
6:3	114	

Numbers		
20:11	89	

Deuteronomy		
4:31	91	
31:6	91	
31:8	91	

Joshua		
1:5	91	

1 Kings		
19	155	
19:15-16	112, 114	
19:16	112	
19:19	113	
19:19-21	113	

2 Kings		
8:7-15	113	
8:13	113	
8:15	113	
18:31	243	

1 Chronicles		
28:20	155	
	91	

Ezra		
8:21-23	240	
9:7-8	235	

| 9:9 | 244 |
| 10:1-12 | 247 |

Nehemiah	
9	235
9:36	235, 244

Psalm	
15:2	92
17:1-11	187
23	155
23:6	231
36:5	231
51	155
57:10	231
59:17	231
77:20	101
103:11	231

110		53	159, 194	Amos	
112:2	91	61:1	236	7:1-6	55
146:7-8	236	Jeremiah		9:11-12	187
Proverbs		3	225	Micah	
8:27, 29-30	179	18:1-3	182	4:1-5	243
12:17	92	31:31-34	218	6:8	236
30:24-28	248	32:6-15	182	Habakkuk	
Isaiah		38:24-26	187	2:4	225
2	247	Daniel		Zechariah	
2:2-4	248	3	241, 244	1:4-5	55
11	53	4	237	3:10	243
11:6-9	51, 54	6	241–242, 244	9:12	236
19:24-25	247, 248	6:10	244	11:12	181
32:1-2	89	7-12	239	11:13	182
36:16	243	11:14	245	Malachi	
40:3	184	11:34	245	3:1	181, 184
41:10	91	Hosea			
42:7	236	2	225		
45:1	113	8:7	20, 208		
49:6	247, 248				

New Testament

Matthew		8:19-21	125	8:1	91
5:34	67	9:23-24	92	8:38-39	220
5:39	68	John		16:1	85
6:19	67	1:1	179	1 Corinthians	
10:8	101	1:3	179	1:30	220
10:16	247	10:8	209	2:8	220
12:46-50	125	15:26	30	10:4	89
27:3, 5	182	21:1-14	227	11:1-15	105
27:9	181	Acts		11:5	99
27:9-10	181, 182	2	105	14:34-35	99
Mark		2:3	56	15:20-22	220
1:2	181, 183	2:16-18	16, 105, 110	15:25	220
1:3	184			15:31	92
3:31-35	125	9:4-5	89	2 Corinthians	
10:5	47	Romans		5	204
10:25	226	3:22	149	8:9	165
12:36	164	3:24	220	Galatians	
13:32	167	3:25	220	3:28	47, 106, 110
Luke		5:9	220	Ephesians	
1:47-55	239	5:12-21	220	1:10	37
2:52	167				

Bibliography

Philippians			Hebrews			1 Peter	
2:6-7		165	1:1		217	2:9	92
3:8-9		149	2:17	166, 167, 219			
Colossians			6:4-6		61	1 John	
1:16		179	6:13-20		221	2:27	101
1:17		167	8:13		218	Revelation	
2:15		220	9:28		38	1:1, 9	191
1 Timothy			10:8-10		219		
2		47	10:26		61		
2:11-14		48	13		219		
2:12		47	13:5		91		

Subject Index

A

Abelard, Peter, 11, 35, 41, 159

abolitionist movement, 14, 79, 81

Ackworth Friends School, 150

Adrian, Michigan, 140

agnosticism, 121, 130, 192

Albany, New York, 87

All Friends Conference, 174

America, 9, 15, 17, 25, 62, 79, 120, 131, 133, 134, 151, 169, 234. See also United States of America

American Academy of Religion, 233

American Friends Service Committee, 140, 191, 196

American Society of Christian Ethics, 233

American Standard Bible Committee, 198

Amish, 238

Anabaptist, 21, 119

Anderson, Bernhard W., 119

Anderson, Paul, 149, 192

Andes, 78

Andover Theological Seminary, 191

Anselm, St., 10–11, 35, 137

Antioch College, 34

Apocrypha, 179, 211–212, 239

Apostles Creed, 212

Appalachians, 196

Arch Street Meeting House, 216

Arts and Entertainment Network, 232

Associated Mennonite Biblical Seminaries, 232

Astleford, Margi, 227. See also Margi Macy

Athanasian Creed, 123

atonement
Covenant theory, 11, 37, 38, 41, 44, 173

forensic theory, 10–11, 16–17, 19, 21, 37, 136–137, 143, 145–146, 149, 189–190, 194, 221

moral influence theory, 11, 12, 16, 19, 21, 35, 41, 43, 107, 138, 144, 147, 159, 161, 174, 221. See also subjective theory ransom theory, 16, 21, 159, 221

satisfaction theory, 10–11, 13, 14, 16–17, 19, 21, 35–37, 39, 62, 87, 107, 136, 143–149, 189, 194, 205–206, 221. See also substitutionary theory

subjective theory, 11, 19, 35, 43, 159, 161, 174. See also moral influence theory

substitutionary theory, 10–11, 12, 14, 17–19, 21, 36–37, 40, 42–44, 127, 136, 150, 158, 189, 194, 204–205, 221. See also satisfaction theory

Attleborough, Pennsylvania, 51

Auburn, New York, 80

Augustine, 137

Aulén, Gustaf, 11, 19, 35, 111, 139, 158, 190

B

Babylonian Exile, 20, 234–236, 243

Bailey, Lettie, 222

Bailey, Mabel, 224. See also Googins, Mabel

Bailey, Melvin, 222

Bailey, Moses, 222–225

Bailey, Moses Omar, 223

Baillie, Donald M., 167–168

Baltimore, Maryland, 50, 124, 130, 172

Baltimore Yearly Meeting, 34

Bancroft, Elizabeth, 87

Bancroft, Joseph, 87

baptism, 15, 98, 109, 167, 168

Baptist, 15, 98, 201, 202, 211, 212, 223

Barbados, 26, 28

Barbour, Hugh, 158

Barclay, Robert, 7, 9, 11–13, 17, 26, 27–28, 29, 33, 36–39, 51, 59, 62, 75–76, 85, 106, 122, 148–149, 154

Barclay, William, 229

Barnard, Hannah, 84, 129

Barth, Karl, 119

Bates, Sarah, 109

Battey, Thomas J., 115–116

Behmen, Jacob, 117–118

Benedict, Saint, 119

Benezet, Anthony, 38, 238

Bergson, Henri, 226

Berkeley, California, 227

Biblical Theology Movement, 37, 119, 200, 228–229

Bill, Brent, 104–105

Birmingham, England, 18, 131, 132–133, 201

Bluffton College, 232

Boehme, Jacob, 119, 122

Boobyer, Dorothy, 213. See also Keirle, Dorothy

Boobyer, George Henry, 20, 212–216

Bootham School, 150

Boston, Massachusetts, 78, 80, 116

Boston University School of Theology, 223

Bournville, England, 132

Bownas, Samuel, 54

Braintree, England, 150

Braithwaite, William Charles, 19, 120, 128, 129, 137

Brazil, 78

Bristol, England, 38, 150

British and Foreign Anti-Slavery Society, 79

British and Foreign Bible Society, 211

British Isles, 58

Brown, Lydia, 191. See also Cadbury, Lydia

Bryn Mawr College, 191

Bucks County, Pennsylvania, 51

Buddha, 171

Bunyan, John, 118

Burkitt, 186

Burrough, Edward, 7, 12, 17, 28, 30, 37–38, 45, 50, 88, 104, 154

Burton, 188

Bushnel, Horace, 19, 159–160

C

Cadbury, Anna Kaighn Lowry, 132, 191

Cadbury, George, 131, 133

Cadbury, Henry Joel, 20–21, 191–212, 217, 223

Cadbury, Joel Jr., 132, 191

Cadbury, Lydia, 191. See also Brown, Lydia

Cadbury, Richard, 131, 132

California, 227

Calvinist, 11

Calvin, John, 10, 35, 137

Cambridge, Massachusetts, 121, 132

Cambridge University, 47, 119, 124, 201, 249

Cambridge University Press, 211

Canada, 130, 140

Canterbury, England, 35, 167

Catholic, 123, 233, 239, 240

Catholic Worker Movement, 240

Chase, Pliny Earle, 116, 119

Chelten Hills, Pennsylvania, 79

Chester, Pennsylvania, 87

Chicago, Illinois, 131, 134, 170, 174, 188, 190

Chile, 78

Christopher, David, 232. See also Smith, David

Christus Victor, 11–12, 16, 21, 35, 36, 37–39, 49, 93, 111, 136, 147, 158, 173, 190, 221, 239. See Atonement

Churchman, John, 13, 54, 56, 238

Church of England, 123, 211

Church of Rome, 123

Church of Scotland, 211

Church of the Brethren, 21, 237–238

Clark, Asenath, 109

Clark, Dougan, 109

Clark, Dougan, Jr., 15–16, 96, 99, 107, 109, 109–116, 125, 141–142, 168

Clarkson, Thomas, 117

Coeymans Monthly Meeting, 87

Coffin, Anna, 78

Coffin, Lucretia, 78. See also Mott, Lucretia Coffin
Coffin, Thomas, 78
Collins, Lydia, 57
Comly, John, 8, 11, 12, 38–42, 47, 194
Congregational Church, 124, 211
Connecticut, 57
Constantine, 21, 237
Coole, Benjamin, 47
Cooper, Wilmer, 216
Coutant, Sarah (Sallie), 120
Cox, Lieuetta, 169
Craig, Clarence T., 198
Crosfield, George, 58–59
Crosfield, Margaret, 58
Croydon, England, 151

D

Davie, Martin, 127–128, 177
Day, Dorothy, 240
Delaware, 87
Denck, Hans, 119
Devonshire, England, 124
Diatessaron, 178
Dibelius, Martin, 212
Dodd, C. H., 198
Douglas, John Henry, 168, 170
Dreiser, Theodore, 177
Duke Divinity School, 175. See also Duke University School of Religion
Duke University, 175, 190

Duke University School of Religion, 174. See also Duke Divinity School
Durham, North Carolina, 175
Dymond, Jonathan, 12, 13, 63–78

E

Earlham College, 15, 109, 168–172, 188, 216–217, 223, 228
Earlham School of Religion, 216, 221, 227–228
East Anglia, England, 150
Eastern Orthodox Church, 30
Egypt, 30, 180
Eichrodt, Walther, 119
Elkhart, Indiana, 232
Emerson, Ralph Waldo, 18, 116–120
England, 17–18, 38, 50, 58, 62, 63, 77, 79–80, 84, 87, 120, 121, 123, 124–125, 127, 129, 131–134, 150, 169, 174, 201, 211, 212, 232
Enlightenment, 8
Epiphanes, Antiochus IV, 245
eschatology, 189, 198, 208
Europe, 120, 132
Eutaw Street Meeting, 172
Evangelical Friends Church International, 98
Everard, John, 119
exile, 20, 22, 234–248

Bibliography

F

Fell, Margaret, 7, 14, 45, 82, 85, 106, 154

Fénelon, Archbishop François, 122

Finger Lakes region, New York, 80

First Friends Church, 232. See also Reedwood Friends Church

Fisher, Samuel, 129, 249

Five Years Meeting, 15, 98, 221. See also Friends United Meeting

Florida, 175

Flounders Institute, 150

Flounders, Jonathan, 58

Forbush, Bliss, 51

Fosdick, Harry Emerson, 177

Fothergill, Samuel, 13, 38, 54, 56, 61, 238

Fox, George, 7–23, 26–44, 45–50, 51–53, 75–77, 82, 88, 93, 104, 117–123, 131, 136, 147–150, 154, 215, 219

Frame, Esther, 170

Frame, Nathan, 170

France, 109

Franck, Sebastian, 119

Free Will Baptist Church, 223

Friedrich, G., 229

Friends Home Service Committee, 214

Friends Meeting House at Braintree, 150

Friends Meeting House at Scarborough, 201

Friends School, 18, 109, 115, 116

Friends United Meeting, 98, 214. See also Five Years Meeting

Friends University, 228

Friendsville, Tennessee, 169

Friends World Committee for Consultation, 140

Fry, Elizabeth, 80. See also Gurney, Betsy

Fuller, Reginald H., 191

G

Gandhi, Mahatma, 244–246

Garrison, William Lloyd, 79–80, 173

George Fox Evangelical Seminary (Portland Seminary), 11

George Fox University, 227, 232

Germantown, Pennsylvania, 97

Germany, 208, 212

Glasgow, Scotland, 120

Glens Falls, New York, 140

Glover, T. R., 225

Gomes, Peter, 119

Googins, Mabel, 223. See also Bailey, Mabel

Goose Creek Meeting, 51

Gorringe, Timothy, 37, 206

Graham, John William, 128

Grant, Frederick C., 198

Great Britain, 15, 18, 25, 63, 85, 109, 120, 124, 129, 140, 151, 211

Great Separation, 10, 34, 79

Great Separation, the. See Hicksite-Orthodox Separation

Grebel, Conrad, 119
Green, Donald, 25
Greensboro, North Carolina, 175
Gregory I, Pope, 119
Grellet, Stephen, 8, 77, 79
Grotius, Hugo, 47
Grubb, Edward, 19, 128, 150–168, 174, 185–186, 194, 202
Grubb, Elizabeth, 150
Grubb, Emma, 151. See also Horsnaill, Emma M.
Grubb, Jonathan, 150
Guilford College, 109, 175, 199
Gummere, Amelia M., 137
Gurney, Betsy. See also Fry, Elizabeth
Gurneyite Friends, 10, 13, 15, 18, 34, 63, 95–98, 109, 115–116, 120–121, 126
Gurney, Joseph John, 9, 11–12, 25–28, 33, 35, 36, 39, 45–50, 62–63, 80, 105, 107, 128, 141
Gurney, Samuel, 80
Guyon, Madam, 118, 122

H

Hamm, Thomas, 95, 111, 171
Harris, J. Rendel, 17–18, 19, 119, 124–129, 131, 132, 133, 134, 170, 177–188, 189, 199, 201, 202
Hartford Monthly Meeting, 224
Hartford Theological Seminary, 216–217, 223–224
Hartford YWCA, 224

Hartshorne, Charles, 177
Harvard Divinity School, 191, 223
Harvard Graduate School of Arts and Sciences, 227
Harvard University, 132–133, 191
Haverford College, 18, 97, 109, 116, 119–121, 124, 132–133, 170, 191, 207, 210
Haverford Friends Meeting, 140
Haverford, Pennsylvania, 120, 131–133, 134, 192
Heidelberg University, 212
Hertfordshire, England, 152
Hicks, Catharine, 51
Hicks, Edward, 13, 14, 51–56, 61
Hicks, Elias, 8–9, 11–12, 13, 25, 34, 39, 42–44, 51, 53, 54, 57, 84
Hicks, Isaac, 51
Hicksite Friends, 9–10, 12, 13, 34, 44, 53, 79, 81, 87, 115, 129, 174, 197
Hicksite-Orthodox Separation, 57. See also Great Separation, the
Hicks, Thomas, 51
Holiness movement, 15–17, 95–175, 177
Hopkinton, Rhode Island, 57
Horsnaill, Emma M., 150. See also Grubb, Emma
House, Zsa Zsa Janine, 232
Howard Association, 151
Howgill, Francis, 30, 104
Hudson Monthly Meeting, 87
Hudson, New York, 84
Hudson River, 87, 132

Bibliography

Hull Monthly Meeting, 136
Hurtado, Larry, 187

I

India, 244, 246
Indiana, 98, 140, 169, 232
Indianapolis, Indiana, 169
Indiana Yearly Meeting, 15, 109, 140
Inskip, John, 97
Ireland, 79, 109, 131, 140, 211
Irenaeus, 183

J

Jackson, F. J. Foakes, 194
John Rylands Library, 134
Johns Hopkins University, 124, 172–174, 188–189
Johnson, Sherman E., 181
Joint Committee on the New Translation of the Bible, 211–212
Jones, Ann, 58
Jones, Edwin, 116
Jones, Eli, 120
Jones, Elizabeth Bartram Cadbury, 132–134, 191
Jones, Lowell Coutant, 120, 132, 133, 134
Jones, Mary Hoxie, 116, 134
Jones, Rufus M., 17–19, 22, 116–121, 126–128, 130–134, 136–140, 170, 177, 191, 196–197, 216
Jones, Sybil, 120

Jones, T. Canby, 158, 232
Josephus, Flavius, 186, 193

K

Karl Barth, 119, 221–222
Keirle, Dorothy, 212. **See also** Boobyer, Dorothy
Kempis, Thomas à, 122
kenosis, 166–168
Kierkegaard, Søren, 226
King, Martin Luther, Jr., 119
Kirkbymoorside, England, 136
Kittel, G., 229
Kuenan, 161

L

Lake Cayuga, 120
Lake, Kirsopp, 194
Lamb's War, 12, 14, 22, 37, 44, 92–93, 104, 158, 239, 245
Lawn, Evan, 224
Lawn, Marguerite, 224
Lawn, Marguerite Bailey, 223
Lawton, Abraham, 12, 14, 87–93
Law, William, 122, 134
Lay, Benjamin, 85, 142
Leiden University, 134
Letchworth, England, 152
Letter to the Governor of Barbados, 26, 28
Locke, John, 47

Lollards, 119

London, England, 62, 79, 80, 130, 151, 213

London University, 150, 201, 212

London Women's Yearly Meeting, 50

London Yearly Meeting, 17, 50, 79, 126–127, 129, 131, 133, 205, 214, 232

Loudon County, Virginia, 97

Love, Gregory Anderson, 19, 37, 139

Loyola, Ignatius, 119

Loyola Marymount University, 232

Lutheran, 11, 35

Luther, Martin, 117, 137

M

Maccabees, 22, 245

Maccabeus, Judas, 239

Macgregor, G. H. C., 217

Macy, Hazel, 227

Macy, Howard R., 20, 225–232

Macy, Mahlon, 227

Macy, Margi, 227. See also Astleford, Margi

Magdalene, Mary, 16, 142

Mahoney, Roger, 233

Maine, 116, 120, 222, 223

Malone, Emma, 168

Malone, Walter, 168

Manchester Conference, 17, 18, 127–130, 141, 151

Manchester, England, 17, 127, 134

Martin, Josiah, 47

Martyr, Justin, 180

Marx, Karl, 239

Massachusetts, 78, 132, 227

Meeting for Sufferings, 34, 50

Mekeel, Arthur, 28

Memphis, Tennessee, 119

Mennonite, 11, 21, 232, 237, 238

Merswin, Rulman, 119

Methodist, 11, 97, 117, 169, 175, 211

Michigan, 140

Middle East, 124

Middletown Monthly Meeting, 51

Military Service Act, 151

Milton, 117

Mitchell, Eliza, 97

modernist movement, 15, 17–18, 95–175, 177, 195–197, 233

Mohammed, 171

Molinos, 122

Morgan, Arthur, 34

Moses, 10, 16, 30, 32, 64–65, 89, 101, 102–103, 119, 153, 162, 165, 187

Mott, James, 14, 78–81

Mott, Lucretia Coffin, 12, 14, 78–87, 109, 115, 116, 129

Mount Pleasant, Ohio, 97, 98

Mount Sinai, 102, 124, 180

mysticism, 8, 18–19, 116–122, 127, 131–133, 134, 136, 139, 189, 196–197, 200

Bibliography

N

Naish, Constance M., 130. See also Rowntree, Constance

Nantucket Island, Massachusetts, 84

Nantucket, Massachusetts, 78, 227

Napoleon, 171

National Bible Society of Scotland, 211

Nayler, James, 12, 37–38, 104, 117

Netherlands, 134

Nettleton Chair, 223

Nettleton, Reverend, 223

Newberg Friends Church, 227

Newberg, Oregon, 232

Newcastle Meeting, 213

New England, 57, 63

New England Yearly Meeting, 13, 34, 57, 63, 223, 227

New English Bible, 20, 211–212

New Garden Boarding School, 109

New Garden, Indiana, 140

new humanity movement, 21, 221

New Jersey, 199

Newport, Rhode Island, 62

New Testament, 13, 20–21, 46, 64–66, 70, 73–74, 76–77, 83, 100, 109–110, 149, 156, 161–165, 173, 174, 178, 180, 183–186, 188–190, 192, 198–204, 206, 208, 211–212, 212–216, 216–217, 223, 225, 229

Newtown Preparative Meeting, 51

New York, 78, 80, 87, 120, 131, 134, 140, 216, 233

New York City, New York, 54

New York Yearly Meeting of Friends, 9, 34, 57, 87, 233

Nicene Creed, 30, 212

Nine Partners Meeting House, 78

Nobel Peace Prize, 191

No-Conscription Fellowship, 151

North Carolina, 109, 175, 189, 199

North Carolina Yearly Meeting, 34

Northwest Yearly Meeting, 232

Norway, 191

Norwich, England, 62

O

Oak Grove Seminary, 120, 223

Oakwood Seminary, 120

Ohio, 96–98, 214, 232

Ohio Yearly Meeting, 15, 34, 63, 97–98, 109

Old Testament, 20, 46, 65, 76, 83–84, 112–113, 135, 161–164, 166, 168, 180, 182, 184–187, 188, 192–193, 195, 199, 203, 206, 211–212, 218, 223, 224, 228–229, 230–231, 232–233, 234, 239, 240–241

Op-den-Graeff, Abraham, 97

Op-den-Graeff, Dirck, 97

Oregon, 227, 232

Orthodox Friends, 9–10, 12, 33–34, 42, 44, 53, 57, 79, 140, 174, 191

Oslo, Norway, 191

Oxford University, 47, 131, 232, 249

Oxford University Press, 211

P

Palestine, 223, 235, 242, 244
Papias, 186
Parker, Theodore, 83
Pascal, 118
Pastorius, Francis Daniel, 97
Paul (apostle, saint), 21, 47–48, 53, 85, 88–90, 99, 105–106, 108, 110, 117, 125, 149, 159, 163, 173, 179, 184, 192, 194, 204, 209–210, 213, 217, 220–221, 240
peace testimony, 230
Pendle Hill, 174, 199, 221
Pendle Hill, Pennsylvania, 191
Penn Charter School, 191
Pennsylvania, 51, 55, 64, 87, 97, 120, 131, 132, 192, 216
Pennsylvania Anti-Slavery Society, 79
Penn, William, 9, 15–17, 29, 36–37, 46, 51, 53, 64, 103, 141, 147–148
Pentateuch, 153–155, 161, 170
Pentecost, 16, 56, 102–104, 105, 111–112, 141
Philadelphia, 8, 13, 33, 50, 53, 78–79, 87, 97, 98, 133, 174, 191, 196, 216
Philadelphia Female Anti-Slavery Society, 79
Philadelphia Women's Yearly Meeting, 79
Philadelphia Yearly Meeting, 9, 34, 63, 87, 173
Philo, 179, 180, 186
Pickard, Irene, 185
Pickering Monthly Meeting, 136
Pinkham, William P., 171
Pius X, Pope, 233
Plato, 118, 180
Pliny the Elder, 186
Plotinus, 117
Plymouth, England, 124
Porphyry, 117
Portland, Maine, 222–223
Portland, Oregon, 227, 232
Poughkeepsie, New York, 132
Presbyterian, 32, 97, 139, 211
Price, Rebecca, 97
Pritchard, Esther Tuttle, 168, 170
Providence, Rhode Island, 18, 109, 115, 116, 120
Purdy, Alexander C., 21, 61, 216–222, 222–224
Purdy, Ellison, 216, 222

Q

Quaker Peace and Service, 232
Quaker Religious Thought, 63, 228, 234
Quaker Theological Discussion Group, 229
Quietist Friends, 8, 17, 26, 38, 104

R

Ramallah Friends School, 223
Ramallah, Palestine, 223
Reedwood Friends Church, 227, 232. **See also** First Friends Church

Bibliography

Religious Education Committee of Friends General Conference, 216, 224, 276, 284

Revised Standard Version of the New Testament, 20, 198

Rhode Island, 18, 57, 62–63, 109, 115, 120

Rhode Island Quarterly Meeting, 57, 63

Richards, Leyton, 151

Richardson, John, 54

Richmond Declaration of Faith, 10, 15, 34, 98

Richmond, Indiana, 98

Roberts, Arthur O., 22, 231, 235

Robinson, Theodore H., 219

Rome, 106, 117, 123, 184, 209

Rowntree, Antoinette, 129

Rowntree, Constance, 133, 134. See also Naish, Constance M.

Rowntree, John Wilhelm, 18–19, 128–139, 150, 169

Rowntree, Joseph, 129

Rowntree, Joshua, 129

Rowntree Trust, 137

Royce, Josiah, 132

Russell, Elbert, 19, 21, 168–177, 188–191, 194, 216

Russell, Eliza (Sanders), 169

Russell, Eva, 169

Russell, Josiah, 169, 174–177

Russell, Marcia, 169

Russell, Ruth, 169

Russell, William, 169

S

Saint Catherine's Monastery, 124, 180

Sandiford, Ralph, 64, 103

Saranac Lake, New York, 132

Scalby, England, 132, 133, 136

Scarborough, England, 129, 132, 133, 150

Schweitzer, Albert, 200

Scipio, 117

Scotland, 79

Scott, Job, 13, 27–28, 39, 54, 56, 64

Second Vatican Council, 233

Selly Oak Colleges, 201

Selly Oak, England, 133, 201

Selly Oak Meeting, 213

Seneca Falls Convention, 14, 80

Seneca Falls, New York, 80

Shackleton, Abraham, 84, 129, 146

Sharpless, Isaac, 137

Shelton, R. Larry, 11, 37, 41, 147, 173

Shillitoe, Thomas, 57–58

Short Creek Monthly Meeting, 97

Shrewsbury Friends Meeting, 199

Shrewsbury Lecture, 199, 274, 285

Sidcot, England, 213

Sidcot Meeting, 213

Sidcot School, 150

Silver Bay, New York, 233

Simons, Menno, 119

Simpson, James, 54

Smith-Christopher, Daniel L., 20, 21–22, 232–248, 250

Smith, David, 232. See also Christopher, David

Smith, George Adam, 170

Smith, Joseph H., 96, 99

Smith Neck Friends Meeting, 227

Smith, R'Dean, 232

Smith, R'Dean, Jr., 232

Smith, Virginia, 232

Socrates, 117, 173

South Africa, 244

South America, 78

South Dartmouth, Massachusetts, 227

Southern Methodist Church, 175

South Kingston Monthly Meeting, 57, 63

Southport, England, 150

Staines Meeting, 213

Stanton, Elizabeth Cady, 80

Stanton, Henry B., 80

Stephen, Caroline E., 17–19, 121–124, 126

Stephen, Leslie, 121

Stephenson, Isaac, 57

Stoke Saint Gregory, England, 212

St. Petersburg, Florida, 175

Studiorum Novi Testamenti Societas, 202

Sudbury, England, 150

Suso, Henry, 119

Swarthmoor Hall, 131

Swarthmoor Women's Monthly Meeting, 50

Swarthmoor Women's Quarterly Meeting, 50

Swarthmore College, 81

Swarthmore Lecture, 21, 205

Swarthmore, Pennsylvania, 174, 216

Swedenborg, 117

Switzerland, 18, 131

Syrus, Ephrem, 178

T

Tatian, 178–179

Tauler, John, 119, 122

Temple, William, 167

Tennessee, 119, 169

Tennessee Valley Authority, 34

Tertullian, 137, 201

Theological Commission of the Archdiocese of Los Angeles, 233

Theresa, St., 122

Thomas, Richard H., 128–129

Thurman, Howard, 177

Tolstoy, 173

Townsend, Elvira, 140

Treaty of Versailles, 20, 207

Trudeau, Edward, 132

Trueblood, Elton, 225–227

Tuke, Henry, 8, 46, 64, 129

Twelfth Street Meeting, 191

Twining, David, 51

Twining, Elizabeth, 51

Bibliography

U

Union Springs, New York, 120
United States of America, 14, 78, 81, 124, 130, 140, 151. See also America
University College of Rhodesia, 213
University of Birmingham, 202, 210
University of Bristol, 212
University of Chicago, 174
University of Chicago Divinity School, 170, 188–189
University of Chicago Libraries, 189
University of Newcastle upon Tyne, 213
University of Pennsylvania, 109
University of St. Andrews, 202
Updegraff, David Benjamin, 97
Updegraff, David Brainerd, 15–17, 96–111, 115, 125, 141–142, 168
Updegraff, Rebecca Taylor, 16, 97, 106
Upper Holloway Baptist Church, 201
Usher, Charles, 130
utilitarian, 13, 238

V

Valparaiso, Chile, 78
Vassalboro, Maine, 120, 223
Verdi, Giuseppe, 234, 236
Virginia, 51, 97
Virginia Yearly Meeting, 34

W

Wales, 211
Wallis, Dorothea, 201
Ward Lecture, 199
Washington, George, 51
Wayne County, Indiana, 140
Weaver, J. Denny, 11, 37, 145, 147, 158, 173
Webb, Richard, 83
Wellesley College, 223
Wesley, 117, 137
Westbury-on-Trym, England, 150
West Chester, Pennsylvania, 64
West Laurens, New York, 216
Westminster Abbey, 211
Westminster Confession of Faith, 32
West Newton, Indiana, 169
West Richmond Monthly Meeting, 171–172
Westtown School, 55, 64
Whitehead, George, 28
Wilburite Friends, 13, 63, 97
Wilburite-Gurneyite split, 63, 97
Wilbur, John, 12–13, 57–63
Wilbur, Mary, 57
Wilbur, Thomas, 57
Willhausen, 161
William Penn College, 216
William Penn Lectures, 173
Williams, Walter, 22, 42
Wilmington College, 214, 232

Wilmington, Delaware, 87
Wilson, Henry Lloyd, 133
Withy, George, 58
Woodard, Cader, 140
Woodard, Luke, 15–17, 140–150, 161–163, 166–167, 168, 170
Woodard, Rachel, 140
Woodbrooke, 18, 133–134, 151, 174, 201, 213
Wood, Ellen, 132
Wood, Henry George, 20–21, 201–212, 213
Wood, John Roskruge, 201
Woodman, Charles, 222
Wood, Samuel, 57
Woolman, John, 8, 13, 54, 56, 154, 156, 157, 238
Woolman School, 174
World Anti-Slavery Convention, 79, 85
World War I, 20, 151
World War II, 213
Worstall, Sarah, 51
Wren, Frances Anne, 201
Wright, G. Ernest, 32–33, 119
Wright, Martha Coffin, 80

Y

Yoder, John Howard, 237
York, England, 129, 131, 150
Yorkshire, England, 136, 150

www.ingramcontent.com/pod-product-compliance
Lightning Source LLC
Chambersburg PA
CBHW030851170426
43193CB00009BA/565